DISCARDED

By Sir Lewis Namier

★

ENGLAND IN THE AGE OF THE AMERICAN REVOLUTION

THE STRUCTURE OF POLITICS AT THE ACCESSION OF GEORGE III

CHARLES TOWNSHEND
A mezzotint after a portrait by Sir Joshua Reynolds
National Portrait Gallery

CHARLES TOWNSHEND

by

SIR LEWIS NAMIER

and

JOHN BROOKE

LONDON
MACMILLAN & CO LTD
NEW YORK · ST MARTIN'S PRESS
1964

MACMILLAN AND COMPANY LIMITED
St Martin's Street London WC 2
also Bombay Calcutta Madras Melbourne

THE MACMILLAN COMPANY OF CANADA LIMITED
Toronto

ST MARTIN'S PRESS INC
New York

PRINTED IN GREAT BRITAIN

FOREWORD

by

LADY NAMIER

EARLY in the 'fifties my husband began to talk of Charles Townshend as a fascinating subject for a full-scale biography. We were motoring about England, Scotland and Wales — from one great muniments room to another — in search of materials and documents relevant to the lives and political activities of eighteenth-century Members of Parliament. Here and there, often quite unexpectedly, he found tantalizing references to the brilliant, indispensable, unreliable or exasperating Charles Townshend. In no time the allusions had rekindled his old interest in the man who had played so unfortunate a part in the prelude to the American Revolution.

As work on *The History of Parliament* developed and gathered momentum, boxes of hitherto unpublished — sometimes even unsorted — documents were brought or sent by their generous owners to its offices for study by Lewis and his staff. Perusal of those from Raynham Hall and Dalkeith Palace made it clear that the biography Lewis had pondered, on our long drives, could be written. In the Raynham MSS. was a most important batch of letters from the young Charles to his father, and a smaller one to his mother; both revealed a family situation disastrously formative of Townshend the 'weather-cock' politician. As for the MSS. from Dalkeith, they made possible at last the disentangling of Charles Townshend's Parliamentary and political career.

For *The History of Parliament* Lewis was to write a biography of Charles Townshend 7000-words long. Much of the new material obviously had to be left out; yet to waste it was unthinkable, and the time for the full-scale biography seemed ripe. When the University of Cambridge asked Lewis to deliver the Leslie Stephen lecture for 1959, he chose to speak on Townshend's character and certain aspects of his career — making, in fact, of this lecture a preliminary sketch to the large biography.

So it came about that at his death in August 1960, there were three works on Townshend by Lewis's hand: the unfinished full-length biography, the completed short biography (for *The History of Parliament*), and the Leslie Stephen lecture which had been published by the Cambridge University Press in the previous year. The full-length biography broke off at Townshend's appointment as Chancellor of the Exchequer, leaving the last chapter — planned to cover the most eventful year of his life — still to be written. Besides, some isolated events in Townshend's life and career were covered neither by the short biography, nor by the lecture; nor were they as yet incorporated in the large biography where none of the written text had been revised and much of the material was arranged in sequences of paragraphs headed by Roman numerals, each sequence starting with 'I'.

During his last years, devoted chiefly to *The History of Parliament*, Lewis had been closely associated with Mr. John Brooke, his principal assistant, who says: 'Throughout, while writing the biography, Sir Lewis had consulted me, and I had read each section after it had been written. He had also talked over with me how he proposed to write the final chapter; and when he died Lady Namier asked me to complete the work. I had finished my revision of the manuscript and was about to begin the final chapter, when a fresh batch of letters from Charles to his father was discovered among Lord Townshend's papers. This necessitated the rewriting of the first two chapters; and it is no longer possible to state precisely which parts of the book are by Sir Lewis and which by me. In the section that I am almost wholly responsible for (Chapter VIII) I have followed the outline he discussed with me, and have incorporated phrases of his from the Leslie Stephen lecture.'

There is in the book an even more subtle blending of two scholars' work, since Lewis in the last year of his life came increasingly to rely upon Mr. Brooke's precision and agility of mind, and often modified his own views to suit the conclusions they had reached together. For my part, I was (in the matter of Charles Townshend as in much else) the repository of Lewis's surmises, doubts, and deliberations with himself in my hearing — a position that makes me able to judge how inextricably the two writers' minds had to blend before this biography of Charles Townshend could be published. It has also enabled me to write the last paragraphs of the book, those following the asterisk. They are based on our discussions in the last year of my husband's life.

But the book owes much to others, too, without whose ready help it could never have been written. In the first place thanks are due to the Marquess Townshend and the Duke of Buccleuch, owners of the two most important collections of Charles Townshend papers; Mr. T. S. Blakeney, who searched Lord Townshend's MSS. for material relating to Charles; Mr. Ian Gilmour, M.P., through whom access was obtained to the Duke of Buccleuch's MSS.; and Dr. Lucy S. Sutherland, who kindly read the book in typescript.

We extend our thanks also to all owners whose MSS. have been used in the book:

The Duke of Bedford
The Marquess of Bute
The Duke of Devonshire
Lord Egremont
The Earl Fitzwilliam and the Trustees of the Wentworth Woodhouse estates
The Duke of Grafton
The Earl of Harrowby
Mr. David Holland
The Marquess of Lansdowne
The Earl of Malmesbury
Sir John Murray, K.C.M.G.
Mr. Humphrey FitzRoy Newdegate
The Marquess of Salisbury

CONTENTS

CHAPTER I

Early Years
1725-1747

(i)

In the summer of 1765, Lord Rockingham, taking stock of his Government's position in the House of Commons, marked a list of its Members with 'pro', 'contra', or 'doubtful' against their names.[1] Two only eluded classification: William Pitt and Charles Townshend. Not made for team-work, they could not be fitted into any political system. Yet so transcendent were their gifts as House of Commons men that neither could be neglected for long. Townshend, while lacking Pitt's grandeur and undaunted courage, was unsurpassed for brilliancy: 'if there was something more awful and compulsive in Pitt's oratory, there was more acuteness and more wit in Charles Townshend's,' wrote Lord Waldegrave about 1758.[2] And he thus explained the omission of Townshend in November 1756 from 'more active employment': 'Pitt did not choose to advance a young man to ministerial office, whose abilities were of the same kind, and so nearly equal to his own.' This, though written before Pitt's greatness as War Minister was fully revealed, is significant.

By the time Townshend had reached his thirties, his character, private and public, had impressed itself on contemporaries: its various facets were described and discussed; and there is enormous material to cover the last decade of his short life. But no serious biography of this seemingly protean personality has been attempted. Yet his impact on relations between Britain and America was momentous, its effects are still felt, and an attentive, backward glance at his brilliant political performances reveals at least one curious consistency: his fatal American measures of 1767 enacted, at the end of his career, a programme he had formulated at its

[1] Rockingham's list of the House of Commons, Fitzwilliam MSS. Northamptonshire Record Office.

[2] Waldegrave, *Memoirs*, 86–7.

start; and there was a strong emotional colouring to that programme, derived from his early impressions of family life.

Charles Townshend was born on 27 August 1725, second son of Charles, 3rd Viscount Townshend. The Townshends were closely connected with the ruling Whig families of Walpole and Pelham. Lord Townshend's step-mother was the sister of the great Sir Robert Walpole, and Henry Pelham and the Duke of Newcastle, Walpole's successors, were his uncles. Charles Townshend's mother was Audrey, daughter of Edward Harrison of Balls Park, near Hertford (M.P. 1717–26), sometime Governor of Madras and director of the East India Company. Besides Charles, there were four other children of the marriage: George, who succeeded his father as 4th Viscount in 1764 and was created Marquess in 1786; Edward, who died an infant; Roger, who was killed at Ticonderoga in 1759; and Audrey, who married and had children.

Charles's family background was unhappy. He was the son of a formidable father, intelligent yet primitive, suspicious, vehement, and oppressive, and of a mother, fastidious and intellectual, famed for her wit and promiscuity. They separated when Charles was fifteen, and he remained with his father, professing the greatest attachment to him and indifference or even contempt for his mother. But for his father Charles felt no love either: much rather fear seeking relief in mockery, a weapon of the intelligent under oppression. Nor was he ever really attached to any other member of his family; even his attitude to his brother George, with whom in later years he professed the closest relations, was subject to extreme changes: critical and uncertain, it produced quarrels followed by periods of fervent devotion. Wonderful abilities, inordinate vanity, and poverty of heart explain a great deal in the pattern of his life.

Townshend suffered much from ill-health — 'my crazy constitution' and 'weakness of body'. After puberty, epilepsy set in, which at times incapacitated him for weeks. There are detailed accounts of these fits and of their after-effects in Charles's letters to his father, and a good many references in letters from relatives and friends. The fits seem to have started in adolescence. In June 1745, when Charles was twenty, his father refers to 'those disorders you have laboured under for some time past'. The latest, discreet yet unmistakeable, references to fits which have been found, occur in 1761: on 5 July Horace Walpole wrote to Lord Strafford that Townshend had had 'a bad return of his old complaint'; and on

4 December a debate which he was to have opened and which attracted much attention, had to be postponed because of 'a severe fit of ill health' which, he said on the 9th, had left him 'in a very weak condition'. Sir Charles Symonds, a foremost authority on epilepsy, has very kindly examined my material on Townshend's fits, and thinks that there can be little doubt that they were epileptic; that the seizures had probably a focal origin in the left hemisphere, and were due to injury at birth; that Townshend had also inhibitory motor seizures of a minor kind; and that a succession of such minor attacks accounted for periods of malaise and misery of which Townshend complained. Sir Charles further writes: 'The presumed organic basis for the attacks makes it quite possible that some psychological abnormality may have existed in association with the epileptic liability, i.e. due to the same organic cause.' Lastly, Townshend's 'crazy constitution' may very well have been associated with his epileptic liability. One is struck, following him month by month and year by year, by the frequency and diversity of ills from which he suffered. Still, with incredible pertinacity and drive he struggled on, giving his life a brilliant and amusing appearance. The tragic side was usually overlooked.

Townshend did not go to Eton with his brother George, but he did go to some school: in his letter to his father of 30 December 1744 he mentions, 'when I left school'. He matriculated at Clare College, Cambridge, in 1742, and being expected to make his career at the Bar, was entered at Lincoln's Inn. About this, as about most of his early life, the information derives from his correspondence with Lord Townshend.[1] It makes painful reading; in letters of portentous length a constant struggle is waged: Charles and his father dissect as under a microscope what has been said, manœuvre for position, and find fault by putting forced constructions on what the other has said (a technique Charles was to use all his life). There was self-damaging torment on both sides. This alternates with feigned submission on Charles's part and flattery so extreme as to render both unconvincing—which sets the tone in fervency as in non-performance for later professions of devotion to political chiefs.

(ii)

The first extant batch of letters from Charles Townshend to his father covers the period from December 1744 to February 1745,

[1] MSS. of the Marquess Townshend at Raynham.

when Charles was in residence at Cambridge; only one from Lord Townshend to Charles has been traced for these few months; and some of Charles's, mentioned in the correspondence, are missing. Those that survive deal mainly with a message received from Lady Townshend in which she offered to settle some money on him.

> A clergyman, who is an attendant on courts and courtiers, [Charles wrote on 7 December], called on me yesterday with a message from Lady Townshend, in which she kindly offers me £750, which she adds was overlooked in the settlement made on her marriage. An act of this nature by so inveterate an enemy surprised me. . . . I deferred my answer for two reasons, both as I recollected that she was formerly entrusted with the management of some money belonging to me which if I am not mistaken is near this sum she offers me, and as I would not proceed in this affair without your directions. If I have a claim to this money it would come to me in a good season, and therefore I would not reject the offer until I had consulted you; if on the contrary this is a voluntary kindness in her, I would not before I knew your opinion either accept or refuse it. As to my own inclinations, such has been her behaviour to me and so fixed is my contempt for money, that if I can do it without lessening my reputation, I should choose to acknowledge her goodness without accepting her favours. This is a patriotism I shall always act through life, having less regard for wealth than honour, more desire of being a good than a rich man.

His father, after some sharp remarks about Lady Townshend and her conduct towards him, proceeded to advise Charles:

> If you were to accept this first present and to refuse any further attempts, the talk of the settlement would be then thrown off and it would be told everywhere that you had accepted of a sum of money from her and you would be charged with ingratitude. And indeed I think she might hurt your character by saying that though you will not desert your father yet you will take money of her without obeying the conditions and intent of those gifts. In short, I would not on any account, were I in your case, accept of this artful present which she now offers or take any money from her. Besides, considering what has passed with respect to her behaviour with regard to you, without considering those other very important considerations relating to me and my family, prudence I think forbids you to trust her at all. I do really believe that if you was to take this money you would be unhappy with it.

With this reply Charles professed to be content:

> I have only time to assure you, [he wrote on 9 December], that I shall observe your advice with strictness and give such an answer to Lady Townshend's message as shall yield you satisfaction and myself credit.

Charles's elder brother George, who in May 1743 had gone out to serve as a volunteer with the British Army in Germany, was coming home with a view to securing rank in the Army, and possibly also to settle financial matters connected with his coming of age. His attitude in the conflict between his parents was undetermined. Whereas Charles professed to side completely with his father and avoided any contact with his mother, George, according to Horace Walpole, was 'governed' by her; and after his return in February 1745, she 'made a great ball' to celebrate his 21st birthday.[1]

Charles wrote to his father in his letter of 7 December:

> I have just received a letter from George, written in a style and temper which proves the alteration we have so long wished in his disposition all but accomplished. Instead of declaiming with passion against your relations, he forces an opportunity of pressing his desire of deserving their esteem, declares himself attached in the strongest manner to the *real* interest of his family, and promises in explicit terms that we shall all in a little time acknowledge him our sincere and firm friend. As far as his temper will suffer him he confesses his past misconduct, and I think in many paragraphs he hints to me that he has detected the designs of his concealed enemies, and at length unmasked the hypocrites, who, under the specious show of affection for him, have reduced him into such conduct as must in the end have destroyed his character without even defending their conduct.

'This account', replied Lord Townshend, 'gives me great satisfaction, and raises a happy expectation in me that I may now find that his eyes are open, that he sees through the designs of his concealed enemies, and that there is a perfect and lasting change in his conduct.'

> But when I recollect that it is now almost one quarter of a year since I heard from him, though I desired in my last to him that he would let me soon hear from him; and when I observe in your description of his letter that there is no mention made of me but only expressions of his desire to deserve the esteem of *my relations*, I do confess that I have

[1] Walpole, *Memoirs of George II*, i. 39; Walpole to Mann, 4 Mar. 1745.

> some difficulty in raising my expectations at present so high as I wish I could and that there was foundation for the most certain expectation of so happy an event.

Charles, discussing George's attitude in his letter of 9 December, shows much perturbation — fear of misinterpreting George, or of being accused of having done so:

> One mistake in my letter to you remains to be corrected, my brother was not wanting in his professions of duty and affection, nor did I represent him with justice when I omitted them. I expressed his whole intentions in too cold a manner, I am afraid, for indeed his letter convinced me that he is desirous of joining with you and your friends. I must desire that what I have said relating to him may be known only to ourselves, for if my hopes are false and his position unchanged, he will condemn me for making him thus talk in a strange language, and profess intentions he never designed.

Another letter of 30 December shows strain and exasperation in Charles's dealings with his father:

> I have never felt any return of my passion for cricket since you objected to it, nor has my attendance on the tennis court been either prejudicial to my time or my purse. For want of better exercise in the late frost I went once every week and stayed one hour, which in a course of years cannot consume either much time or money. I lost my relish for the diversions of a schoolboy when I left school, and now choose tennis more as an exercise necessary for my health than as an amusement, always following it under such restrictions as that I have never spent four shillings or four days on this article. I shall obey your orders in discontinuing this exercise, which I assure you never was or shall be dear to me.

And next he reverts to the refusal he was going to send to his mother's 'offer'. But three days later, loth to refuse the money, he professed to have mistaken her intention and to have misrepresented it to Lord Townshend. She had not the sole disposal of the money which she offered to settle on him; and as Lord Townshend's concurrence was required, acceptance — such was Charles's view — would impose on him no obligation towards her. He laboured the point with copious assurances that if his father thought differently, he would refuse, fully satisfied with having conformed to his will.

The discovery did not impress Lord Townshend; and on 24 January 1745 Charles reported having replied to his mother's offer in the 'style and temper which you advised'.

If she complains of the indifference with which I speak to her, my coldness is justified by her behaviour, if she abuses me for having refused her favours without respect, I can easily bear her hatred whose kindness I denied; in short, my obligations to her are not very binding, those which I owe to you are insuperable.

Charles sent his father a copy of the letter he transmitted to her through the intermediary. Written to please Lord Townshend, it goes to the length of saying: 'It is improbable the same person should be my friend and enemy within a few years, especially when there has not been any change in my conduct to explain this alteration in her.' And the covering letter to his father of 3 February concludes:

I thank you for the kind reproof you gave me in your last letter, and will remember to avoid the puerilities you blame in my future letters.

There follow five letters of 18 to 27 February 1745, three from Lord Townshend and two from Charles, dealing with his further studies and profession. The subject seems to have been previously touched upon by Lord Townshend, as appears from Charles's same letter of 3 February:

My fondness for the profession you recommend to me increases every day, and I am not less resolved to undergo the drudgery, than willing to enjoy the advantages of it. My whole study is now directed to that end.

Next, on 18 February, Lord Townshend wrote to Charles in a simple and friendly letter that he wished to see him soon at Raynham (the family home in Norfolk), and, in view of the time he had been at Cambridge and his age, to talk with him about Lincoln's Inn and determine his future scheme of life: but he specifically stated that he did not mean Charles to take his leave of Cambridge before they jointly had reached a decision.

Charles's reply on 20 February starts by mentioning a return of his illness; and proceeds to give an account of how he had spent his time at Cambridge, as if his father had charged him with idleness and demanded his leaving immediately. In his first year he applied himself entirely to the study of Greek and Roman historians; in the second, he also 'learnt algebra, with some books of Euclid, and made some progress in astronomy'. 'I am now employed in the civil law'; he has already studied Grotius and Puffendorf, and is reading Justinian. He next means to study Common Law 'and be a punctual attendant on our courts and Westminster Hall'.

That I have been diligent in the prosecution of my design and made few allowances of my time for diversions or company, all I believe who know me will bear witness, nor do I imagine that I have ever had it in my power to increase my application without endangering my health.

He is not likely to find another opportunity so well to prepare himself for his profession, and pathetically pleads with his father to let him spend 'two or three months more without interruption in this place —

But if my reasons appear to you insufficient, I will order my books to be sent to London and be at Raynham on the day you appoint.

Charles's mention of his illness worked as intended. His father was 'truly concerned':

You do not mention in what manner or in what degree it returned, so that I am really under apprehension that you have had it in the severe manner it came upon you before you went to Scarborough. . . . I know very well that you are affected in a different manner when under this indisposition . . . and therefore I cannot venture to say anything in justification of my last letter without some fear lest your spirits may be affected by the few words I shall write on this head. And beg you will interpret what I say in a favourable light.

But next the 'few words' fill five closely packed pages, repeating and expounding what he had clearly said in his previous letter, and showing that Charles had put a wrong construction on it — all this 'though explanations as I have found by experience have seldom their desired effect'. And two days later, he wrote again begging Charles not to suffer the matter to give him 'any further uneasiness but forget it'. He also agreed to Charles continuing at Cambridge — 'that shall be as you shall think proper and like best'.

On 27 February, Charles gratefully acknowledged the kindness of these two affectionate letters; and thus encouraged, proceeded to give a reassuring yet harrowing account of his illness:

My last relapse was attended with a very troublesome and general eruption of a scorbutic humour in my head, which Heberden[1] says was a very favourable circumstance which possibly prevented an immediate epilepsy. My face was never convulsed, and what few symptoms I felt of my old disorder were very slight and momentary.

[1] William Heberden sen. (1710–1801), 'one of the most eminent English physicians of the 18th century (*D.N.B.*); fellow of St. John's College, Cambridge. 'He resided in Cambridge until 1748 or 1749, practising as a physician' (R. F. Scott, *Admissions to St. John's College, Cambridge*, iii. 377).

> These bad attendants were all prevented by the vent the humour found from my head, but in return for this benefit, my whole countenance was changed, my appetite taken from me, and my body shrunk very much. I continued in this state almost a fortnight, and my head is yet so much covered with this humour that I am not well able to bear this piercing weather.

And as he still suffered from a want of spirits Dr. Heberden advised 'opening an issue in his arm', which Charles did not wish to have done without his father's consent.

There follows a gap in the extant correspondence. Then on 19 May 1745 Charles reported yet another severe return of his 'convulsive disorders' with lasting effects. Lord Townshend, replying on 29 May, asked Charles not to make any arrangements for entering Lincoln's Inn at present. 'Between this and your return from Scarborough I shall consider of what I mentioned to you relating to Leyden.'

(iii)

Charles was now about to leave Cambridge. His letter of 5 June 1745 which deals with the subject, starts with a dismal account of his condition:

> My health has . . . of late been very infirm, and my convulsive disorder both quick in its returns and violent in its effects, yet Heberden still promises me a perfect cure from Scarborough waters, if I go there in the beginning of next month and stay till the end of the season . . . but I confess that I believe that not this nor any other spa can shake my illness, which seems to have taken root in my constitution beyond the reach of art or power of medicine. The tremor of my nerves increases very visibly, and I have often a lifeless stiffness in my right arm which entirely deprives me of the use of it.

And next he asks for directions how to settle his affairs on his departure from Cambridge: if he continues his name on the register, this will cost but £2 per annum, whereas he could not 'go through the usual ceremonies upon taking a final leave . . . at a less expense than £20'. While stating that it would be the usual thing for him to take a degree, 'and as my uncle[1] is our representative the University may expect it', he assured his father, with copious repetition and great show of submission, that he did not intend 'to create for you any new expenses' — 'I wait to know your choice, to which I

[1] Thomas Townshend sen., M.P. for Cambridge University 1727–74.

shall conform with pleasure.' He also spoke of a visit to Raynham before starting for Scarborough.

The prospect of possible expense, however carefully wrapped up, touched Lord Townshend on the raw, and it was now his turn to be unreasonable. His reply of 8 June opens with a discourse of about 500 words on the importance of Charles's setting out for Scarborough without delay 'to eradicate entirely all the causes of those disorders you have laboured under for some time past'. There follows another discourse of about 1000 words on Charles's leave taking from Cambridge: his name is to be 'struck out of the buttery boards or register', but the cost of ceremonies on this occasion should not exceed £5. 'I do remember very well that some out of vanity did make a great éclat and parade in their form of taking final leave of their college', while others, some of ancient families, made no such parade. 'I desire that you will not make any', for it would 'be a mark of want of prudence and quite out of character in one who is preparing for a profession'. And two days later, on Monday 10 June, followed a further letter of over a thousand words labouring the same points with even greater urgency: restoration of Charles's health is the supreme concern; he should set out for Scarborough by the end of the week or beginning of the next; and as for leave taking:

> Neither myself nor my brother Tom nor the Colonel[1] ... gave any other treat upon leaving their college than some wine in the evening to the fellows and fellow commoners of the college.... Five pounds will buy more wine than is necessary to make them all drunk, if they can be supposed to be of such a disposition.

Charles replied in a letter misdated 'the 5th 1745', and endorsed by his father: 'Received 13 June 1745.' It deals with his past expenditure at Cambridge, which his father had not impugned.

> Three hundred pounds must certainly be granted to be a considerable income, and should be sufficient to defray every expense ... and enable me to live not only with ease, but with some splendour; yet ... though it would be abundant in any other place, rather straitens me in this. You would ... have a better opinion of my frugality if I should mention a few of those charges to which I am indispensably subject.

He enumerates: commons £86 per annum; tutor £24; chambers £19; laundress, fire, etc., about £12; 'wages and clothing of my

[1] Roger Townshend (1708–60), Lord Townshend's youngest brother.

servant . . . £36, with the annual cost of my own linen and plain dressing'; pocket money never above £4 a quarter — which leaves not above £55 a year for extraordinary expenses.

It should be considered too that my crazy constitution is no small charge to me and I find upon inquiry that my illness and the lameness of my servant have cost me more than £80 within these last two years. . . . My life has been always temperate, and my views here too much confined to be expensive, and therefore I am the more sorry to be suspected of loving either parade of show or the false pleasures of an extravagant taste; no student with the most narrow fortune has feasted his friends less, been more moderate in his apparel, or more careless of all external splendour. . . .

Your orders about my journey to Scarborough shall be obeyed in every circumstance.

Lord Townshend's reply on 15 June starts with a minute analysis of the wrong dating of Charles's letter; proceeds with criticism of an unimportant remark — 'the fault may perhaps lie in me, but as they [the words] appear to me obscure I could not avoid mentioning it to you'. (Picking to pieces single sentences and expressions, and commenting on them at wearisome length, became a habit in the family, which Charles never lost.) Next, he points out the irrelevancy of Charles's past expenditure to the subject now discussed; but tries 'for curiosity's sake' one article, the £36 for his servant's wages and clothing: 'if you had been so communicative to me before the time was over and past . . . I should have told you and proved to you that . . . these articles should not have exceeded £31.14.0.'

This is as I said before a new point, and I shall not say one word more about it now as I am not willing to fall into an epistolary controversy with you. Disputes of all kinds should always be avoided as much as possible between father and son, and though disputes have too often arose between us even in matters which relate to myself entirely and in which you were no ways concerned, yet I am satisfied your own sense will tell you how improper this is, and consequently that they will not happen any more hereafter.

Charles did not reply till 21 June —

It was sickness which prevented your hearing from me. . . . This last disorder was a flux which continued upon me above six hours without the least intermission, which, with the evacuation from my stomach (which began and ended with the other) weakened me so much, that it brought on a slight return of my fits and has left the piles with me.

And next another show of obedience, with a sting in the tail:

I have followed your orders in every article upon leaving this place and shall neither take my degree or make an entertainment, though the former was what I once wished to do, and the latter a custom seldom omitted.

To this Lord Townshend did not fail to reply that he had not forbidden 'an entertainment', but said that one for £5 was sufficient.

Charles arrived at Scarborough towards the end of June, and a fresh squabble broke out over money. Before he left Cambridge, his father had sent him £20 to cover the expenses of his journey; in a letter of 2 July Charles said that he had not three guineas left, begged for a further remittance, and asked that it should be deducted from his account. Lord Townshend in his reply of 6 July argued that seventeen guineas was a great deal too much for the expenses of the journey and denied that he was making Charles an allowance: the £300 a year he had received while at Cambridge was to end when he left the university. However, he sent Charles a remittance of £50.

It is your business to take care that your servant's charges, horse, and lodgings are moderate, and I hope in future I shall not find these articles in your letters. For this is making me your servant, and when the case is really that I have done what all the world would think in my circumstances of income is generous and more than could be expected, I hope you will in return treat me as your father. . . . I hope you will be prudent and careful in your expenses, when this [the £50] is out you will let me know and I will send you a further draft. Be careful to keep good hours and to drink the waters regularly; according as your health requires, the time of your stay must be determined. . . . The oftener I hear from you relating to your health the more agreeable it will be to me, and in these cases I think you should not always expect an answer from me.

Charles's health was causing Lord Townshend serious concern, and he wrote on 21 August:

I cannot forbear mentioning to you that I hope you will not leave Scarborough until your physician, Dr. Heberden or Dr. Dealtry, whichever it be you advise with now, does with his own hand write and sign to this effect: *that Mr. Townshend has perfectly recovered and re-established his health and may therefore leave off the use of the waters*; or else *that Mr. Townshend has received all the benefit from the use of the waters for this year, they not being capable of being of any further service to him this year*. The reason why I am so minute on this head is because that you can now without any inconvenience allow what time shall be necessary for the care and perfect recovery of your health, which is a matter of the highest importance to you and on which your success in future undertakings and happiness in life do depend.

Charles replied on 1 September:

> My want of health arises I believe more from natural infirmities than any uneasiness of mind; because I feel the same illness in the same degree in every different state of my mind. Few things have occurred to vex me since I came here and yet, even in this regimen, I can't escape [pain], where if my body was sick, only as it partakes of my mind, I should have been free from every complaint. Every accident which disturbs the one may perhaps increase the other, but I am convinced I often suffer illnesses which have no other source than a constitutional weakness of body. Dealtry . . . advises me to discontinue these waters, and try a foreign air which with much exercise may perhaps work a cure.
>
> As to Leyden, your inclination is my rule, as your judgment must be best able to promote my interest in the best manner.

There follows a paragraph of gross flattery, 'the result of much cool reflexion', which concludes with the flourish, 'your choice will always be productive of my happiness'. It does not appear from the correspondence when Charles left Scarborough, but he cannot have spent much time with his father that summer and autumn.

(iv)

In November 1745 Charles set out for Leyden, the leading Continental university for the study of Roman Law. His correspondence with his father that winter is a prolonged and tedious dispute about money. It began before Charles left England, for on 9 November, while he was waiting at Harwich for a favourable wind, he had to ask his father for permission to draw the first payment of his allowance immediately on his arrival. Lord Townshend's unreasonableness and irascibility were increasing, and Charles seems to have despaired of ever satisfying his father. He hardly mentions his studies except on one occasion, when he had to ask his father's permission to engage a private tutor in law.

On 3 March 1746 Lord Townshend informed Charles that he expected him to return to England at the end of April or beginning of May. This seems to have surprised and disconcerted Charles, who replied in a letter of 22 March (New Style):[1]

> As you have fixed April for the time of my return to England, I ought not perhaps to allege any reasons for my longer stay here, but as you have always given me a liberty to speak my mind on such occasions I hope you will forgive me if I mention one inconvenience which will arise from my returning so soon, without presuming to determine you in your final resolution.
>
> The course of civil law in the public colleges as well as in the private one in which I am engaged with Professor Schwartz will not finish before July, and therefore if I leave Leyden in April my knowledge of that science for which I came will be imperfect and the end in some measure unanswered. If my residence here is prolonged to July, I shall have gone through the whole system and all business will then be ended here, whereas if I come to England next month my advantages expected from this place will be lost.

In an angry and sarcastic letter of 20 March (Old Style) Lord Townshend agreed to Charles remaining at Leyden until the end of May, provided he did not have to draw for more money — 'otherwise you must return in the first week of May next.'

> You now know clearly what my orders are: that you should return to England in the first week of May next or towards the later end of May at furthest, but you must be here before May is over. These are my final orders and therefore I do expect they should be obeyed without further argument on this head.

On 14 April he relaxed his severity to the extent of permitting Charles 'to take a little tour to The Hague and other places in Holland' provided he had enough money; and Charles was not now expected to return before the end of May.

> I have found by your letters and do find it confirmed by your brother, that you are in a very bad state of health, which will I hope receive some benefit by motion and changing the scene.

As for Charles's request that he should be allowed to complete his course in law — 'I think you have been there long enough to gain

[1] At this time England had not completed the transition from the Old Style of dates to the New Style. The New Style had long been used on the Continent, and it was therefore natural for Charles to adopt this system during his stay in Leyden.

as much knowledge in the civil law as may be necessary for a basis to your future study of the laws of your own country.'

The tour in Holland, replied Charles on 8 May (New Style), would be 'very agreable' but he did not have the money to make it: 'my health is indeed yet more infirm than I ever knew it, nor have I hopes of its re-establishment, but it is some comfort to me that if any air is particularly suited to my constitution it is my native air.' A short and simple note was the answer:

May the 6th 1746

Dear Charles

I received yours of the 8th instant N.S. last night, and do desire that you will return to England.

I am

your affectionately

Townshend

Charles did not reply until 5 June (New Style) — more than a fortnight after Lord Townshend had sent him this positive order to return home. 'A violent fit of sickness' had made it impossible for him either to leave or even to write.

> I have had five convulsive fits, severe and of a long continuance, and my body has since thrown out a humour, which, if neglected, may have bad consequences, and for which therefore, with your permission, I will go through one course of physic before I begin my journey. This will delay me but one fortnight at most, and I hope as it is so necessary to my health it will have your approbation.

In fact, this fresh attack of epilepsy delayed Charles's homecoming for more than a month. On 2 July (Old Style) Lord Townshend's steward, 'my Lord being very busy and not having time to write to you himself', sent Charles a second, positive order to return home. It was answered by Charles on 12 July (New Style): he had been unable to write because of his illness, but hoped before the end of the week to make the journey. His letter contains an attempt to propitiate his father, and indicates what sort of welcome he expected to receive in England:

> At the latter end of next week I hope to arrive at Raynham, where I shall endeavour by the dutiful behaviour I shall observe and by my constant attention to your will, to remove what objections you have to my conduct and to deserve your affection and your esteem.

At Leyden, Townshend was a contemporary of John Wilkes; of William Dowdeswell, subsequently Chancellor of the Exchequer in the first Rockingham Administration and leader of the Rockingham Whigs in the House of Commons; and of the Rev. Alexander Carlyle, the Scottish divine, whose *Autobiography* is a source of information on Townshend at Leyden.[1]

In the art of shining, writes Carlyle, Wilkes 'was much outdone by Charles Townshend', whose person and manners were more engaging.

> He had more wit and humour, and a turn for mimicry; and, above all, had the talent of translating other men's thoughts, which they had produced in the simple style of conversation, into most charming language, which not only took the ear but elevated the thoughts. No person I ever knew equalled Charles Townshend in this talent but Dr. Robertson.

Carlyle further recounts:

> An unlucky accident happened at the end of January [1746] which disturbed the harmony of our society.... At an evening meeting, where I happened not to be, Charles Townshend, who had a great deal of wit which he was fond to show ... took it in his head to make a butt of James Johnstone, afterwards Sir James of Westerhall.[2]

He did it in a hurting manner. Johnstone, who had taken it in good part, had his attention subsequently called by one of the company. Next morning,

> I was sent for ... to Charles's lodgings, who looked pale and undone.... He was liable at that time to convulsion fits, which seldom failed to attack him after a late supper.

He told Carlyle that he had been up late, and had been ill; and showed him a letter from Johnstone, with a challenge.

> 'And what answer are you to make to this?' said I. 'Not fight, to be sure,' said he, 'for I have no quarrel with Johnstone, who is the best-natured man in the world.' 'If you can make it up, and keep it secret, it may do, otherwise you'll be dishonoured by the transaction.' ... He seemed quite irresolute.

And he made it up in a manner that hurt him.

[1] 1860 edn., pp. 170, 179–82, 352.

[2] Eldest brother of William Johnstone (afterwards Pulteney), Governor George Johnstone, and John Johnstone. All four sat in Parliament, but after Townshend's time.

After Townshend had married Lady Dalkeith, John Home, the dramatist, took Carlyle to see Townshend.

> He received me with open arms, and was perfectly familiar, but not a hint of having seen me before . . . and in spite of our intimacy afterwards in Scotland, he never made the most distant allusion to anything that had happened at Leyden.

(v)

In September 1746 Charles Townshend went into residence at Lincoln's Inn, and spent the next year studying for the Bar. For this period six letters are extant between Charles and his father — the last dated 31 December 1746 — and one from Lord Townshend's steward to Charles. In the first two letters Charles addresses his father as 'Dear Papa' — an unusual form of address from a young man who had just attained his majority. Hitherto he had used the styles 'Dear Father' or 'Dear Sir'.

Their correspondence continues in the customary strain but their relationship seems to be approaching a crisis. The mounting irritation, one feels, cannot endure. In his letter of 27 September Charles asked what he should do about candlesticks 'and other necessaries': 'I borrow all these conveniences at present at a small premium, for having expended a great part of my money in law books . . . I have not money for those other demands.' Lord Townshend, in his reply of 6 October, asked Charles what had become of the things he brought back from Cambridge. He would supply whatever furniture was necessary for Charles's rooms, but it would be plain and simple. 'As you know that I eat upon pewter, I think my son should not blame me because that I do not throw more foppery upon him than I can possibly afford for myself.' As for Charles's expenditure on books:

> I cannot conceive it necessary to buy a great many books at once, for no one can read more than one law book at a time, and a beginner in the profession must I imagine find it necessary sometimes to read the same book over more than once. So that I should have thought that two or three would have been enough to buy at once.

The next letter extant is of 25 October, from Lord Townshend's steward to Charles:

> My Lord having been very much out of order for above this week last past and not being yet very well able to write himself, has ordered

me to acquaint you that he did not dare, particularly under his present situation of health, to open the letter which he received from you this morning, and has ordered me to return it to you here inclosed. That his Lordship finds more and more every day that ease and quiet are necessary for his health, and orders me to mention that he has done everything on his part towards you which could have been expected from the most fond of fathers, yet your letters are always filled with complaints and uneasiness . . . he is determined not to venture to open any letters from you until he has gained reason from experience in other respects to think that your letters are wrote with a more sincere and ingenuous temper of mind towards his Lordship, and with a disposition easy and contented with regard to what his Lordship has done for you and ready to comply with his Lordship's advice without the necessity of any controversial letters as have been the case in times past.

Poor Charles's attempt (in his letter of 4 November) to placate the angry master of Raynham seems to have been unavailing. The next letter, of 27 December, also from Charles to his father, begins:

Dear Sir,

Having been informed by many relations that you are recovered from your illness, I take the liberty again to write to you, to confess my satisfaction in the re-establishment of your health and my wishes for its continuance. Give me leave to entreat you to believe the truth of these professions, and to forget such errors in my past conduct as may lessen your opinion either of the sincere affection or duty which I bear to you. Many and too notorious faults I have done as I both confess and recollect with shame, and I now most submissively and with the utmost concern beg you to forget the various mistakes of my past life, to credit my declarations of grief in having fallen into them, my resolution to make you every return a forgiven, affectionate, dutiful son can, by obedience to your will, affection for your person, gratitude to your kindness, and steadiness to your interest. I mean to lay my uneasy thoughts before you, and I hope you will again give me hopes of your esteem. My views are at last contracted within a small and proper compass, to the being successful in the law by strict application and happy in life under your protection, and I can now truly say that I desire no other province and would rely on no other friend. I wish I had thought thus earlier, but I have seen my error and beseech you to forgive it.

Parental authority may extort professions of repentance and declarations of future good behaviour, but affection, gratitude and loyalty must be spontaneous. How far Charles Townshend's declarations in this letter were sincere will be seen in the course of his biography; here it is sufficient to note that conflicts with his father produced a mental attitude towards authority which he carried over into the field of politics — now about to be opened to him.

CHAPTER II

Member of Parliament 1747-1754

(i)

At the General Election of 1747, on 30 June, Charles Townshend was returned for Great Yarmouth, a borough where the Townshend and Walpole families had considerable influence. Lord Townshend paid the election expenses, which, judging by subsequent correspondence, did not come to much. It also appears that Lord Townshend was reluctant to allow Charles to stand, fearing that attendance in Parliament would distract him from his legal career. No correspondence about the election has survived, and we do not know how Charles overcame his father's objections.

On 18 October Charles wrote to Lord Townshend in a smooth and deferential style:

> Term is now coming on very soon and therefore I must beg leave to ask your advice and take your directions about my being called to the Bar. My friends tell me I may engage in as much business as at my first appearance I can possibly have, upon the knowledge I have already gained in my profession, and it is upon their testimony I presume to say I am ready to begin my profession as soon as you approve of it. If you resolve that I come to the Bar in the approaching term, I will inform myself what will be the expense of it and report it to you.

Further expense being at the root of the inquiry, it provoked a typical reaction from Lord Townshend:

> I find by experience, [he replied on 19 October], that whenever there is an imaginary want of money my advice is called for and a great show of submission and resignation to my opinion is made, and this seems now . . . to be the cause of your calling on me again to repeat my desire that you should follow that profession which I have often advised and so strongly encouraged you to pursue. . . . I have put myself often to inconveniences that you might feel none, the allow-

ance you have lately had is what you have seemed *contented with*, and is as much as is consistent with the study of the profession.. . . Since May last you have already cost me above £364 [this presumably includes Charles's election expenses]. You will consider that . . . and will not trouble me about so trifling a matter as that of the expenses of your being called to the Bar. You have already given me your solemn promises that the House of Commons shall not divert you from the pursuit of this profession, and it was upon receiving these promises and assurances that I did comply with your desire of being in Parliament.

Charles replied on the 24th that his inquiry related merely to the date of starting, not to the continuance in his profession.

My past diligence I hope shows my resolution to persevere. . . . Whatever I have promised upon this head will be faithfully performed, and the Parliament shall never occasion a neglect of the Bar. The expense of being called amounts to £60, which is a sum I am far from being able to save out of my income, which is at least as little as any student in this inn lives upon.

And next he placed before his father an accomplished fact: to avoid losing another six months, he proposed himself as a candidate for the Bar and on 28 October was accepted; he must now pay the fees, he wrote on the 29th, or else

become a public debtor . . . and incur a disgrace very uneasy and lasting among a society with whom I am to live and practise. . . . I am very sensible how much your estate is encumbered, and how much you do for us all . . . but what can I do in this case? Until this expense is borne I cannot have the profits of my profession, and it is so large I cannot bear it myself.

Lord Townshend replied on 31 October with a most violent letter, starting with 'Sir' and rating Charles with ingratitude; referring to him as a 'genius', and to himself as 'the turnip merchant at Raynham'. Had he foreseen how much it would cost, he would have told Charles that the expense of his election to Parliament and his being called to the Bar 'would be too great for me to bear' — a delay would have given Charles an opportunity 'of preparing yourself more fully both in law and *arithmetic*'.

Charles's answer on 10 November was cringing and tasteless:

Some of my family [i.e. his mother] have I know often laid ingratitude to my charge, but as I always industriously and invariably declined

> every way of deserving their praise I was not surprised upon incurring their censure, and I hoped that, whatever they might say, I had your esteem . . . by my habitual endeavours to make a suitable return for your great kindness. . . . When very young and more unthinking, I was guilty of a very improper freedom in a very imprudent letter, but I had reason to hope this fault had been forgiven, and that my age, situation, and prejudices had excused in your mind what I said.

The letter is endorsed by Lord Townshend: 'Not answered.'

Charles once more found refuge in illness — Thomas, younger brother of Lord Townshend, wrote to him on 29 December:

> My nephew Charles has been for some days ill, but is recovering apace by the care of Dr. Hardinge, who has attended him with the most affectionate diligence. His disorder was of the epileptic kind, and such as, I am told, he has often had, but less violent than some attacks which he has had. I came from him about an hour ago, and left him very cheerful, and with hardly any remaining symptom of his distemper.

This produced the usual response from Lord Townshend who on 2 January 1748 wrote to Charles much concerned to hear 'of your late dangerous illness'. Charles replied on the 5th:

> I received your letter by the last post, and give me leave to assure you I never was made more happy by any incident than I was by the receipt of it. During some time I have suffered much, very much, from my apprehensions that I had displeased you and some expressions I have had of your dislike, and therefore you may well imagine that a letter like your last, wrote in so kind and affectionate a style, gave me, upon my recovering out of a very violent and painful illness, the greatest satisfaction and spirits. Indeed it has made me extremely cheerful and settled in my mind, and it shall ever be my study to deserve the same letters and the same kindness from you.
>
> My illness in this attack appeared in a very bad and dangerous shape; my first warning of it was by a sort of paralytic insensibility in my right arm and side which, even upon large and frequent bleeding, moved very slowly. Afterwards the usual symptoms all followed, and both my pain and variety of evacuations have been very great. This evening I am tolerably well, and have only two blisters upon me, and if the weather is not very severe I shall in this week go abroad.

When a few days later Lord Townshend was asked by a friend to desire his sons to attend the Westbury election petition on the 18th, he replied that Charles, having 'now just got free from a very dangerous fit of illness . . . I imagine he must still be so weak as not to be capable of attending the committee of election without the greatest hazards to his health'. Moreover —

> I did oblige him to make me a promise when I first told him that I would endeavour to bring him into Parliament that he would not attend any of the committees of elections. The reason why I demanded this promise from him [was] because that it would take him too much from the study of his profession to attend the House both morning and evening. He likewise was obliged to promise me that he would not attend the House but on particular days. These promises I insisted on from him that I might be in some degree secure that his being brought into Parliament so early might not divert him from pursuing his studies in that profession which I had always designed he should follow and had fixed him in.

During 1748 Charles Townshend suffered several relapses; made the most of them in sweetly affectionate letters to his father; and was allowed to give up practise at the Bar. Some time before the end of May Lord Townshend waited on his uncle the Duke of Newcastle, Secretary of State; asked him to take Charles under his protection; acquainted the Duke 'with the necessity I had been under, on account of his infirm state of health, to take him from the profession of the law which he had entered upon'; expressed his great desire to see Charles 'fixed in some place of business'; and named the Board of Admiralty.[1]

On 2 June Charles wrote to his father:[2]

> The illness, of which I complained in my last, is entirely removed; it was some return, but a slight one, of my usual disorder, but care and continual temperance in diet and hours have entirely restored to me that health and freedom from pain which you left me with. It has been, and shall be, my study to discover and avoid every inadvertency or irregularity which can delay or prevent my perfect recovery, and I shall be the more diligent and punctual in this, as it is your desire, as well as my interest, I should.

And next on 19 June:

> I have hitherto been kept in London, or rather from my journey to Scarborough, by solicitations from Yarmouth . . . which are material on account of the persons desiring them. My business is near done

[1] Lord Townshend to Newcastle, 14 December 1748, Add. MS. 32717, f. 444.
[2] The letter is dated by him '2 July', but endorsed by his father: 'It ought to have been dated June the 2nd 1748.'

> and in the next week I shall set forth. When I am there I will, as you desire I should, be regular both in diet and hours, giving every aid I can to the waters and taking the whole benefit of their powers and effect. I will too stay the whole season.

After this he expected to spend a few months at Raynham, happy in 'that very great kindness and affection I receive from you'.

His first letter from Scarborough is of 17 July: 'Though it is a great while since I set out, it is but a few days since I came here', having been unable to bear the fatigue of long stages. This is also the first extant letter dealing with the question of office: a vacancy having occurred at the Board of Trade, Lord Townshend apparently urged Charles to apply for it to Henry Pelham, First Lord of the Treasury and Minister in the House of Commons. But Charles still hankered after a place at the Admiralty, though acknowledging with fulsome compliments and deference his father's arguments in favour of the Board of Trade, 'where only one can learn what ought perhaps for its importance to be the first thing learnt by all who would deserve great offices in this state'. Besides: 'Your present allowance to me is a very large one, larger not only than what I as your younger son could have asked, but than perhaps you can out of your encumbered estate conveniently pay.' It would therefore be a very great satisfaction to him if he could maintain himself 'out of any office which you recommend or raise me to'. Yet he continues to harp on the way in which a seat at the Admiralty would 'strengthen and establish immoveably' his interest at Yarmouth, and speaks with a touch of contempt about that at the Board of Trade: he will write to Pelham — 'the vacancy is not engaged nor likely to be so, few persons in Parliament being willing to renew their elections for it'. And next he makes a great show of attachment to his father in preference to his mother, and of the financial losses he will gladly suffer because of it.

> When I was [in June] in Craven Street [George Townshend's house] Lady Townshend never came to the house or the street, nor, if she had, would she have made any change in my opinion or behaviour by her appearance. She knows this to be true from much trial and repeated temptations, which I ever have slighted and overcome as one resolved consistently to support my first resolution and attachment to you, be the consequences of it to me what they will. I have been often told what I might expect from the regard of her and my grandmother if I would deserve it, and that nothing was required but outward

> complaisance and sometimes a visit, but I have always refused any testimony of affection which I knew you disapprove, and have upon this view and with this satisfaction contentedly seen all the expectations I had from them fall away, and borne all the injury their ill-will and misreport has been able to do to my interest and my honour.

Charles was learning how to get the better of his father: to hint at the possibility of a reconciliation with his mother, and to claim credit for having refused it. There is something pitiful in Lord Townshend's obvious need for affection and in his failure to inspire it.

Another letter from Scarborough, 19 August, followed, full of flattery to his father, concluding:

> I was far from supposing you pressed the Board of Trade to me against my own choice, your manner of advising me had very little the air of authority or constraint, and I am sensible in how friendly a manner you have transacted this whole matter. I only prefer the Admiralty as it is a full shop for my customers at Yarmouth, and wish to make those gentlemen all possible return for their long regard to you.

In September Charles was in London to press on the Treasury the claims of some of his constituents. 'Dr. Hardinge', he wrote on the 17th,[1] 'thinks me the better for Scarborough but . . . I doubt whether I have made any advance towards general health.' Nothing more appears about the place at the Board of Trade; Sir Thomas Robinson, the later Lord Grantham, was appointed to it. On 19 November, the day Parliament reassembled, George Townshend wrote to Lord Townshend from Craven Street: 'My brother Charles was this evening taken very ill . . . Doctor Hardinge . . . hopes he will soon be better . . . my brother was in such pain that when I arrived he could utter but very little.'[2] And Charles wrote in a letter which he misdated 2 November, but his father marked as written on 1 December:[3]

> I should have wrote to you by the last post to inform you of my safe arrival in town, but illness and dangerous illness prevented me. When I came here I found my letters of notice from my friends whom Mr. Pelham had desired to advise me of his intention to give me the seconding our address, but I came too late and lost the opportunity in

[1] *H.M.C., Townshend MSS.*, 364. [2] Ibid., 366.
[3] Ibid., 365, prints it under 2 November, which is patently wrong, as it refers to the opening of Parliament as 'on Tuesday last'.

> despite of his endeavours, who delayed naming any other person until Sunday night when Mr. Charles Yorke was appointed. Mr. Pelham told me on Tuesday how sorry he was this had happened and added he was the more sorry as my appearance on this occasion would have given him an opportunity of honourably mentioning me to the King, who would have been by this means prepared to grant readily what Mr. Pelham said he every day thought of asking for me.

Stanhope, a Lord of the Admiralty Board, was dying, and Charles felt confident that, had he seconded the Address, he would have succeeded on the vacancy, and therefore begged his father to apply once more to Pelham on his behalf — 'a seat at the Admiralty will at once put me out of the necessity of being of further expense to you as long as I have it.' (And Charles undoubtedly pined for an end to his dependence on his father.)

Lord Townshend replied the next day with a letter which picked out any points in that from Charles which might be construed into a reproach; and having said that he would rather forego stating his case than run any risk of hurting Charles's health when it was weak, proceeded with a most lengthy and detailed analysis of what had at various times passed between them; reproached Charles with having avoided an open and sincere talk with him; with having doubted Pelham's goodwill, and having urged a renewal of solicitations. He concluded:

> I think it will be improper for me to write to him — but I will lay aside my own judgement according to custom and will comply with what your very young judgement had determined, and will write to Mr. Pelham this post.

Charles wrote back on 8 December disclaiming in the most controversial manner all controversy with his father; and thus described his own position, with implied reproaches against Lord Townshend:

> I have asked Mr. Pelham for the vacant seat in the Admiralty, but he tells me he cannot promise it to me, that he will mention me among the candidates to the King, and say that it is your request that I may have it. Sir Peter Warren insists upon it and I believe will be complied with, as I am not only not advantageously known, but not even personally, to his Majesty, it is little likely I shall have his preference, and it is the less probable now as my competitors are all men of families in great favour with him, pushed by great interests and by friends assiduous in their solicitation.

And the next day:

> I have had a meeting with Mr. Pelham since I wrote to you last in which he mentioned the letter he has lately received from you. His manner of speaking of it was very short and I thought that he appeared in this last conversation less warm and expressive of affection than before . . . the only thing I can conclude certainly from what passed between Mr. Pelham and myself is that I have no chance of the preferment asked and that Mr. Pelham found not the kindness he hoped for in your letter. I hope I take no improper liberty in mentioning this to you . . . but I think at present I have reason for what I say and therefore I have presumed to say it.

The letter is endorsed by Lord Townshend as answered on the 14th: 'But I did not keep any copy' — hardly a matter for much regret; the previous letters suffice as a sample of how correspondence was carried on between the two, whose style and modes Charles reproduced in many another correspondence in later life. Lord Townshend, however, made a further attempt, and on that day, 14 December, wrote to Newcastle, putting him in mind of his previous application on behalf of Charles, and asking that he should succeed Stanhope.[1] Newcastle replied on the 21st with a polite refusal and assurances that his brother (Henry Pelham) and he would in future be extremely glad to show their regard to one so deserving in himself 'and so very nearly related to us'.[2]

On 27 December George Townshend reported to Lord Townshend 'a very severe relapse' which Charles had 'just when he proposed to set out'; and on the 29th Lord Townshend begged him not to come to Raynham.[3]

After this a gap of four years intervenes in their correspondence extant at Raynham, and nothing appears about the steps which finally brought Charles into office: he was appointed to the Board of Trade in June 1749 — his re-election at Yarmouth was on the 19th, and the commission under the Great Seal naming the new Board is dated 23 June.[4] But during his first six months Townshend attended only about half its meetings, more probably owing to ill health than slackness; especially as during the next year he attended 110 out of a total of 140 meetings.[5] Lord Halifax, President of the Board 1748–61, was most active in its affairs and on its

[1] Add. MS. 32717, f. 444.
[2] *H.M.C., Townshend MSS.*, 367.
[3] Ibid., 368.
[4] *Board of Trade Journals, 1742–49*, 429.
[5] A. H. Basye, *The Lords of Trade and Plantations*, 221.

behalf, and Townshend became a favourite of his, and 'distinguished himself on affairs of trade, and in drawing plans and papers for that province'.[1] He worked hard and he worked quick, and during these five years at the Board became acquainted with colonial problems and formed his ideas concerning America. In the House, according to Horace Walpole,[2]

> Townshend's speeches for four or five years gave little indication of his amazing parts. They were studied, pedantic, and like the dissertations of Burke, with less brilliancy. When he attained his maturity he exceeded everybody.

Again, there was application and endeavour which at first made his speeches appear 'studied', but greatly added to their quality once he had found the way to master his material and had developed a style of his own. In the didactic letters which he later wrote to his step-son Henry, 3rd Duke of Buccleuch, when on his grand tour 1764–6, there are relevant autobiographical touches.[3] Thus on 23 July 1765:

> If you continue your diligence and persevere in your improvement, you will not only commence where most men conclude in knowledge and capacity, but you will find the same pursuits which to others are a labour, and the same business which to others is a science, an exercise and an amusement to yourself. If I may venture to recommend any one part of your present system of application to your particular attention, it should be the forming your language and habit of expression to some model which you shall yourself think suited to your temper and feel you can command readily. It is incredible how much the possession of this easy qualification tends to bring out a young man's ambition as well as his talents.... May I go one step farther, and tell you how much benefit I have found from translations[4] and still more, from occasionally preparing short speeches upon such incidents in history as have struck me and seemed analogous to events likely to occur in our own kingdom.

There follows a critical list of selected speeches and writings by ancient and modern British orators and authors, concluding with this somewhat elaborate peroration:

> Out of these several manners, make one for yourself; avoid the lavish ornament so vicious in Cicero; reject the frequent interrogatory too

[1] Walpole, *Memoirs of George II*, i. 340. [2] *Last Journals*, i. 82.

[3] Buccleuch MSS.

[4] Among his papers at Dalkeith House there are translations of Demosthenes and Cicero.

> habitual in Demosthenes; shun the obscure brevity and studied contrast of Tacitus; and having first, by the study of Lowth and a consideration of our best writers, laid the ground of a simple and accurate style, cover and adorn it with the tropes of Demosthenes, the amplification of Cicero, the bold moral of Tacitus, and the language which shall result from a careful perusal of the English writers I have named [Dr. Middleton, Locke, Harrington, Milton, and Clarendon].

As to Townshend's way of seeking information, it can be found in a sketch of him by William Knox — an expert on colonial matters in touch with Townshend 1763–7:[1]

> His manner of reading a book was curious. He turned over the leaves at the beginning extremely quick, first glancing at the middle of each page. 'That's all preface', says he. He then ran over the facts with more attention, and when he had gone through them, turned over the remainder of the leaves as he had done the beginning, saying, 'That's all conclusion, I can do that myself'; and he received oral information in the same manner, always confining the narrator to the fact.

(ii)

During Townshend's first six years in Parliament several speeches by him are recorded: he moved the Address at the opening of the session, 16 November 1749; spoke in favour of the subsidy treaty with Saxony, 22 January 1752;[2] and on Jamaica, 8 March 1753.[3] On a number of occasions he spoke on the business of his department.[4] But none of these speeches is reported at any length; his earliest noted by Horace Walpole, either in letters or the *Memoirs*, was on the Clandestine Marriage Bill, 21 May 1753. An avowed personal element entered into it. 'He spoke long and with much wit', wrote Walpole,[5] 'and drew a picture, with much humour at least, if not with much humility, of himself and his own situation, as the younger son of a capricious father who had already debarred him from an advantageous match. "Were new shackles to be forged to keep young men of abilities from mounting to a level with their elder brothers?" ' According to another report,[6]

[1] *H.M.C., Various Collections*, vi. 279–81.
[2] Walpole, *Memoirs of George II*, i. 243.
[3] Report from the French Embassy in London; Quai d'Orsay Archives, 'Correspondence Politique, Angleterre', vol. 436, ff. 10–18.
[4] L. F. Stock, *Proceedings and Debates of the British Parliament respecting North America*, v. 384–5 (6 February 1750), 430 (26 March 1750), 507 (23 May 1751), 509 (4 June 1751), 543 (9 May 1753).
[5] *Memoirs of George II*, i. 340–1.
[6] *Parliamentary History*, xv. 51–2.

he spoke of clandestine marriages between parties unequal in fortune: 'When the gentleman or lady of quality so marrying has no estate but what depends upon the goodwill of their parents, we know that parents are often by their pride and avarice rendered so cruel as to leave their child to starve rather than seem to approve of such a marriage.' Even marriages between equals 'such as parents ought to approve of, and would approve of if not governed by some whim or caprice', were often forbidden by the father's dissent.

In January 1753 Townshend had planned to marry — whom it does not appear — and turned to his father (in Lord Townshend's words) 'to make up the fortune of this match'. Lord Townshend replied on 20 January:[1]

> I am thoroughly sensible from what I have experienced from your constant and uniform conduct towards me that nothing I can offer on this occasion to dissuade you from your present scheme will or can have any effect. But give me leave to remind you that if your income in your present situation is so strait and severe as you represent, what a melancholy situation must you and your lady be in if you marry with the additional income of only £700 per annum at the most. . . . Advice from me is never agreeable to you nor would you ever throughout the whole course of your life hitherto attend to it, so that I shall not detain you long even on this occasion. . . .
>
> [The] scheme and project . . . is your own and I will have nothing to do with it.

Charles's own case was not really analogous to the cases covered by the Clandestine Marriage Bill; but the fact that the Bill increased the powers of parents or guardians over the marriage of their children or wards (if minors) sufficed to rouse him — and such was his performance that Horace Walpole makes it the occasion for introducing Townshend into his *Memoirs of the Reign of King George II*:[2]

> Charles Townshend [was] a young man of unbounded ambition, of exceeding application, and, as it now appeared, of abilities capable of satisfying that ambition, and of not wanting that application.

Not rising, however, 'in proportion to his ambition', he resorted to little arts, falsehoods, and stratagems. 'His figure was tall and advantageous, his action vehement, his voice loud, his laugh louder.

[1] *H.M.C., Townshend MSS.*, 381. [2] Vol. i, pp. 340–1.

He had art enough to disguise anything but his vanity.' Walpole thought him marked by nature for leadership (wherein he was wrong); he had 'quickness of genius', foresaw himself 'equal to anything', had no passion but ambition, and was impetuous, unsteady, yet indefatigable.

Townshend, having now stepped into the limelight, seems to have paid less attention to the routine work of his office. Even earlier his rate of attendance at Board of Trade meetings had dropped from nearly four-fifths in 1750 to just above half in 1751 and 1752; and in 1753 to one-third; and during the first three months of 1754 he attended only 12 out of 40 meetings. Henry Pelham died on 6 March 1754, and in the reshuffle of offices, undertaken before the General Election, Townshend ambitioned a seat at the Board of Treasury, 'stuck out for some time', but finished by accepting one at the Admiralty.[1]

At that election Townshend met with a strong opposition: John Ramey, a Yarmouth attorney, who in the past had acted as agent for the Townshend-Walpole interest in the borough, having been refused a place in the Customs, developed a grievance, primarily against Sir Edward Walpole, Townshend's colleague. He started building up his own party at Yarmouth, and the opposition soon turned against both Members. John Morse, a supporter of Townshend, wrote to him on 4 December 1753[2] that for days there had been a report that William Browne (a wealthy Yarmouth merchant and father-in-law of Ramey) would be a candidate.

> Today after a very pompous procession to the New Hall, Mr. Fuller [a neighbouring squire] made a speech to the freemen and recommended to their choice a townsman, and Mr. Browne was accordingly declared. I think this measure must fully convince you and put it out of all doubt who are your real friends and will most serve you . . . the whole force of the party against you will be united to give a majority both to Mr. Browne as well as to Mr. Fuller.

And Thomas Martin, another Townshend supporter, wrote to him on 26 January 1754:

> The enemies employ all their engines to produce a separation of your friends. . . . I know their cry is to turn out Sir Edward but I am not such a stranger to their policy but they would also drop you tomorrow, if they could have assurance of bringing in their men.

[1] Walpole, *Memoirs George II*, i. 421. [2] Buccleuch MSS.

Still, even in Newcastle's electoral survey, compiled about the middle of March, only Fuller is mentioned as contesting the borough against Townshend and Walpole.[1] But both went to the poll and after a hot and expensive contest Townshend received 541 votes, Walpole 518, Fuller 397, and Browne 342.

As was to be expected, Charles and his father quarrelled over the election. Lord Townshend, on the basis of information he had received from Yarmouth of Sir Edward Walpole's extreme unpopularity, advised Charles to break off the junction with him and stand singly; to which Charles replied on 17 November 1753, in a polite and friendly letter, that his father had been misinformed and that to break with Walpole would lose him more votes than he could possibly gain. Lord Townshend, who could never let slip an opportunity for contention with his son nor bear to appear to be in the wrong, claimed in a letter of 24 November that he had based his advice on what Charles had told him the previous summer and had acted, however mistakenly, in Charles's best interest.

> What is the return I receive from you? I am treated by you throughout the course of three sides of paper as if I had acted in a manner highly criminal and this treatment you give me to prove the truth of your declaration in the first part of your letter which is that *you must so far do justice to your constant endeavours to deserve my affection and good wishes as to declare with the utmost sincerity that receiving my love and regard for you has ever since you came into life been the chief though unsuccessful object of your ambition and care.* I shall not enter further into particulars upon so disagreeable a subject . . . more especially as I have found by a severe experience that nothing which I can say or do will be understood or received by you in a true light.

Despite this, and Charles's attack upon him in the House of Commons, Lord Townshend paid Charles's share of the election expenses. In January 1754, as he claimed at great inconvenience to himself, he had put £1000 at Charles's disposal but had stated in the most categorical terms that he would pay no more. Yet Charles's expenses came to £1900[2] and it seems that Lord Townshend was called upon for a further contribution — 'I cleared the whole charge of your election before I left London in November last', he wrote to Charles on 18 August 1755.[3]

[1] Add. MS 32995, ff. 75–80.

[2] John Morse to Charles Townshend, 2 June, 11 November 1754, Buccleuch MSS.

[3] Raynham MSS.

Another contest at this General Election indirectly impinges on Charles Townshend's future. At Great Bedwyn the dominant interest was in Lord Bruce and Lord Verney; and in the election lists as settled by Henry Pelham, Robert Brudenell and Lascelles Metcalfe appear as their candidates. 'They join in interest', wrote Newcastle about the two patrons in his electoral survey, 'and yet an opposition is apprehended'. And on 20 May:

> Mr. Brudenell and Lord Verney to be supported.
> Mr. Huske, General Huske's relation, makes a great opposition.
> General Huske to be spoken to by my Lord Cardigan [eldest brother of Robert Brudenell and Lord Bruce].

The Opposition candidates were William Sloper, whose family had an old interest in the borough and had repeatedly represented or contested it, and 'Captain Townshend', without doubt Roger Townshend, Charles's younger brother. In a further memorandum on 21 March Newcastle records that Brudenell 'declines joining in the expense', which 'will be £1600 each'; and again, 'That Mr. Huske is gone down making a great expense'; and lastly on 25 March,[1] 'It is supposed the two last [Sloper and Townshend] are supported from an unknown hand.'

Whose was that hand? Sloper's candidature was not surprising, and he was finally returned at the General Election. But mystery attaches to Roger Townshend's candidature, and to its promoter, John Huske, a tough adventurer of American origin, who came over to England in 1748 and was later closely associated with Charles Townshend. It seems certain that neither George nor Charles Townshend could have been his secret backers: it would have cut across their current alignments, and neither of them could have afforded the money. Nor would Lord Townshend have put it up. The 'unknown hand' is most probably Lady Townshend's: she had money of her own; Roger was her favourite child; and in the summer of 1757 she quite openly tried through Huske to secure Roger's election at Hull. Lastly, it is probable that Huske's connexion with the young Townshends started through his uncle General Huske who was their friend.[2] But Roger's candidature vanished as mysteriously as it had started.

Charles Townshend's notes for speeches on the Marriage Act of

[1] Add. MS 32995, f. 126. [2] *H.M.C., Townshend MSS.*, 309.

1753[1] include a paper on the legal position of minors in Scotland, on that of tutors and guardians, etc. He may have wanted the information solely for the purpose of Parliamentary debate, but possibly he was already contemplating marriage with Lady Dalkeith, eldest daughter of John, 2nd Duke of Argyll, widow of Lord Dalkeith (who died in 1750), and mother of Henry, 3rd Duke of Buccleuch (who succeeded his grandfather in 1751), a woman by nearly eight years his senior, but possessed of an ample fortune and further expectations. Lord Townshend, in a letter of 18 August 1755, reminded Charles that when he was

> at Raynham October last I told you I had heard a report that you was going to be married to Lady Dalkeith and the answer you made to me was that that affair was entirely off and that you should think no more of it, for that you had just before you had then left London received an offer of marriage from the relations of a Miss Warren who had a very large fortune in possession, I think you said upwards of £60,000, and who must have a lesser sum come to her on the death of her mother. This is all I ever heard you say of your marriage with Lady Dalkeith.

By July 1755 the match had again become the talk of London. Still, it was not till 16 August that Charles approached his father on the matter: his letter has not been traced, but some passages from it are quoted in his father's of the 18th:

> You inform me by your letter [wrote Lord Townshend] that the lady you have contracted with is Lady Dalkeith. She is certainly I acknowledge a lady of high rank and fortune and that an alliance with a family of such great rank is what must be very desireable. You further inform me that her present jointure and income is £3000 net receipt, which will be increased to £5000 net receipt at the death of the Duchess of Argyll now 78 years of age, and that she has besides to dispose of in money and personal estate about £46,000, £30,000 of which you are empowered by her to say she will settle on you if the marriage takes place, and that she has besides very large and probable expectations from the Duchess of Argyll.... You write that the Duchess of Argyll and the Duke of Argyll[2] gave *their consent to you last week and desired you to wait on me, and at the same time that you expressed their consent to inform yourself of my opinion and disposition upon this matter.*

What Charles wrote to ask of his father was such a settlement 'as will prevent the opportunity from being lost'.

[1] Buccleuch MSS. [2] Archibald, 3rd Duke, uncle of Lady Dalkeith.

Financial demands from Charles usually exasperated Lord Townshend, and the present stung him to the quick. His reply starts with a page of reproaches:

> I have done everything in my power to deserve your affection, esteem, and regard, but . . . have not ever received any grateful return from you. The compliances I have at any time made to your requests have not in your opinion . . . arose from a generous and good natured disposition in my temper but from the magic quality of your great abilities. . . . All the returns I have had has been that of finding that my thoughts and actions have been made the subject of your ridicule and supposed wit.

Charles, he argued, only came to him when wanting money. After he had cleared Charles's election expenses in November, from then 'to the present time I have not been worthy of your notice'. And as for the new claim: his income is 'so narrow and reduced' that it is not in his power to comply with the request — 'if you had common humanity towards me you . . . would not ask me to do it.' He has 'a power to raise £20,000 for fortunes for my younger children'; one-third is 'in round thousands no more than £6000'. Even if circumstances allowed him to assume that charge

> this £6000 . . . would be no more than a mere grain of Norfolk sand to Lady Dalkeith's great affluence of fortune. . . . But however that be I say again that I cannot give anything and that I will not give anything, and shall conclude my answer to your letter with this observation, that out of nothing nothing can be had.

And in a postscript: uncertain of Charles's London address he directs this letter to him 'at Lady Townshend's at Richmond in Surrey'. This is the first sign so far found of Charles having drawn closer to his mother.

Charles replied a week later from the house of the Duchess of Argyll at Adderbury in Oxfordshire.

> My present situation cannot but be a state of extreme anxiety, as, upon the event of this affair absolutely depends the future comfort and colour of my life, but I am also sensible I have already expressed myself as fully upon every part of this subject as I have any pretence to do, and therefore I will not add anything further upon it.

In the end Charles received £8000, out of the £20,000 available for Lord Townshend's younger children: £6000 plus the £2000 remaining from a division of £20,000 between the three younger children. In return Charles gave his sister Audrey a deed of indemnity for her share of the £2000 'in case her fortune from Lord Townshend should not be equal to mine' (no such indemnity to Roger, his younger brother, is mentioned). The marriage took place on 18 September 1755, and on 25 September Lord Townshend wrote to congratulate Charles — presumably he had not been present at the ceremony. It marks virtually the end of all attempts to maintain friendly relations between father and son. In a bitter letter to his mother of 29 December, Charles wrote that the haggle over his marriage settlement 'has made me firmly resolve to withdraw from every family transaction as a sort of business in which I never act unhurt, be my conduct ever so exact or careful'; further, 'Lord Townshend refuses to see me and the reason he gives for it is my having had more fortune from him than he designed to give me, to the prejudice of my sister.'

Horace Walpole wrote to Richard Bentley, 17 July 1755, 'Charles Townshend marries the great Dowager Dalkeith: his parts and presumption are prodigious. He wanted nothing but independence to let him loose: I propose great entertainment from him; and now, perhaps, the times will admit it.'

CHAPTER III

Junior Minister
1754-1760

(i)

In August 1753 instructions of a rather unusual character were issued to Sir Danvers Osborn, Governor of New York[1] — Horace Walpole, writing about 1755, described them as 'better calculated for the latitude of Mexico and for a Spanish tribunal, than for a free, rich British settlement'.[2] These instructions Charles Townshend subsequently avowed in the House to have 'advised', that is, to have drafted.[3] They charged the New York Assembly with trampling upon the royal authority and prerogative by assuming 'to themselves the disposal of public money'; directed it to make permanent provision for the salaries of the Governor, judges, and other officials; and for the security of the province and any foreseeable charges. The money was to be applied by warrants from the Governor advised by the Council, the Assembly being merely permitted 'from time to time to view and examine... accounts'. In short, the royal executive was to be rendered financially independent of the colonial Assembly. A re-modelling of colonial government was Townshend's aim, to which the raising of a revenue by Act of the British Parliament became a necessary corollary.

In 1754 undeclared war between the British and French in the backwoods of North America raised the problem of how to muster against the centralised power of the French Governor the strength of the numerically much superior but disunited British colonies. On 19 June, with Lord Halifax's approval, commissioners from seven northern colonies met at Albany, and in July voted a plan of union which was not, however, submitted to the Board of Trade

[1] For their text see *Gentleman's Magazine*, 1754, pp. 65–6, and L. W. Labaree, *Royal Instructions to British Colonial Governors, 1670–1776*, i. 190–3.
[2] *Memoirs of George II*, i. 397.
[3] Ibid., ii. 173; debate of 20 February 1756.

till 24 October, and was not accepted by the colonial Assemblies. But a day before the Albany Congress met, on 18 June, a letter from the Secretary of State, Sir Thomas Robinson, was read at a meeting of the Board of Trade, directing them 'to prepare and lay before his Majesty a plan of general concert to be entered into by the American colonies for their mutual defence'.[1] This, with a representation to the King and a letter to the Secretary of State, was ready on 9 August,[2] and on the 15th Halifax communicated them to Newcastle, to avoid the delays of official circulation and to enable him to consult Hardwicke, the Lord Chancellor, who was about to leave London.[3] Newcastle hastened to do so;[4] but he also consulted Charles Townshend — a curious step seeing that only some four months earlier Townshend had been a junior member of Halifax's Board.

The Board of Trade's plan was for the colonies to appoint commissioners to meet and consider the needs of their joint defence and estimate the cost. 'The commissioners are then to agree on the proportion to be paid by each colony, having regard to the number of inhabitants, trade, wealth, and revenue of each colony, as shown in their accounts.' The Commander-in-Chief, appointed by the Crown, would be responsible for the expenditure of the money, and would present fresh annual estimates to the commissioners. The proceedings of the commissioners were to be laid before the King, and their actions to be subject to the approval of the Governors, Councils, and Assemblies of the provinces.

'It is my opinion', wrote Townshend on 13 September,[5] 'that the plan begins a great work in a wrong manner'; and he concluded his letter with an effusive declaration of attachment to Newcastle:

> It is always a great satisfaction to me to be employed by your Grace, and I shall think it the honour of my life if in anything I shall be thought by you to be of any degree of service or deserve your notice.

His 'Remarks upon the Plan for a General Concert', together with his covering letter, are an early exposé of his guiding ideas on the policy and measures to be pursued in America. He explains the delay in sending the enclosed papers to Newcastle by having waited 'for a perfect copy of the bill designed to have been brought into Parliament in 1710 for raising a permanent revenue in America by the act of the British legislature'. This he quotes

[1] *Journal of the Board of Trade*, 1754–68, p. 49.
[2] Ibid., p. 65.
[3] Add. MS. 32736, ff. 243–5, and enclosures, ff. 247–56.
[4] For Hardwicke's reply of 25 August, see ibid., ff. 340–3.
[5] Ibid., ff. 508–13.

> as a precedent of what the Administration of that time had resolved to have done if the province of New York had not been induced, by the fear of incurring such an act of Parliament, to provide for the public security and service in a manner the Crown approved. The articles of trade specified in that bill were ill chosen, because it is certainly bad policy to encumber with duties those exports which facilitate and extend our American commerce, but the plan of the bill is doubtless right as it professes to regulate a disordered colony and obliges them by the authority and necessary superintendency of the mother country to provide for their own safety and our interest in it.

He enclosed a rough sketch of how best to employ the British forces in America.

> I have also thrown together with more heat and less accuracy than I could have wished some of the many objections I have to the scheme of a general union which your Grace has done me the honour to entrust me with.

'Whatever is done, can only be done by an act of Parliament', which the colonies were more likely to accept than to form a plan in any meeting of their deputies or in their Assemblies. 'I shall endeavour to prepare such a plan for your Grace against your return with a fund which all the provinces will, I am certain, approve and cheerfully pay.' No such plan has been found among the Newcastle MSS. But here are the most telling of Townshend's objections to the plan submitted by the Board of Trade — and this did not go by any means the length of the Albany plan of union:

> It makes the duty of the commissioners so very expensive and intricate that it makes the commission itself almost impracticable. . . . It is not probable that the number of men required in the commission will be found in all the colonies in themselves and from their capacities proper for the execution of it. . . . It is . . . impossible to imagine that so many different representatives of so many different provinces, divided in interest and alienated by jealousy and inveterate prejudice, should ever be able to resolve upon a plan of mutual security and reciprocal expense. . . . Some of the least peopled and considerable colonies are most connected with large tribes of Indians and most exposed to an invasion, while the most peopled and more flourishing are most remote from the danger. . . . It will be difficult to persuade the more wealthy colonies not immediately interested to take upon them the charge of defending their neighbours upon their own allegation of their own inability.

Even if the commissioners were able to reach agreement, Townshend had a telling argument against entrusting them with the raising of a revenue in America:

> I am certain the Assemblies of the provinces will never pass the act of supply requisite to support the scheme of union in such a manner as his Majesty may confirm it. It is well known to those who have attended to the affairs of America that the provinces have for many years been engaged in a settled design of drawing to themselves the ancient and established prerogatives wisely preserved in the Crown as the only means of supporting and continuing the superintendency of the mother country, and their manner of doing this has been by their annual bills of supply, in which they have appointed all the officers of the Crown by name to be employed in the Exchequer, substituted warrants for drawing out public money in the place of the Governor's, and in one word dispossessed the Crown of almost every degree of executive power ever lodged in it; it is as certain that whenever the bill of supply to follow this scheme of a general concert is passed, the same provinces will insert into it the same scheme of encroachments, and then the Crown will be reduced either to purchase this security to the colonies by sacrificing our only security for their dependence upon us, or to have a partial supply in consequence of a general fund to be settled, or to drop the whole design of a union upon this plan.

Townshend understood earlier than most of his contemporaries that sovereignty went hand in hand with the power of the purse, but in 1754 the time was not yet ripe for his plan to maintain the supremacy of the parent country over its American children.

Townshend's two speeches recorded by Horace Walpole during the session 1754–5 hardly bear out the declarations of fervent attachment to Newcastle which he made when flattered by being consulted on American affairs: he followed his own inclinations and views for the future without regard to the line adopted by the Government.

The first speech, on 11 December 1754,[1] was in a debate on the new clause in the Mutiny Bill subjecting the regiments to be raised in America to the military discipline of the British army: which was deemed unsuitable by opponents in view of the very different type of men expected to enlist over there for the defence of their homes. Lord Egmont, though about to take office, 'could

[1] Walpole, *Memoirs of George II*, i. 421–2.

not resist the impulse of haranguing against a Mutiny Bill'; and Charles Townshend,

> hurt at a new promotion over his head, started up, and not considering how indecent it was in him, a little Minister, to discourage renegades, fell with warmth and insolence and eloquence on Lord Egmont . . . then panegyrized the Board of Trade, defended all their acts, even the instructions to Sir Danvers Osborn; and, turning again to Lord Egmont, bade him take the poor American by the hand, and point out his grievances; his lordship was able, and used to be willing to bring out grievances; he had threatened he would; yet he defied him — if that would not do, he beseeched him — to point out one grievance; for his part, he did not know of one; he should be glad to learn why his lordship did not intend to mention one *now*; and then, in the most provoking manner, and in terms most intelligible, he attacked him on the place he was going to accept.

The second speech, on 26 February 1755,[1] was in direct opposition to a Ministerial measure, and forecast the interest Townshend was shortly to acquire in Scotland and its affairs. It was proposed that the Act, passed seven years before and about to expire, subjecting the Scottish sheriffs-depute to the King's pleasure, should continue some time longer. Townshend warmly opposed it; argued that their independence as judges 'was a case connected with everything sacred, and hoped that the most habitually-attached to a Ministry, who are generally the most unfeeling, would think on this'; called the measure 'a breach of faith to Scotland'; and claimed that he himself 'neither meant ambition nor courted popularity, but looked upon himself as an executor of those who had planned the Revolution'.

(ii)

As Horace Walpole had forecast, the times were ripe for Townshend's parts and presumption to be revealed to their fullest extent. The Duke of Newcastle, who in March 1754 had succeeded his brother Henry Pelham as head of Administration, was running into difficulties; and in October 1755, in order to meet Pitt's attack on his foreign policy, secured the appointment of Henry Fox as Secretary of State and Leader of the House of Commons. Even George Townshend, who in March had taken an active part in the House on the side of Administration, was put off by the new

[1] Ibid., ii. 5.

arrangement;[1] and Newcastle, in a letter to Hardwicke of 18 October, when reviewing 'our line of battle in the House of Commons', classed the two Townshends as 'doubtful'.[2] But apparently he still made an attempt to retain Charles's support by promoting him to the seat at the Treasury Board he had previously asked for. Audrey Townshend wrote to her father on 26 October:

> My brother Charles has been a week in town. He returns to Adderbury this morning very far from well. He has refused the Treasury which the Duke of Newcastle offered him, but it is his opinion that things will be made up before the meeting of the Parliament. If so, I suppose Charles may be so good as to accept of the office.

Although this offer is nowhere directly mentioned in the Newcastle MSS., it appears from a note from Robert Nugent to Newcastle, 6 November 1755, that the Duke must have considered promoting Townshend:[3]

> Mr. Nugent . . . takes the liberty to inform his Grace of a circumstance relating to Mr. C. Townshend, necessary for him to know. Mr. Nugent has been told that a re-election at Yarmouth will be attended with great difficulty and hazard.

Things were not 'made up'; Charles Townshend did not appear at the meeting of Government supporters at the Cockpit on 12 November, the night before the opening of Parliament; and on 13 November, on the division on the Address, both Townshends voted with Pitt against the Government. On 20 November Pitt and his associates in the House of Commons, Legge and George Grenville, were dismissed from the King's service. Thereupon, wrote Horace Walpole, 'Charles Townshend made an offer to Mr. Pitt (which being offered could not be accepted) of resigning; Mr. Pitt . . . thanked him, but said he desired nobody to resign on his account'.[4]

During the first fortnight in December Charles Townshend, while still retaining his place at the Admiralty Board, took a prominent part in debates on the Opposition side. On 2 December he 'spoke severely and admirably on the long acquiescence of the Administration under the insults of France, and on the similar acquiescence of Parliament'; 'submission, miscalled moderation'.[5]

[1] George Townshend to Newcastle, 15 October 1755, Add. MS. 32860, ff. 54–5.
[2] Ibid., f. 89.
[3] Ibid., f. 389.
[4] *Memoirs of George II*, ii. 62–3.
[5] Ibid., 80–1.

On the 5th he described 'the melancholy state of America', where 'the plan of Lord Halifax, so singular in his attention, had been embraced', but not supported; and French encroachments had been tolerated; if measures were not changed, the situation would become 'incapable of amendment by honester hearts and wiser heads'. According to Walpole, Townshend in fact planned a campaign against the Ministry 'for their tame and negligent administration of the plantations'.[1] In the crucial debate of 12 December on the subsidy treaties with Hesse and Russia, Townshend spoke against the Ministry for three-quarters of an hour 'with infinite rapidity, vehemence, and parts'; reviewed the international situation, with a hit against Newcastle when referring to 'the little petulant mechanic activity sometimes seen in the persons of some Ministers'; and apostrophised the House in his peroration: 'Show that you are not under any one man; show you are not part of his retinue; that you are without *superiors*.'[2] According to Charles Yorke, abuse of Hume Campbell and the Duke of Newcastle was the purpose of Townshend's speech.[3] Hume Campbell, replying to Townshend, remarked that 'the former adulation' of some 'was turned to run the race of invective'; while Pitt, refusing the description of invective for everything 'that had not the smoothness of a Court compliment', said that Charles Townshend 'had displayed such abilities as had not appeared since that House was a House'.[4] Parliament rose for Christmas on 23 December; and in the changes made during the recess, Townshend was dismissed from his office.

At the end of this session, Horace Walpole wrote when discussing the foremost speakers in the House:[5]

> Charles Townshend astonished; but was too severe to persuade, and too bold to convince.... Neither caring whether himself or others were in the right, [he] only spoke to show how well he could adorn a bad cause, or demolish a good one. It was frequent with him, as soon as he had done speaking, to run to the opposite side of the House, and laugh with those he had attacked, at those who had defended.

He was admired 'without the least mixture of esteem'.

> Charles Townshend had such openness in all his behaviour, that he seemed to think duplicity the simplest conduct: he made the innocence

[1] Ibid., 94, 96. [2] Ibid., 121–5.
[3] Charles Yorke to Hardwicke, 13 December 1755, Add. MS. 35353, f. 183.
[4] Walpole, *Memoirs of George II*, ii. 125–6, 132. [5] Ibid., ii. 147–8.

of others look like art. But what superiority does integrity contract, when even uniformity of acting could exalt so many men above the most conspicuous talents that appeared in so rhetorical an age! Mr. Townshend was perhaps the only man who had ever genius enough to preserve reason and argument in a torrent of epigrams, satire, and antithesis.

And on 4 March 1756 in a letter to Henry Seymour Conway:

> Nothing is luminous compared with Charles Townshend: he drops down dead in a fit, has a resurrection, thunders in the Capitol, confounds the Treasury bench, laughs at his own party, is laid up the next day, and overwhelms the Duchess and the good women that go to nurse him!

About Charles's treatment of his wife and his wife's family, Walpole wrote to Conway on 22 January 1756:

> You will be entertained with the riot Charles makes in the sober house of Argyll: t'other night, on the Duchess's bawling to Lady Suffolk, he in the very same tone cried out 'Large stewing oysters!' When he takes such liberties with his new parent, you may judge how little decency he observes with his wife: last week at dinner at Lord Strafford's, on my Lady Dalkeith's mentioning some dish that she loved, he replied before all the servants, 'Yes, my Lady Dalkeith, you love it better than anything but one!'

When Parliament re-assembled, Townshend, 'a perfect master of our West Indian affairs and history',[1] and knowledgeable on America, took again a prominent part in debates on measures for their defence.[2] The Newcastle–Fox Government proposed to raise four Swiss battalions to be blended with colonial levies, and in that connexion on 10 February 1756 brought in a Bill enabling foreign officers to hold commissions in America for the duration of the war. This Charles Townshend opposed at every stage; on 18 February presented a petition from William Bollan, agent for Massachusetts, against it, alleging that the measure would 'in a great degree prevent his Majesty's natural subjects from entering his Majesty's service';[3] and according to Walpole, on 18 February would have produced 'a detail of grievances that he had prepared on American affairs' had not Fox pinned him down by an apposite reference to his challenge to Egmont on 11 December 1754 to

[1] Ibid., ii. 157.
[2] Ibid., 154, 157–8, 162–3, 170–6.
[3] *Commons Journals*, 27, 457–8.

name a single such grievance. On the third reading of the Bill, 26 February,[1]

> Charles Townshend, in a fine, animated, and provoking speech, tried to make them break silence, taunting the majority with following leaders who would not vouchsafe to give them reasons, reproaching the Ministers with the insult of their silence, and calling on the new placemen to give some proofs of being fit for their posts.

After the Bill had passed the Lords, Temple and Talbot signed a protest, according to Walpole 'in words drawn by Charles Townshend'.[2] If so — and the statement is probably correct — their protest shows how Townshend could speak for the colonies when it suited his book: they blame Administration for 'the present neglected, defenceless, and calamitous state of our American colonies'; fear that 'not only the defence, but the civil liberties of America would be entrusted to foreigners'; and when 'this measure shall be thoroughly known and considered in America' expect it to prove impracticable for it will excite 'a deep and universal disgust and apprehension in the minds of his Majesty's most loyal and deserving American subjects, where such eminent services have lately been voluntarily performed by several of the northern colonies'.

When the Newcastle-Fox Government was brought down by the loss of Minorca, and Pitt, at the end of October and beginning of November 1756, was forming a new Administration with the Duke of Devonshire at the head of the Treasury, Charles Townshend naturally expected office commensurate with the prominence he had achieved in the House. James, 2nd Earl Waldegrave, an eminently fair-minded, level-headed, and disinterested man, who as the King's confidant was in the thick of negotiations 1756–7, says in his *Memoirs*,[3] written shortly after the events, that Pitt provided for his friends 'in proportion to their interest or their abilities'.

> There was, indeed, one exception; Charles Townshend being made Treasurer of the Chambers, though he seemed fully qualified for a more active employment.

[1] Walpole, *Memoirs of George II*, ii. 174, dates it 'two days' after the debate of 20 February, which is impossible: 22 February was a Sunday; see also *Commons Journals*, 27, 481, and James West's report to Newcastle, Thursday, 26 February, 5 o'clock: 'Mr. Charles Townshend is now calling on persons to justify the bill, declaring their silence is insolence to the House and will be meanness in the majority to follow' (Add. MS. 32863, f. 107).

[2] *Memoirs of George II*, ii. 176.

[3] Pp. 86–7.

> But Pitt did not choose to advance a young man to a ministerial office, whose abilities were of the same kind, and so nearly equal to his own.
>
> Both had fine natural parts; both were capable of great application: which was the greater master of abuse could not easily be determined: and if there was something more awful and compulsive in Pitt's oratory, there was more acuteness and more wit in Charles Townshend's.

Horace Walpole records a story which, even if not accurate in every detail, illustrates the spirit of the transaction.[1] Pitt, he says, in discussing the future Government with Devonshire,

> seemed solicitous to provide only for his allies the Grenvilles. . . . He even affected to have forgot Charles Townshend, and, as if recollecting himself, cried, 'Oh! there is one that will not like to be at the bottom of the list.' The mediator-Duke took care this neglect should not be a secret.

At an early stage in the negotiations Pitt seems to have decided to make Townshend Treasurer of the Chamber, a Court sinecure: his name appears against it already in Pitt's list of his Ministry enclosed in Fox's letter to Devonshire of 1 November[2]— how Fox obtained it is not known, but the list is singularly accurate.

On 2 November Richard Lyttelton, a relative and friend of Pitt's, wrote to him about Charles Townshend's intrigues and manœuvres:[3]

> He . . . goes out of town tomorrow not to return unless his brother should send for him; professing support and attachment to you, but a *determination* not to accept any office . . . that is not an office of business; and represents his conversation with you this morning as explicitly left upon that footing for your guidance with the Duke of Devonshire. . . . In short, it appears to me that he does not like his situation in the arrangement; is determined his brother shall not like it, either for him or for himself; and hopes by holding back and intimidating you from undertaking, to get a higher thing, Treasurer of the Navy at least, six weeks hence.

A week later, 9 November, Temple reported to Pitt 'a very disagreeable scene' between Richard Lyttelton, James Grenville, and the two Townshends,

[1] *Memoirs of George II*, ii. 264.
[2] Devonshire MSS.
[3] *Chatham Correspondence*, i. 180–2.

in which Charles was a principal actor, which ended, however, very peacably, and promises to go on still better provided the place of Cofferer can be procured for Charles. This is now made by them (the Townshends) a *sine qua non*, and reclaimed as a promise, the breach of which is to be deemed a violation of our private honour. . . . If the Cofferer's place can be obtained, the Townshends are to be most friendly, etc.

And on 11 November, twelve at night:

The great difficulty of the Cofferer subsisting, Lord Bute took upon himself to go to Mr. Charles Townshend, who was gone to Sudbrooke, it seems: not finding him, he then proceeded to George's, and enforced with him in the strongest manner every argument for his brother's acceptance of Treasurer of the Chamber, which is, in every respect, exactly equal to the Cofferer. At last, the Prince of Wales's name was used, and with such effect that George Townshend is determined to push it with his brother to the uttermost, not to break such a public measure upon so slight and unjustifiable foundation, etc. Charles's answer is not yet come.

Pitt certainly showed not much esteem, trust, or affection for Charles Townshend, and could hardly expect from him much gratitude, which anyhow was not his strong suit.

Next there was the question of Charles's re-election in case he took office. His brother George wrote to him about it at length on 24 November.[1] He was invited to stand for Norwich, 'but this will most probably be a most expensive and precarious undertaking — and *où trouver tant d'argent?*'[2] Lord Orford had hoped to bring him in at Callington, but the patronage was in his mother. And George concludes:

With respect to your acceptance of a place, do whatever you like. If the Government can't bring you in elsewhere and you think your re-election at Yarmouth precarious, tell them at once in plain terms your situation and let the sole motive of your declining it appear to arise from that difficulty, which may annihilate you as a Member of Parliament. If on the contrary you can come in again for Yarmouth, I will bear any part of the expense and borrow money to pay you directly, for I think it a pity it should really happen, or a disgrace that it should be said that we were instrumental in defeating the efforts of this or that Administration for the difference of this or that office.

[1] Buccleuch MSS.

[2] On Norwich see also letter from N. Thompson and others to Charles Townshend, 28 November 1756, ibid.

And Lord Orford, in a letter dated 'Monday',[1] told him that Lady Orford had already made her choice at Callington; thought Charles's re-election at Yarmouth 'very insecure, unless we can bring over Browne and his party'; and anyhow advised Charles 'to push the Ministry ... for a Government seat, as I hope you will have frequent occasions to be re-chosen'.

In the end, Townshend was returned for the Admiralty borough of Saltash on 14 December 1756. He undoubtedly expected further promotion, and, not over-keen on the post allotted to him, could at least insist on this additional advantage.[2]

George Townshend was passionately interested in the militia, and in the Bill he was promoting to establish it: wherein he had Pitt's support; and he hated the Duke of Cumberland and his political agent, Fox. Charles, writes Walpole,[3] bore no 'inveteracy to Fox; he left all bitterness to his brother; and was content with promoting confusion'. He assisted George, who acted with Pitt's knowledge, in managing the Parliamentary inquiry into the loss of Minorca; together with him met a representative body of Tories to settle the method of carrying it on;[4] but whereas George and the Tories meant to direct it foremost against Fox, Charles was attacking Newcastle — his reason for doing so is not apparent. On 7 February 1757 he took independent action which the others disliked, fearing it might drive Newcastle to unite with Fox: he attacked the victualling contracts for the troops in America concluded by the Treasury with Alderman William Baker, M.P.; put the loss on them to 1756, at over £72,000, and at more for the future;[5] and fell severely on Newcastle 'whom he abused, with more outrage than wit, in a very florid strain of satiric irony'.[6] But when the inquiry into the contracts was concluded James West wrote to Newcastle on 14 March:[7]

[1] Ibid. Its date must have been 22 November: George Townshend in his letter refers to Orford having written to Charles.

[2] See also Fox's letters to Devonshire (Devonshire MSS., docketed 20 and 25 November — should be 21 and 26) in which the question of Townshend's replacing William Sloper at Great Bedwyn was discussed.

[3] *Memoirs of George II*, ii. 155.

[4] See Sir Roger Newdigate's pocket diary for 1757, under 14 January and 1 February (Newdigate MSS. in the Warwick County Record Office); also George Townshend to Pitt, 15 January, *Chatham Correspondence*, i. 216–17.

[5] For the fullest account of Townshend's contentions, the examination of witnesses, and Baker's reply, see Newdigate MS. B2535.

[6] Walpole, *Memoirs of George II*, ii. 304.

[7] Add. MS. 32870, f. 275.

I wish your Grace joy of the greatest day that ever happened to a Minister out of place. We not only carried the question in the committee but reported it without a division and almost without a negative except the two Mr. Townshends and Alderman Beckford.... Alderman Baker stated his case well and clearly and called on evidence to prove the impossibility of getting the provisions in America, and another to the real price he paid in Ireland for many species of them. Mr. Charles Townshend summed up the evidence and said he brought it before them on the intelligence he had received and moved no question.

And in a postscript:

Charles Townshend has invited Lord Register [Alexander Hume Campbell], Lord Dupplin, Sir Thomas Robinson, Baker, and your humble servant, to dinner. I believe he will not be unwilling to be a manager for the late Ministry in the next inquiry.

Charles, out of humour with Pitt, had recently been steering a more than usually erratic course. He took no part in the heated debates on Byng's trial, but on the last day, 28 February 1757, when after some severe altercations between Pitt and Fox the latter withdrew a motion against the Bill to empower members of Byng's court martial to declare their intentions in pronouncing him guilty, Charles Townshend, according to Horace Walpole,[1]

said, to the surprise of everybody, that he intended to second Fox, but was content too. He congratulated the House on obtaining these grounds for their proceedings by Mr. Fox's means. His brother, offended at this wonderful declaration, told him, if he had been present the first day, he would not have wanted those grounds. Charles appealed to the House if first, second, or third day, they had been so fully explained. Pitt, still more provoked, said, with the utmost contempt, and with the most marked accent, no man of common sense or common integrity could say this matter had been opened on any other foundation — yet he wished Charles Townshend joy that *his conscience* was made easy....

Fox, sneering and insulting, said, he was glad Mr. Pitt had heard commendations of him from Mr. Charles Townshend.

To which Walpole adds the footnote: 'Mr. Pitt, loud enough to be heard by half the House, cried out, "I wish you joy of him!" '

When next the King, vexed by the behaviour of Pitt and Temple over Byng, had Fox sounded whether he would not act with Newcastle, Fox wrote to his brother, Lord Ilchester, on 4 March when

[1] *Memoirs of George II*, ii. 349–50.

outlining his scheme of a new Government:[1] 'I would have Charles Townshend, who has left his brother and Pitt, Secretary at War.' But he added: 'Probably they won't make Charles Townshend Secretary at War.' This is the earliest indication so far found that Townshend wished for that office which, at that time, he could only have obtained and held with the goodwill of the Duke of Cumberland, Captain-General of the Army, his brother's bitter enemy; and it is probably this which made Fox doubt whether the appointment would prove possible. Waldegrave who, as he states in his *Memoirs*,[2] was to be kept fully informed and lay the new scheme of Government before the King, names Charles Townshend among 'the persons who were to have the refusal of the principal employments'; and when showing the list to the King remarked that 'most of them were good speakers in Parliament, and that oratory was now esteemed the first quality of a Minister'. In view of a general disinclination to undertake the task, the scheme fell through.

> Charles Townshend [writes Waldegrave] hated Pitt, and disliked his employment, which was almost a sinecure. Yet did not think it advisable to undertake the defence of an old king, or to be connected with unpopular associates.

When on 5 and 6 April Temple and Pitt were dismissed from office, and their relatives and friends consequently resigned, Charles Townshend hung back. But when a fortnight later a report was spread that he had resigned, he called on Devonshire, who had remained at the Treasury, to communicate to him 'a matter of some delicacy affecting my present situation'. Not having found the Duke at home, he wrote[3] to assure him, 'however I may think upon this subject, that I should never take such a step without your knowledge'. The letter, in spite of its elaborate involutions and effusive declarations of attachment to Devonshire, clearly showed that Townshend was thinking of resigning; and three days later, on 22 April,[4] he wrote again, this time asking the Duke to obtain for him permission to do so.

> The considerations upon which I presume to make this request are so far disagreeable to me as they carry me from his Majesty's service . . .

[1] Lord Ilchester, *Letters to Henry Fox*, 103.
[2] Pp. 102–5.
[3] Devonshire MSS.
[4] Ibid. There is a copy of this letter in the Buccleuch MSS.

> but at the same time they are such as do, from the nature of them, oblige me at this juncture with all humility to solicit his Majesty's favourable acceptance of my resignation.

Walpole may be right when saying[1] that Townshend in his letter to Devonshire

> avoided as much as possible to have it thought that he quitted from attachment to Pitt. Resigning with him, and yet not for him, Townshend thought entitled him to be restored with Pitt, yet would not subject him to the King's displeasure.

During the next two months of entangled, kaleidoscopic negotiations to find a way out of the *impasse* of Cabinet crises, the two Townshends played no part, and, indeed, are hardly ever mentioned. Charles was without a friend among the chief negotiators to press his claims: neither Pitt nor Newcastle nor Fox was under any obligation to him; and in his rather forlorn condition he seems to have clung to Devonshire whose chief desire was to be released from active office. It was not till the negotiations carried on by Pitt and Bute with Newcastle and Hardwicke were nearing conclusion, that the question of office for Charles seems to have come under serious consideration.

Lord Dupplin wrote to Newcastle's nephew, Lord Lincoln, on 16 June 1757, reporting progress made in those negotiations:[2]

> This day . . . Charles Townshend was likewise at Newcastle House, and while he was there Mr. Pitt himself came in. Charles declared to the Duke of Newcastle and Mr. Pitt that if Lord George Sackville was not Secretary at War he would be contented to be Treasurer of the Chambers. But if Lord George Sackville was Secretary at War, he would not take that office and would be displeased if he were Treasurer of the Navy — so ended his private story.

The next day, Friday 17 June, at five o'clock, Charles Townshend wrote to Devonshire asking to see him 'this evening or tomorrow morning' — he had something to tell the Duke 'that you will not be displeased to hear'; he concluded the letter: 'I am, with the most real friendship, even in these times when friendship has so few friends, etc.' What it was he had to report is not clear. For it was only two hours later that Pitt wrote inviting George

[1] *Memoirs of George II*, iii. 2.
[2] Newcastle (Clumber) MSS., Nottingham University Library.

Townshend to call on him the next morning between ten and eleven.[1] Pitt's letter starts:

> Though I can have nothing to inform you of relating to the Duke of Newcastle's transactions, in order to a junction, which you are not acquainted with from his Grace, I should be extremely happy of an opportunity to have some conversation with you on a subject which but just now has taken its final and conclusive turn, and must receive a negative or affirmative answer.

The letter did not mention Charles whom, however, George carried with him to the interview. On 20 June, before leaving London, George Townshend endorsed Pitt's letter with the following memorandum:

> This was the first time for about a fortnight I had heard anything from Mr. Pitt, during which time the negotiation for a Ministry went on in his and Lord Bute's, the Duke of Newcastle's and Lord Hardwicke's hands. On the Friday night, June the 18th, 1757, I received this letter, and the next morning waited on him with my brother, and to our astonishment heard him avow the ridiculous and dishonest arrangement of men which is now to take place — not the least adoption of any public system of measures being declared or even hinted at by him.
>
> Upon this occasion I without hesitation declared my resolution to be no part of it — my brother did the same.

The fullest account of the interview appears in a newsletter from Richard Rigby to the Duke of Bedford:[2]

> Now a word concerning the Townshends, who were (both brothers) this morning with Mr. Pitt. He told them how matters were settled; that he was going to the King; asked George Townshend if he might name him to his Majesty for any employment, and hoped things had his approbation. His answer was that he would take nothing; that he had *a friend or two* by whom he would make his sentiments known to his Majesty; that he had not been consulted till it was too late; that he had neither approbation or disapprobation, or anything left but admiration. And then, turning to Charles, the new Secretary said he hoped he might mention him again for Treasurer of the Chambers. He replied that he already was Treasurer of the Chambers; that he had no thoughts at this time of resigning that employment; but that

[1] *H.M.C., Townshend MSS.* 393. The letter is dated by Pitt 'Friday 7 o'clock', which is erroneously expanded in George Townshend's endorsement into 'Friday night June the 18th 1757' — 18 June was a Saturday. The wrong date is accepted by the editor.

[2] *Bedford Correspondence*, ii. 251–2.

> he should not go to Court on Monday with the new Administration, but retire into Norfolk tomorrow with his brother. George approved of his language, and they left Mr. Pitt equally dissatisfied. Lord Anson's promotion it has made these shuttlecocks play so ill, I am told.

Rigby's report, which is fully compatible with George Townshend's endorsement, on two points finds confirmation in collateral evidence. In a copy of the 'paper delivered to the King by Lord Hardwicke' on 18 July 1757[1] the initials of both brothers appear among those to be considered for office. Further, a letter from Charles Townshend to Devonshire dated 'Saturday noon', i.e. 18 June,[2] explains the remark attributed to him by Rigby 'that he already was Treasurer of the Chambers'. Townshend apparently went straight from Pitt to Devonshire but —

> I forgot to mention to your Grace how very desirous I am that as I shall have no new appointment, my name may not be in the Gazette as being named to the Treasurer of [the] Chambers a second time. I should hope I may remain as never having been out, his Majesty not having accepted my resignation.

The matter being accepted on that footing saved him the trouble and expense of a re-election, and seems to have added colour to the notion he apparently cherished of being in the new Government but not of it.

The two Townshends, and especially George, having managed the dreary Minorca inquiry to its meaningless conclusion on 3 May, the re-instatement of Anson (the man they charged primarily with responsibility for the loss of Minorca) was an obvious and plausible ground for their indignation; which, as Horace Walpole suggests in his *Memoirs*,[3] was really roused in George by the 'amnesty for Fox', and in Charles by 'not being promoted himself'.

Charles retired to Adderbury in high dudgeon. From there he wrote to his mother on 23 June:

> The post is come in and brings no account of the declaration of the Ministry I thought I left unalterably settled. Has any untoward accident prevented even this last submissive incorporating plan? To that his Majesty surely cannot have been perverse enough to object? The Duke of Newcastle cannot, I should imagine, be jealous of an union which levels others to himself. Mr. Fox's friends could not have hoped anything so favourable to him. It is too late for Mr. Pitt to

[1] Devonshire MSS. [2] Ibid. [3] Vol. iii, p. 34.

> repent, and as to the public and the people, they have long been set aside in settlements which relate to them.

And next, in a bucolic passage, flowery yet not altogether insincere (for it expresses a deeper hankering after peace), he writes:

> My whole grounds are a bank of perfumes; my cattle are fat; my child is handsome; and why should I fret that mankind, whom I did not make, cannot be made better?

A week later he wrote again to his mother about the pleasures of his retired life: 'I read many hours every day, and . . . I ride every evening'; yet studies and exercises leave him time for 'offices of affection' and 'lesser acts of friendship . . . reviving those more amiable qualities of the heart, which the ruder intercourse and habitual neglects of the world gradually efface in almost all men'. But next about politics:

> The ship is at last launched; the crew are at last completed and on board; and the crowd upon the shore have at last got something to gaze at. I dare not write my thoughts upon this last Ministry . . . lest my letters should be opened, and thereby an opportunity be given to anybody of saying I have taken an hostile part in the course of this summer, or laboured to create events which are too likely to happen of themselves.

A remark reminiscent of caution, avowed and not observed, in earlier correspondence on family matters.

Moreover the very same day, 30 June, Charles wrote a political epistle to the Duke of Devonshire of about 1200 words:[1] 'As little reason as I have myself to be anxious for either the personal situations or general fate of those who are now taking upon them the government of this unhappy country', he wishes them duration and success, for the financial and economic burdens, 'the experienced insufficiency of our navy . . . and, above all, the extent, distance, and divisions of our American colonies, make it impossible for us to survive either the factions of another divided, or the inability of another incapable, Ministry'. The nature of the war is disadvantageous to us, its course unfortunate, its present state 'in some parts fatal, in all unpromising'; continued as carried on hitherto, it will be 'our disgrace, our ruin'. But can sincere union or a uniform system of measures be expected 'from the present coalition of men',

[1] Devonshire MSS.

with their 'inveterate jealousies and confirmed mutual distrust'? And having once more expressed his wishes of success to whatever rulers are 'set over us', he gloats over Pitt's supposed decline:

> Here, and in this county [Oxfordshire] (which by the by is one of the few counties still belonging to those called the people), the flame of adoration is already strangely abated: but very few fires burn at the altar; and incense boxes are not in every man's hands as they lately were, and the god is rather solitary. Eloquent vows, the rather remembered for their eloquence, made in full senate, of a perpetual disunion from the very persons now joined, are everywhere repeated.

He rejoices at the Duke being

> relieved from an office . . . which in these times can bring to an amiable mind little peace or satisfaction. Even in my confined walk of life, I can derive real comfort from the truth of this reflection, which at this moment disarms every disappointment I may be supposed to have met with, gives an additional cheerfulness to the leisure I live in, and effectually puts me out of the reach of everything not within my direction.

And after further discourse about men and women, spiced with laboured jokes, he concludes: 'Good spirits and more leisure have led me into a longer letter than I ought to have writ.'

Like so many 'patriots' before him and after him, Charles Townshend was consoling himself with the prospect of an unfortunate war, i.e. Pitt's failure and discomfiture. 'Indeed, Lady Townshend, we are undone', he wrote to his mother on 13 July, 'and, as Mr. Fox says in his obliging letter to me, no genius is equal to the distress and danger of the times.' And in a letter of 25 August he ascribed the anti-militia riots to

> the temper of the times, for there is throughout all ranks a deadness and an indifference to all public matters, the natural effect of habitual disappointment and constant oppression, and every man in this kingdom who is not a candidate for office or power, has not confidence enough in Government to excite him to lend his name or his time to the assistance of any measure it undertakes. If this be the temper of the people and the condition of the Government of England, who would be eager to have a share in the administration of such a Government?

And on 18 October, having thanked his mother for supplying him at Adderbury with the latest intelligence from London, he wrote:

> As this year, though under the direction of genius and public spirit, has turned out very like its predecessors, and every month in it has been distinguished by some new defeat and some additional misfortune, I can have had no very good news to tell, and by being the first to publish the bad I have wonderfully conciliated the good wishes of the Roman Catholics and the old interest, who in this county are very considerable and in themselves very agreeable people. Indeed, language can not describe to you the resentment or the dismay which is visible among all orders of men. . . . The Whigs, who never loved Mr. Pitt, affect a respectful silence; the Tories, who gave him popularity for their own purposes, are secretly happy to find, I hope, talents which were so irresistable in opposition, which is their own point, so ineffectual in Administration, which it is presumed is Mr. Pitt's point more than their's; while sober and thinking men admit that this country has run its race; that, as in other past monarchies, the genius of our people has undergone a change, and we are no longer capable of being successful through our own councils or arms.

He was vexed by his brother's single-minded efforts to serve, in the first place by promoting his scheme of a militia. In his letter to Lady Townshend on 23 June Charles called George 'that honest instrument of the deceit and . . . success of other men'; in an undated letter, written some time in October, he desired her to put George 'upon his reserve towards some little agents . . . employed by those who had rather govern him . . . by such concealed instruments than gain him by open friendship'.

By 1758 Charles Townshend was once more Newcastle's affectionate nephew, and when his first son was born, 22 June, asked the Duke to stand godfather to him,[1] which Newcastle did on 18 July; and the boy was christened Thomas Charles. Two days later Charles thanked Newcastle from Lady Dalkeith and himself for 'the very agreeable testimony' of his goodness;[2] and went on in a style reminiscent of some contrite letters addressed by him to his father:

> I cannot pass over so natural an opportunity of assuring you that, in every passage of my life, I shall wish and endeavour to deserve your Grace's favourable opinion and the honour of your friendship; from which if I have sometimes been too much diverted by errors and indiscretions, they are errors which I ever remember with regret, and indiscretions I flatter myself I have had the sense to discover and correct.

[1] Newcastle to George Townshend, 15 July 1758, Add. MS. 32881, f. 337.
[2] Ibid., f. 394.

This mood continued for some time — 'a sincere desire of manifesting my zeal for your personal service'.[1]

(iii)

Charles Townshend's Scottish escapade of 1759 shows what he could imagine and make others believe, if only for a short midsummer night. He spent July and August at Dalkeith with his wife, mother of the young Duke of Buccleuch; and wrote from there in an undated letter to Lady Townshend:

> We see an infinite variety of company here. The whole neighbourhood have dined with us. . . . All the lords of session, all the resident gentlemen of estate, the gentlemen of the law, the presbytery, and every order of men have been to see us, and continual as the hurry has been, I own it has nevertheless been agreeable to me. The women are lively, the men are learned, and both are well bred. Curiosity too has had some merit in my amusement, and the face of this part of the kingdom, so very new to me, has pleased me, independently of the very great civility and personal favour I have met with.

As one of Buccleuch's trustees, he concerned himself with improvements on the estate; and gave orders for planting trees, making walks, and beautifying the park. He also toyed with the idea of playing a major part in the political affairs of Scotland.

On 18 July the city of Edinburgh presented him with its freedom, 'for many good services done to his country, and in particular to this part of the United Kingdom'; and in his speech Townshend appealed to national sentiment by his fervent advocacy of a Scottish militia. For an Englishman to show concern for Scottish affairs was something new, and Townshend appeared eager to become acquainted with them and sympathetic to Scottish grievances. He dazzled the literary and political society of Edinburgh by his 'shining talents and elegant flattery',[2] and his connexions with the great families of Campbell and Scott made him much less of a stranger in Scotland. 'No man', wrote John Dalrymple to Townshend on 29 August 1759, 'did surely ever make himself so popular in so short a time as you did in this country.' There was talk of his standing for Edinburgh at the forthcoming general election, and even of his succeeding the aged Duke of Argyll, his wife's uncle, as

[1] Charles Townshend to Newcastle, 5 December 1758, Add. MS. 32886, f. 179.

[2] Carlyle, *Autobiography*, 389.

Government manager for Scotland. When Townshend departed, he left behind him a group of friends prepared to push his interests.

A change was shortly to be expected in the management of Scottish affairs, for Argyll, the uncrowned King of Scotland, was 77. Who would succeed him depended on the life of another old man, George II, now 76. For when the King died, Lord Bute was expected to assume power both in Scotland and in England. What place then would there be for Townshend? Dalrymple wrote to him on 18 October 1759:

> The relation betwixt the Duke of Argyll and Lord Bute, and the partiality of the future sovereign to this last, makes the transition (I speak of Scotland) of power from the one to the other almost imperceptible. Yet, a stranger in a good measure to this country, his lordship must find some person better acquainted with it . . . than himself, to co-operate with him in the management of it. . . . You take advantage while the Duke of Argyll lives of the advantages which your connection with him gives you to know the country and strengthen yourself, and when he dies (which cannot be far off) you make use of these either to make yourself useful or terrible to his lordship. . . .
>
> In the course of nature Mr. St. George [George II] must soon die. Then follow violent factions in which men of abilities will have an opportunity of showing their parts, and men of abilities and integrity will succeed. Yet with all his prince's favour and all his own character of honour on his side, Lord Bute will be glad of a man of your eloquence, activity, and English connexion by relation, on his side. His condition as a peer will prevent you from vying for particular offices, and the great strength he will derive from your eloquence, as well as his difficulty to find men fit for great offices in the House of Commons, will make him glad to throw the greatest into your hands; and then the show and gaudiness of power will remain with the Scotch lord, the friend of the sovereign, while the reality will remain with the English commoner, the friend of the nation.

It is difficult to say how far Townshend himself shared these ambitious dreams (so remote from reality), or whether he had only prompted them in others. But it is clear that by about November 1759 he had lost interest in Scotland. Alexander Carlyle wrote to him on 4 January 1760: 'If we had not reason to believe that you have been very busy, we should entertain fears that the Court and the Parliament had made you forget us, for I cannot learn that any of your friends have heard from you for two months.' The enthusiasm Townshend had aroused in Scotland remained and bore fruit, when the man who planted it there had forgotten all about it. Lord Elibank wrote to Townshend on 21 December 1759:

> I can now give you joy of the success of your endeavours to rouse the benumbed genius of this country. We have at last resolved to apply for a militia. . . .
>
> History can hardly produce so strong an instance of the force of persuasion, and though you had only the opportunity of exerting it among a few of us, the spirit you infused on that occasion has been able to get the better of the servility of some, the envious selfishness of others, and the timidity of all.

But it was Gilbert Elliot, not Charles Townshend, who on 4 March 1760 moved for a committee to consider the Scottish militia laws, and in the debate on the second reading of the Bill, 15 April, Charles Townshend appears not to have spoken. Nor did he ever visit Scotland again.

At the end of August 1759 there was a possibility of Henry Bilson Legge relinquishing Parliament and the Exchequer to take up a sinecure in the Customs of which he had the reversion. Newcastle was worried about whom to choose for his successor. Determined not to have George Grenville at his Board, who would reduce him to a cipher, he thought of transferring Lord Barrington from the War Office — 'but then Charles Townshend must be made Secretary at War, and there will be no going on in the House of Commons', Newcastle wrote to Hardwicke on 31 August.[1] '. . . If Charles Townshend had not such a character, I would make him Chancellor of the Exchequer at once, but there is no depending upon him, and his character will not go down in the City nor anywhere else.' And again on 5 October 1759:[2] 'Will Charles Townshend do less harm in the War Office or in the Treasury?' Hardwicke replied the next day:[3]

> I do not believe there is anyone else in the kingdom who would approve of that nomination [Charles Townshend for Chancellor of the Exchequer]. That office should be filled by somebody who may in a particular manner be depended upon, of some gravity, known veracity, whose word may be taken and relied upon. These qualities, though very material in every station, are not quite so essential to a Secretary at War, and therefore if the King could be brought to yield to that the *less harm* would be there.

[1] Add. MS. 32985, f. 76.
[2] Add. MS. 32986, f. 300. [3] Ibid., ff. 322–5.

Meantime Townshend wrote to his mother in a letter dated 31 September [sic] (and mainly concerned with his brother George, then on the expedition against Quebec):

> As for myself, I am as you can suppose me to be in my situation, restless, angry, and wretched. If I could see anything to comfort either of us I would, but we do not seem designed for comfort, and, I know not whence it is, everything and everybody conspires against us.

The rumour of his appointment to the War Office even reached the Press.[1] In the end, Legge, having secured the Customs place for his son, remained in the House; and there was no vacancy for removes. But Townshend, restless and ambitious, yearned for a place of business; and American affairs had a peculiar attraction for him. On 17 December 1759 Newcastle reported to Hardwicke a talk he had had with Pitt about the choice of peace plenipotentiaries:[2]

> He . . . told me Charles Townshend had spoken to him; that he had told him that he never imagined he, Mr. Townshend, would think of being a third plenipotentiary for *America*. That there must be *a Lord* at the head. One for foreign affairs: as he explained to me, Major-General Yorke; and another for America. That Mr. Charles Townshend should speak to the Duke of Newcastle. Charles Townshend accordingly spoke to Mr. West to speak to me; that he, *Charles*, had the ear of the Prince of Wales more *now* than anybody; that he wished I would bring him into business. . . . Pitt said this might be so; that he, Pitt, thought we should have one to the taste or approved by Leicester House; that that might be tieing them down to our peace. That if Charles Townshend was now in the situation, it was not so formerly. That was all he could say; but that if Leicester House really approved, and his uncle the Duke of Newcastle would answer for him, he, Pitt, would acquiesce; but he could do no more.

Hardwicke replied on 18 December:

> I suppose Mr. Charles Townshend, by desiring to be a plenipotentiary, means to be the *sole plenipotentiary*. By Mr. Pitt's saying *if his uncle the Duke of Newcastle will answer for him*, it is plain to me that he don't like it.

No plenipotentiaries were appointed, and the question of employing Townshend in that capacity does not seem to have arisen again.

[1] Alexander Carlyle to Townshend, 16 October 1759, Buccleuch MSS.
[2] Add. MS. 32900, ff. 120–1.

What degree of favour he enjoyed at Leicester House at this time is uncertain; but much trust was not placed in him even there. Although never mentioned in the letters from the Prince of Wales to Bute, he appears after George III's accession among their candidates for office. Newcastle, in his 'Heads for my conference with my Lord Bute', dated Claremont, 14 December 1760,[1] wrote about the office of Secretary at War: 'This, I apprehend, will create great difficulty, and much distress me. Mr. Charles Townshend told me positively that in all events he could not remain any longer in his present employment.' Newcastle was afraid that 'to secure Mr. Charles Townshend' Bute might try to push out Barrington, an excellent Secretary at War, and 'of great service to my friends'; he could not expect the same from Townshend. And Dodington writes in his *Diary* on 16 January 1761 that Bute had said to those who proposed to him to unite with Newcastle 'upon conditions', that he would agree to none

> till he saw Talbot, Dashwood, and Charles Townshend (which last, he said, had sworn allegiance to him *for a time*), had such places as he wished.

[1] Add. MS. 32916, ff. 49–55.

CHAPTER IV

Townshend in the New Reign 1760-1763

(i)

A seat for Townshend in the new Parliament, the first of George III's reign, had been a problem for some time past: it seems to have been assumed all along that the seat he held at Saltash was to revert to an Admiralty candidate. By the spring of 1760 Townshend's bid for the leadership of Scotland and the Parliamentary representation of Edinburgh, if indeed they had been seriously meant, had slumped completely, and his name appeared on 26 July in Newcastle's list of 'persons to be brought into Parliament at the next election'. Not that Townshend left the matter to Newcastle's exclusive management. Two filibustering attempts by him in wholly unexpected regions are recorded.

The first was directed at Pembroke Boroughs, a constituency with which the Townshends had no concern or connexion either before or after, and where the candidate was Sir William Owen, Bt., M.P. for Pembroke Boroughs 1722–47 and for Pembrokeshire 1747–61. Owen's changes of constituency are succinctly explained in a note in Bute's Parliamentary list, compiled in December 1761:

> Joined with Sir John Philipps to turn out Campbell of Calder, afterwards was turned out of the county by Sir John Philipps, and compromised for the borough.

That compromise was presumably reached before the county meeting on 4 December 1760, when, according to the *Public Ledger* of the 11th, Philipps's candidature, having been proposed by William Edwardes, M.P. for Haverfordwest and seconded by Sir Thomas Stepney, Sir William Owen 'thanked the gentlemen for their former services, and joined in the unanimous resolution of the gentlemen at the meeting'; 'we hear', adds the report,

'Sir William Owen will be elected for the town of Pembroke'.

A fragmentary account of Townshend's Pembroke adventure can be pieced together from two letters. Neither gives the date of his first declaring himself a candidate; but his having to begin with received support, or at least encouragement, from Sir John Philipps and Sir Thomas Stepney, places it before the county meeting of 4 December. It further appears that Townshend counted foremost on John Wogan of Wiston, one of the boroughs included in the constituency — Lewis Wogan had stood in 1710 against Sir William Owen's father, and having been defeated on the poll, was seated on petition, having established the right of the freemen of Wiston to vote in Pembroke elections.

On 23 February 1761 Sir William Owen wrote to Newcastle:[1]

> I am well assured that some gentlemen that I never thought friends of the Government have persuaded Mr. Charles Townshend to oppose me at the next election for the town of Pembroke, where every man has promised me, which he knows, but there is a town there called Wiston which the last Parliament of Queen Anne admitted the freemen to vote, though never voted before nor have not since. Mr. Townshend I hear intends trying the validity of those people's votes, and says he will make 1000 votes there and establish them by the House of Commons. This is what I am sure your Grace can't approve of, as it will fix a great weight in people's hands of a sort you don't like. As that is the case I hope your Grace has weight with Mr. Townshend to dissuade him from this bad scheme, and if he likes such new adventures I hope you'll prevail with him to turn his heavy artillery against his enemies and not his friends.

There is no sequel to this letter in the Newcastle papers, while Townshend's letter to John Allen,[2] written on 25 March, by which time Townshend's return had been fixed at Harwich, was a graceful renunciation of Pembroke, worth quoting for its style and the account it gives of previous transactions:

> Dear Allen,
>
> I have this moment read a letter from you to Sir T. Stepney. From that letter I find that you are of opinion that I should have had the honour of being elected for Pembroke if the gentlemen who persuaded me to offer myself had continued firm to their plan.

[1] Add. MS. 32919, f. 222.

[2] Buccleuch MSS. John Allen (c. 1724–67), of a leading Pembrokeshire family, Sheriff 1757–8, married Mary, sister of Sir Thomas Stepney, 7th Bt. of Prendergast, Pembrokeshire.

I agree with you in this: but how could I act otherwise than I did when Sir J. Philipps *changed*, and my friend Mr. Wogan reasoned upon that change as he did on his visit to London? You know how little the first surprized and how much the last circumstance governed me, and that sincerely ambitious of the honour of being elected, I could never think of disturbing the quiet of the boroughs upon any presumption or vain expectation of mine. If the gentlemen and electors have heard the true state of this matter they must approve of the motives upon which I tendered my services and to withdraw.

As the case now stands I am, as I ever have been, at the command of the gentlemen and electors of Pembroke: their candidate, their friend, or their representative, declining nothing from fear of expense, presuming nothing from any claim or situation or pretence of mine, and soliciting nothing but at their command. If Mr. Wogan and the gentlemen and the electors are willing to use my name, I think it an honour to be their servant. I will stand the charge and decision of the election: if not, I have again shown how much I wish to obey their sentiments.

I have never exchanged the least message with Sir W. Owen and therefore I have no explanation to make or measures to keep with him. I have as little to observe with Sir J. Philipps.

I am, my dear Allen, etc.
Ch. Townshend

Owen was returned unopposed on 2 April 1761.

Townshend's other recorded attempt off his own bat, made before the General Election of 1761, was even more perfunctory and concerned Liverpool. Ellis Cunliffe, its representative 1755–1767, reported to Newcastle on 6 April 1761[1] that after he had been unanimously declared a candidate about four months ago, and had at the instance of the principal merchants joined Charles Pole (the other sitting Member), 'Mr. Charles Townshend threatened an opposition but soon declined offering himself'. 'The ferment raised by this disappointment' produced a contested election in which Pole was defeated by Sir William Meredith.

While thus engaging in 'new adventures', Townshend made sure, through Bute and the King, both of office and of a seat in the new Parliament. The Count de Viry, the Sardinian Minister, who was in everybody's confidence and intriguing all round, told Newcastle on 27 January 1761 about the changes in office intended by the new Court and specially mentioned 'Charles Townshend for

[1] Add. MS. 32921, f. 346.

Secretary at War'.[1] It also seems that some time in January Newcastle must have heard that the King desired Townshend's return for the safe Treasury borough of Harwich: why Townshend pounced on that particular borough, and when and how he obtained the King's promise of it, has not been ascertained. But Newcastle, in his 'memorandum for Lord Bute', dated 3 February 1761,[2] and prepared for the much desired and much dreaded conference of 4 February[3] (when Bute was to bring Newcastle the list of men the King wished to see in Parliament), wrote as if already acquainted with the demands he had to expect:

> To show my Lord Bute the list of boroughs.
>
> . . . .
>
> Mr. Charles Townshend. To know the King's intention and what is really wished about him. If the King really wishes it, to endeavour to do it in the least disagreeable manner.

There is no direct account of that conference in the Newcastle papers, which circumstance long gave rise to wildly exaggerated stories of what happened at it. But the Duke of Devonshire, informed by Newcastle, put down some notes about it in his political diary:[4]

> Lord Bute came to the Duke of Newcastle, stayed upwards of three hours, began very unpleasantly. . . . It ended at last in naming Mr. Breton, Mr. Worsley, and Lord Parker to be brought in, and Mr. Charles Townshend to be chose for Harwich. They then came to talk of changes, he said there would be scarce any, the King indeed wished to have Mr. Legge turned out of the Treasury . . . Charles Townshend Secretary at War.

Thus while in the case of the other three candidates whom the new Court billetted on Newcastle's list, the choice of seats was left to him, in the case of Townshend a specific demand was made for Harwich: most embarrassing to the Duke, as John Roberts, secretary to the late Henry Pelham and for many years Treasury manager at Harwich, was importuning Newcastle to return him for the borough, and his claim was pressed on the Duke by the formidable Lady Katherine Pelham, Henry Pelham's widow. Newcastle wrote on 5 February in reply to her expostulations:[5]

[1] Add. MS. 32918, f. 82. On Viry, see Namier, *England in the Age of the American Revolution*, 80–2.
[2] Add. MS. 32918, f. 82.
[3] Namier, *England in the Age of the American Revolution*, 152–5.
[4] Devonshire MSS. [5] Add. MS. 32918, ff. 279–80.

I had a long conference yesterday with my Lord Bute, which almost in every point passed entirely to my satisfaction. The chief disagreeable thing was this point of Mr. Roberts. Lord Bute said that the King had promised to bring Mr. Charles Townshend into Harwich. I disputed it, combated it, and opposed it, as much as I could. I did not prevail, but yet I don't despair but I shall at last be able to get Mr. Roberts in at Harwich.

Next, Newcastle, in his 'memorandums for my Lord Bute', dated Claremont, 8 February 1761,[1] dealt once more with Townshend's office and seat: satisfactory compensation must be found for Lord Barrington 'or . . . otherwise I cannot in honour consent to Charles Townshend's being Secretary at War'. There follows a note on Westminster where Sir John Crosse declined to stand again: Newcastle desired 'to know the King's pleasure', and mentioned Townshend as one of several possible candidates. Whether his candidature at Westminster was his own idea or Newcastle's, eager to ease his position at Harwich, has not been ascertained. But in Newcastle's 'memorandum for the King', 12 February,[2] there is the enigmatic entry:

Mr. Charles Townshend Westminster
Pembroke Town

And in another 'memorandum' of 17 February:[3]

Charles Townshend
Westminster
To do what he will do.

Finally it had to be Harwich, and Newcastle cleared the borough of both previous incumbents in order to be able to return both Townshend and Roberts. He thus explained the matter to Lady Katherine Pelham on 15 March:[4]

Notwithstanding the strong representations and orders from the King to the contrary, I have, from the beginning, invariably insisted upon bringing Mr. Roberts into Parliament *for Harwich*, and that was . . . his great point. I have done so, after all attempts made by me (and I believe by my Lord Bute) to bring Mr. Charles Townshend in at some other place, were, by his trifling and provoking behaviour, become impracticable.

Townshend and Roberts were returned unopposed on 30 March; though, according to Lord Egmont, there was difficulty in choosing

[1] Ibid., ff. 363–4.
[2] Ibid., f. 459.
[3] Add. MS. 32919, f. 50.
[4] Add. MS. 32920, f. 228.

Townshend 'on account of the . . . slight shown to the borough' in not going there himself.[1]

Six days before the election, Townshend was appointed Secretary at War — 'he forced the Secretary at War's place from Lord Barrington, for whom the Duke of Newcastle would have made a better fight, if he had not been the only man he could put into the place of Legge [as Chancellor of the Exchequer]', wrote Henry Fox in his *Memoir* of the events of 1760 to 1763.[2] But so confident did Townshend feel of obtaining the office through his new patrons that on 4 February, the very day Bute first broached the matter to Newcastle, he wrote to John Dalrymple in Edinburgh[3] expressing joy at Dalrymple's brother

> coming into a profession where I can assist him soon and effectually, and if you will name the regiment at home in which you choose he should be commissioned, I will take the earliest opportunity of giving such commission to him. As Lord Granby is not at home I have *as yet* no opportunity of making a recommendation to him, but if his Lordship should come to England soon, or I should have a correspondence opened with him by an event *I believe not distant*, the farther support of the application . . . shall be one of the first points of my letter.

The correspondence with Granby, Commander-in-Chief of the British forces in Germany, opened at the end of March, and commissions and promotions naturally took an important place in it.[4]

On 5 July 1761 Horace Walpole writes in a letter to Lord Strafford that Charles Townshend has had 'a bad return of his old complaint' — apparently the last overt reference to his fits.

(ii)

By the time the new Parliament met in November 1761, Townshend was once more in semi-opposition to the Government of which he was a member: he was offended at the lead in the House of Commons on Pitt's resignation being assigned to George Grenville and not to him, and, according to Henry Fox, at the King's refusal to appoint Lady Dalkeith to the Queen's Bedchamber.[5] On 4 November, at the meeting of the principal men in

[1] Egmont to Bute, 27 February 1763, Bute MSS.

[2] Lady Ilchester and Lord Stavordale, *Life and Letters of Lady Sarah Lennox*, 38–9.

[3] Buccleuch MSS.

[4] *H.M.C., Rutland MSS.*, ii.

[5] Walpole, *Memoirs of George III*, i. 68; *Life and Letters of Lady Sarah Lennox*, 59–60.

the House of Commons to hear the King's Speech and the respondent Address, he 'found fault that there was no mention of the militia' and 'debated the point with much warmth'. Such an attack was much resented as Bute and Newcastle had only with great difficulty overcome Grenville's reluctance and apprehensions and persuaded him to accept the leadership of the House by assuring him of the King's and their own fullest support.[1] The King wrote to Bute on 5 November, 'past five o'clock':[2]

> Both Lord Egmont and the Duke of Devonshire told me of Townshend's improper conduct last night. As to the Duke of Devonshire, he has seen Mr. Townshend this morning and shown him how very improper his conduct was and how the world speaks of his language. He promised he would for the future be more cautious in his conversations, and said it was his firm purpose to support my measures if he did not meet with that treatment that his spirit cannot brook.
>
> My dearest friend will I am sure agree with me in thinking Townshend's conduct must be taken notice of, for if George [Grenville] is not supported in this first instance he cannot go on with that comfort I should wish every man in my service.

Horace Walpole, not knowing how the change in Townshend's language was brought about, continues his account:

> The next night, at a larger meeting at the Cockpit [the meeting to which all friends of Government in the House were invited], Townshend recanted to Grenville all he had said, professed he believed he had been infatuated, begged it might be forgotten, and that Grenville would not take it to himself. Grenville replied, he had not: that for himself he forgot it; as the King's servant, he could not forget it.

But the King wrote again to Bute, on 6 or 7 November, in reply to a report from Bute which is not extant:

> The account my dearest friend sends me is fully convincing of Charles Townshend's intentions. I will undoubtedly show him that reserve that shall either force him to repent or resign.

Throughout November Townshend spoke repeatedly on matters concerning his office; and on Friday, 4 December, James Harris notes in his Parliamentary reports:[3]

[1] Namier, *England in the Age of the American Revolution*, 289–301.
[2] Sedgwick, *Letters from George III to Lord Bute*, 67.
[3] Malmesbury MSS.

> A very full House, not only of Members but strangers and ladies, to hear the subject of the Army in Germany debated. Mr. Pitt, Mr. Fox, Mr. Grenville, Lord Barrington, etc. present. But alas! what a disappointment! We were informed that the Secretary at War was taken ill, and so the matter was postponed to Wednesday next.

When on that day, 9 December, Townshend opened the Army estimates, he expressed his great concern at the delay caused by 'a severe fit of ill health' that had still left him 'in a very weak condition'[1] — which sounds like a recurrence of his epileptic fits.

In this speech Townshend defended British participation in the war in Germany much more than was pleasing to the new Court: which, while discouraging the campaign for the immediate withdrawal of the troops from Germany, really aimed at soon reducing British participation. The German war, argued Townshend, was 'expedient under the present circumstances' and 'consistent with our abilities', honour, and interest. The losses in men were comparatively small, their numbers could easily be maintained, and the necessary financial resources would be found. A change of plan, as desired by some, might be fraught with the greatest danger, and in the long run produce even greater expense. The international situation was such that happy developments could be expected 'if we do not hastily desert the cause we are engaged in'. If we ceased to support our allies, the influence of France would be completely re-established, with alarming consequences. 'This, Sir, must be the effect of a new system here, and it will be fatal to this nation.' And he concluded that 'the more vigorous our resolutions . . . and the more extensive our efforts, by so much nearer shall we be to peace'; whereas complaints of an inability to carry on the war, 'whether true or false . . . can only serve to retard . . . the object of our wishes, a safe, a lasting and honourable peace'. (He did, however, guard himself by saying that we were able to bear the expense 'provided no neutral power shall engage against us'.)

It is remarkable that this, the fullest report of the debate, does not mention Townshend's references to Pitt noted in other much shorter accounts: included among the papers of Charles Jenkinson, Bute's private secretary, it was presumably taken down for Bute, and though not in Jenkinson's handwriting was possibly prepared by him or some other follower of Bute. According to Walpole, Townshend 'concluded with high encomiums on what he called

[1] Add. MS. 38334, ff. 19–20.

Mr. Pitt's divine plan';[1] and James West, Newcastle's Secretary to the Treasury, quotes him saying that 'such a divine spirit has been infused into our councils, that the French were lost in America and hopeless in Europe'.[2] Further, in a letter to Devonshire of 9 December,[3] Newcastle reported George Grenville having complained to the King that no one except himself had attacked Pitt, and that Charles Townshend had plainly spoken in concert with him, and paid him the highest compliments. 'There is,' added Newcastle, 'and perhaps with reason, at Court a settled inveteracy against Charles Townshend. I say nothing to it, but that I should be sorry we should part with him, considering his abilities.' It looked as if the wheel of Townshend's affiliations and views had once more turned half-circle.

But when the King received George Townshend on his return from Germany on 18 December, he said that a fortnight earlier he would have complained of his brother's conduct, but that Charles 'had now perfectly set things to rights by the professions he has made'.[4] A new *éclaircissement* seems to have followed for when Parliament met after the Christmas recess, with war declared on Spain, Charles Townshend went back to a certain extent on what he had said. On 25 January 1762, when Rigby, in preparation for other inquiries, moved for a muster roll of Hessian troops in British pay (among whom serious deficiencies in numbers were alleged), he was seconded by Townshend who, 'to the great surprise of all present', spoke for contracting the German war 'now that the unexpected event of a Spanish war had intervened'.[5] According to James West,[6] Townshend said 'that he did not speak the language of despondency, but would not have us endeavour more than we could support'; and according to Walpole:[7]

> It had been fortunate if our apprehension of Spain had driven us to make peace with France. He feared we should sink from a dream of ambition to a state of bankruptcy.

Townshend now appears to have settled down for a while, and during the next six months little is heard of him. He seems to have devoted himself to the work of his department and refrained from speaking in the House except on War Office business. But even on

[1] *Memoirs of George III*, i. 79.
[2] Add. MS. 32932, ff. 74–7.
[3] Ibid., ff. 78–91.
[4] Sedgwick, 74.
[5] Sir James Caldwell's report, *Cavendish's Debates*, i. 566, misdated.
[6] Add. MS. 32933, ff. 477–8.
[7] *Memoirs of George III*, i. 105.

this his interventions in debate were purely on points of detail and did not touch on larger issues of policy. The outbreak of war with Spain in January 1762 had led to renewed demands in Parliament that the British contribution to the war in Germany should be reduced, and these demands were strengthened when the death of the Empress Elizabeth of Russia later in the month was followed by the opening of peace negotiations between Russia and Prussia. British assistance to Prussia, so the argument ran, should now be reduced, especially since we were committed to help Portugal, which had been attacked by Spain. Grenville openly, and Bute secretly, supported the attack on the German war; and when the vote of credit for Portugal was debated on 12 May 1762, Pitt was almost alone in the House of Commons in pressing for war on all fronts against the Bourbon powers. Townshend did not speak in that debate, though he had already declared for reducing British committments in Germany; and he seems to have sided with Bute against Newcastle on the question of stopping the British subsidy to Prussia.

After having resigned the Treasury on 26 May 1762, Newcastle, to emulate Bute's crowded levees, wished for the greatest possible concourse of friends at his country house Claremont (near Esher in Surrey). Hans Stanley wrote to him on 13 June, presumably in reply to an invitation:[1] 'Mr. C. Townshend and I premeditate a visit to Claremont, but as he is not quite recovered from his cold, we do not know when we shall be able to pay our respects there.' Newcastle wrote back on the 28th:[2] 'I must now claim your kind promise and my nephew's Mr. Townshend; I hear he is perfectly well of his indisposition; and the rains have made this place so pleasant that I am desirous that my best friends should see it in that situation.' But somehow the visit seems never to have come about — possibly not altogether through Stanley's and Townshend's fault.

Meantime Townshend's relations with Bute were deteriorating. Devonshire wrote to Newcastle on 28 May 1762:[3]

> Sir Francis Dashwood [Chancellor of the Exchequer] has turned out Vaughan from being his secretary. Mr. Townshend is outrageous. Last night he talked of resigning, by his own account he treated Lord Bute and Sir Francis very roughly at Court this morning, but he did

[1] Add. MS. 32939, f. 329.
[2] Add. MS. 32940, f. 116.
[3] Add. MS. 32939, f. 56.

not convey anything to them that looked as if he meant to give up his employment.

And the King wrote to Bute on 31 May:[1]

> Townshend by his conduct undoubtedly means ill humour and my heart dictates me to wish such a fellow out of my service unless he will be hearty.

Next, on 18 June, after some differences between Townshend and Bute over Army appointments:[2]

> I wish him out of the War Office and don't see how he can possibly stay there after his present impertinent conduct; but would have no objection to his going into the Board of Trade. My dear friend will I have no doubt agree with me in opinion that yielding to such a man would be only encouraging others to follow his unworthy steps.

And in a second letter on the same day: 'I beg he may be probed to the bottom and if he is as bad as I think him, there must be another Secretary at War.'

In a letter of 15 July Sir Henry Erskine reported to Bute that Townshend was going to resign because of some Army promotions;[3] whereupon the King inquired of Bute whether Townshend had yet wrote to him about it.[4]

> I fancy though that he will think bullying not the way to get anything but the loss of his employment. Besides his character is so very bad that I believe nothing would strengthen the opinion of the present Government in the eyes of the public so much as that vermin being against it.

By October there was a new change of scene. Differences had arisen during the summer between Bute and Grenville over the terms to be demanded from France in the peace negotiations carried on through the Sardinian Ministers in London and Paris, and over the management of the House of Commons. On 6 September the Duke of Bedford started for Paris to negotiate peace; and a month later, on a reshuffle in the Government, Grenville was transferred to the Admiralty, Lord Halifax was made Secretary of State, and on 12 October Henry Fox was 'declared Cabinet Councillor and His Majesty's Minister in the House of Commons'.

[1] Sedgwick, 112. [2] Ibid., 117–18.
[3] Mentioned in the register of Bute's correspondence, Add. MS. 36796.
[4] Sedgwick, 120.

The idea of removing Townshend from the War Office had persisted; and apparently he himself at times wished for the Board of Trade, but presumably with extensive powers over colonial affairs. On 16 September Rigby wrote to the Duke of Bedford:[1] 'The world talks much of me as Secretary at War; . . . I believe Charles Townshend has a promise for his favourite American plan.' The exact nature of that plan unfortunately is nowhere stated, though it can be gauged in broad outline.

When the Duke of Devonshire refused to attend the Cabinet Council on the peace terms, the King, suspecting him of acting in concert with Cumberland and Newcastle, who were now drifting toward opposition, wrote circa 5 October to Bute:[2]

> We must . . . turn our eyes some other way, and see whether by gaining Fox and Charles Townshend, the House of Commons can't be managed without these proud dukes.

Grenville's post of Secretary of State was offered to Fox with the leadership of the House; this Fox was prepared to undertake but refused the secretaryship — 'suppose the seals given to Charles Townshend', he wrote in a memorandum on 8 October.[3] The King would not have it — he wrote to Bute:[4]

> The scheme of giving the seals to Townshend would be very absurd; the changing Halifax and Grenville appears to me the best proposal yet made.

Townshend's transfer to the Board of Trade continued to be talked about — Rigby wrote to Bedford on 13 October:[5]

> In the various lists of changes which are handed about this town, I am told I stand for Secretary at War. I have heard nothing of it from any man in power. . . . Charles Townshend is not pleased and intends to stay at the War Office and not pursue his own plan of going to the Plantation Office [i.e. the Board of Trade].

On 16 October, when dealing with Fox's suggestion that Lords Waldegrave and Gower should be given Cabinet rank, the King wrote to Bute:[6]

> I have no objection [to] Lords Waldegrave and Gower coming to Council, but wish they were counterbalanced by Charles Townshend

[1] Bedford MSS., part printed *Bedford Correspondence*, iii. 122–5.
[2] Sedgwick, 143.
[3] Fitzmaurice, *Life of Shelburne*, i. 120; Ilchester, *Life of Henry Fox*, ii. 193.
[4] Sedgwick, 144. [5] Bedford MSS. [6] Sedgwick, 147–8.

(if he can be depended on) and any others that may not be looked upon as Bedford House men, for else I fear that will be the name the counsellors will get.

Presumably at that time an offer was made to Charles Townshend; and here is his own, undoubtedly embellished, version of what had happened, repeated by Newcastle to Devonshire in a letter of 21 October:[1]

Charles Townshend told Tommy Walpole, and I understand that he was to tell it to me, that my Lord Bute, upon communicating to him the arrangements lately made, said, Now, *Charles*, what shall I do *for you*? Charles answered with his hand to Lord Bute's mouth, *Nothing*. That the King offered him the head of the Board of Trade and Secretary of State for the Plantations, which he refused in the following manner: I beg your Majesty would excuse me; though it is the employment I should like best of any, I cannot support Mr. Fox. I have already attacked him once in Parliament and at the same time *my uncle* [Newcastle himself] was in connection with Mr. Fox, which circumstance grieved me then. (He forgot that he attacked *his uncle* himself soon after.) That now he could not support Mr. Fox, when *his uncle* had no connection with him and that objection was removed. I give it you as I had it from Mr. Walpole, but I really believe he will not join or support those gentlemen.

Thus, incredulous as Newcastle had grown by experience, he still believed too much. A similar story, even more embellished, and coming also from Townshend, was told by Thomas Nuthall, Pitt's solicitor:[2] according to this, Townshend had seen the King three times, had 'spoke out freely', and had 'said things that did not a little alarm'.

In the letter to Devonshire of 21 October Newcastle, having mentioned Legge's high ambitions on a possible change of Government (he looked 'very high', even to becoming head of the Treasury), added:

My nephew Charles Townshend looks as high, and in his own opinion with much more reason. How these great men can be all satisfied I know not, but satisfied they should be. . . .

Charles Townshend sent me word the other day that he was *ready* the moment the Duke of Devonshire and I *called upon him*. He is certainly at work, informing himself and getting materials. I should not be surprized if he proposed in Parliament some plan of peace of his own, and of restitution and satisfaction for the same.

[1] Add. MS. 32943, ff. 332–40. [2] *Chatham Correspondence*, ii. 181–3.

Rigby, reporting the changes in the Government to Bedford, had written on 19 October:[1]

> Charles Townshend, that splendid shuttlecock, veers about with all these different gales. He laughs at the Ministry at night and assures them in the morning that he is entirely theirs. If he could be fixed to any point, it would be for peace; when they talk of equivalents, he says very well, the getting rid of a war which nobody can conduct is equivalent enough for all.

In spite of Townshend's uncertain attitude, and though he was not a member of the Cabinet, he seems to have been consulted on the final terms to be demanded from the two Bourbon powers. Shelburne wrote to Bute also on Sunday 19 October, that Samuel Touchet (who appears here for the first time as connected with Townshend),[2]

> was with Charles Townshend a great while, looking over Spanish treaties, which gave him an opportunity of speaking over other matters. He left him determined to support the King's measures and your Lordship both statedly and steadily and with cordiality. He intends waiting on you tomorrow to tell you so [and to give Bute papers relative to some previous treaties with Spain] with notes and thoughts of his of use in the negotiation.
>
> As to Mr. Fox too, Touchet thinks he [Townshend] will be easily reconciled — but not to change his office, for some reasons he is to give on Monday.

The Government's intention was to demand from Spain either Florida or Porto Rico as an equivalent for Cuba, which had been captured by Britain; and while the matter was under discussion, at a date which it is difficult to fix precisely, Townshend told the King[3] that 'within these few years' one 'of the greatest Spanish merchants in this kingdom'[4] had been offered Porto Rico but thought 'the sum asked too great';

> that it would be very valuable to us, and would easily be obtained as an equivalent for Cuba. Mr. Townshend for all this appeared gloomy and dissatisfied, and very full that a less equivalent could not be accepted for our conquest.

[1] Bedford MSS.
[2] About Touchet, see below, pp. 106–7.
[3] Sedgwick, 142.
[4] By a Spanish merchant, Townshend meant a British merchant trading to Spain.

He also mentioned that he would bring in two or three days important papers from that merchant to Bute; but nothing about these appears in further correspondence.

The day after the Cabinet meeting of 22 October on the final terms of the preliminaries of peace, Townshend imparted to Fox intelligence he had received concerning the pacific dispositions of the French and Spanish Governments, of which he was 'very sure', and which apparently encouraged a very peremptory demand from Spain of a total surrender of her claims to fish off the shores of Newfoundland. Fox desired Townshend to inform Bute about it, which he did, constructing Fox's words into a message supporting his own view of the matter.[1] Whatever the exact truth about that 'message', the transaction shows that Townshend participated in these discussions. With regard to his relinquishing the War Office for the Board of Trade, Fox wrote to Bute in the same letter of 23 October:

> I thought Mr. Townshend resolved to act as his best friends wish, and to change his employment; but what terms relative to that employment he means to have, or your Lordship designs to give, I do not precisely know, but fear his design and yours in that regard is not the same.

On 6 November Townshend was still being considered for the Board of Trade;[2] but although Horace Walpole states that he 'refused to be First Lord of Trade with the same power over the colonies as had been granted to Lord Halifax',[3] and Townshend himself in his letter of 10 November[4] claims to have declined 'the Cabinet and . . . what I think the first office and highest situation in this country', there is no record of any such high offer in the correspondence of those from whom it would have had to come.

On 28 October Fox reported to Bute that Townshend was freely talking against the peace.[5] The peace preliminaries, signed in Paris on 3 November, reached London on the 8th. On the 10th the King wrote to Bute[6] that Townshend had congratulated him 'but coldly on the peace'; described Florida as 'useless territory' and 'ran out in praises of Porto Rico'; objected to the treaty not diminishing French power in the West Indies; and then contradicted himself 'by saying he could make Florida the most advantageous of all our

[1] Bute to Fox, 23 October 1762, Fox MSS; Fox's reply, Bute MSS.
[2] Sedgwick, 159. [3] *Memoirs of George III*, i. 166. [4] See p. 78.
[5] The letter is noted in the register of Bute's correspondence, Add. MS. 36796.
[6] Sedgwick, 161.

colonies' by 'making Pensecola a free port'. Possibly referring to the same conversation, the King told Fox[1]

> that Townshend enjoined secrecy about Pensecola, but Lords Halifax and Egremont followed him into the Closet and that in that minute he had told them both his secret.

An event to which anyone but Townshend might have been expected to react, was the summary way in which the King dismissed the Duke of Devonshire on his refusal to attend the Cabinet. The King wrote to Bute on 3 November:[2]

> Contrary to custom Mr. Townshend came to Council, but when asked whether he wanted an audience, denied it. When I called for the council book, declaring that it was to strike out the Duke of Devonshire, he sunk as if he had been shot and did not stay the levee.

But this was as far as Townshend went — Newcastle's attempts to make him resign were of no avail.[3]

A letter from Townshend, dated 10 November 1762, shows the light in which he saw his own behaviour during this period, or at least wanted it to be seen perhaps by himself and certainly by others:[4]

> It is my firm resolution to act the part of a man of business and a man of honour; to be decided by things and not men; to have no party; to *follow* no leader, and to be governed absolutely by my own judgment with respect to the peace now concluded, the approaching system of measures, and the future Ministry. It was formerly my ill fortune to be much neglected and frequently injured by my uncle, the Duke of Newcastle. I have been twice dismissed from public office in his Grace's and the Duke of Devonshire's Administration. I have been left by Mr. Pitt at the end of a successful opposition in an unpleasant office, without communication or common respect. I have been received with kindness and treated with confidence by his Majesty in the execution of my present office. I have spoke my sentiments in the Closet freely and fully upon the change which has lately been made in the Administration, and therefore no man is so perfectly able as myself to preserve that independence which I sincerely value above either the lustre of popularity or the reward of subservience.

[1] Fox to Shelburne, 13 November 1762, Lansdowne MSS.
[2] Sedgwick, 155.
[3] Newcastle to Rockingham, 27 November 1762, Add. MS. 32945, f. 162.
[4] A copy or draft of the letter to an unnamed addressee is in the Buccleuch MSS.; the concluding part is missing, and has been so for some time, as appears from a note on it.

Unconnected with the Duke of Newcastle, I should certainly have been justly called inconstant if I had adopted his resentments merely as such. You would not wish to see me act *second* to the Duke of Devonshire's personal and private disgusts. No motive on earth shall ever unite me with Mr. Fox; and as to my continuance and conduct in public office, that depends upon measures I can't foresee. In the mean time, to show I am determined and *not inconstant*, Mr. Fox can decide whether I have not gone so far as to decline the Cabinet and the acceptance of what I think the first office and highest situation in this country; and why? not from want of ambition, but from a love of *consistency*. . . . Let me speak the truth to you. It is because I will not be the second of any man that you call me inconstant; it is the voice of party that pronounces this censure; and it is because I will not be the obedient instrument of any set of men that I have not at this instant the crack of party which you call the confidence of mankind. Let me add that if my constancy is to be judged of by any obligations they are all to the Crown; but I shall act upon a still higher obligation than those. . . .

. . . My talents such as they are shall be directed only by myself, delivered up to the views neither of popular nor of Court faction, and exercised at no man's *order*. Time will show how far they are ready at any and at every hour to be exerted with vigour and intrepidity in the full support of those measures which my mind, impartially consulted, tells me are for the advantage and honour of this country. . . . I have taken my part; I have placed myself between the extremes of party; I have refused power and declined faction, and dangerous, delicate, and ungrateful as I know every situation to be that humours the expectations and promotes the interests of no set of men, I am nevertheless resolved to adhere to this one clear principle of being really directed by the measures that shall take place.

There was imitation of Pitt in Townshend's boasts of independence; of regarding measures and not men; and in wishing in his relations with the King to by-pass leaders and parties. There was also a vast amount of unconscious self-deception, both in his view of himself and of events in his past. And one would hardly guess, reading this letter, that Townshend's conduct during the next few weeks was to be more inconsistent and unpredictable than contemporaries had believed possible even from him.

(iii)

Some of the further gyrations of Townshend's 'consistency' can be followed in letters which passed between Bute, Fox, and

Shelburne during the fortnight before Parliament met. Shelburne wrote to Bute on 11 November 1762:[1]

> C. Townshend yesterday, after declaring himself dissatisfied about the peace, angry about the Duke of Devonshire, etc., affirmed however that the King's business might possibly go through, but there would be a difference made between what might be called the King's measures and Mr. Fox's.

And Fox to Bute, the same day:

> Charles Townshend is worse than ever; upon my word, my Lord, we shall not be able to go on with him in his employment and this fickle humour. I hope his brother will come over soon.[2]

Bute replied to Shelburne on 12 November:[3]

> As to Charles Townshend, I believe the best method will be to leave him to himself, and in the meanwhile to take care that the Army promotions be not directed by his caprice. But he dare not oppose, and the day of retribution will come.

There is among the Raynham papers a letter from Charles Townshend to his mother entirely undated, but marked '17 November 1762', and docketed likewise by George Townshend at a later time. Charles wrote:

> I have the favour of Mr. Fox's message to your Ladyship, repeating his desire that I would move the Address. The same circumstances upon which I grounded my former request of being permitted to decline this office still have the same weight with me and oblige me to persevere in my resolution.

It seems unusual for a front bench man to be asked to move the Address at the opening of the session, but in the absence of conclusive evidence to the contrary the placing of the letter by contemporaries has to be accepted, though with due reserve. The same day Fox sent a list of queries to Bute[4] in which he suggested three Members from whom to choose the mover of the Address, but Townshend was not one of them. The same paper contains the puzzling query: 'Whether Charles Townshend should *not go* to Portugal?' In what character or for what inducement is not stated: possibly Charles's cousin, Charles Townshend of Honingham, is

[1] Bute MSS.

[2] George Townshend was away in Portugal on active service, and did not return till February 1763.

[3] Lansdowne MSS.

[4] Bute MSS.

meant, who had been Secretary to the Madrid embassy from 1751 to 1755.

In a letter docketed 'received November 19, 1762', Townshend wrote to Fox:[1]

> I cannot conceal from you how much I am mortified by a report which generally prevails that Porto Rico is not ours. I have ever thought Florida of little importance to us; and I wish you do not find the plan and conditions of the treaty rendered much less acceptable to the public by the want of this island, which in my judgment and in the judgment of all commercial people would in the course of no very distant time have been itself the source of great wealth, navigation, and strength to these kingdoms.

On 20 November the King wrote to Bute:[2] 'I shall be glad if Townshend will remove into the Board of Trade.' On 23 November Fox wrote to Bute:[3]

> Mr. Charles Townshend was [here], and anybody who did not know him would have thought him not only a friend but the most zealous one. I myself think he must be determined on our side for Thursday [25 November, the day Parliament assembled] at least.

And Bute to Fox, later in the same day:[4]

> I have had a long conversation with Mr. Townshend, ending at last in begging to defer his final answer till Thursday morning, which I think has not the most promising aspect.

Possibly the 'final answer' Townshend was to give concerned his proposed removal to the Board of Trade. Fox replied:[5]

> Charles Townshend is intolerable. He will I believe do all he can to ruin you; but he has ruined himself.

And the next day, 24 November:

> I fancy Charles Townshend will be more [forth]coming when you see him next. We shall not only have numbers, but, which I more doubted of and value more, a most eager co-operation of those we have.

Rigby wrote the same day to the Duke of Bedford:[6]

> There is no guessing at Charles Townshend's intentions, but he continues even yet to shuffle and I dare say will resign or be turned out.

[1] Fox MSS.
[2] Sedgwick, 164.
[3] Bute MSS.
[4] Fox MSS.
[5] Bute MSS.; the letter is wrongly docketed, obviously at a later date: 'Mr. Fox, December 1762.'
[6] Bedford MSS.

And some time in the second half of November the King wrote to Bute:[1]

> Mr. Townshend seems resolved to remain where he is, unless he should yet join the Duke of Newcastle (which I can never think impossible).

The House met on 25 November, and practically all extant reports of the debate on the Address record Townshend as commending the peace preliminaries. William Beckford, Pitt's leading follower in the City of London, having vehemently spoken against the treaty and compared it with that of Utrecht, Townshend, according to James Harris's account of the debate, agreed in condemning Utrecht, which had been opposed by his ancestor Lord Townshend, but spoke very differently of the present peace which he highly extolled — 'did well and was well heard'. Similarly in Sir Roger Newdigate's notes of the debate[2] — if the present treaty was like Utrecht, 'he would show his blood was genuine, but believed it very different'. And Rigby in his report to Bedford:[3] Beckford having 'faintly animadverted upon part of the preliminaries . . . Charles Townshend very smartly reprehended him as not combating the whole of it together'. From Walpole's report[4] it appears that the part animadverted upon by Beckford concerned Florida, which he compared 'for barrenness to Bagshot Heath' (very much what Townshend had said to the King): Townshend answered him in 'a trimming speech, though very personal against Beckford'.

When on 29 November the preliminaries were laid before the House, and Bamber Gascoyne, at that time a follower of Pitt, moved that they be read, according to James West's report he was seconded by Townshend, 'who declared that he had never seen them and was ignorant of them':[5] a report one could hardly credit did it not come from a reliable witness and concern Townshend. Nonetheless the next day, Fox, when naming in a letter to Bute[6] possible movers and seconders of an Address that the preliminaries should be considered on 9 December, still asked, 'Will Charles Townshend do it?' But nothing more appears about this suggestion, unless the letter in the Raynham papers dated 17 November should be placed here. Townshend did not speak in the debate of

[1] Sedgwick, 165.
[2] Newdigate MS. B2311.
[3] *Bedford Correspondence*, iii. 159.
[4] *Memoirs of George III*, i. 174.
[5] Add. MS. 32945, f. 194.
[6] Bute MSS.

1 December, nor is he mentioned in a very incomplete division list as voting on either side; but his name appears in the list compiled by Fox during the following week of Members secured in favour of the peace.[1]

On 6 December Townshend addressed a letter to Bute which has not been discovered but is thus summarized in the register of Bute's correspondence:[2] 'Wishes to retire from the office of Secretary at War.' Bute replied the next day:[3]

> I could not observe the anxious state of your mind yesterday without the most sensible sorrow. The affectionate regard I have for you suggested to me every method I could think of to prevent your coming to the resolution you now seem by your letter to have taken. The singular circumstance of my receiving a letter from your brother in the same hour, full of the most cordial declarations of support, with the utmost detestation of the faction now on foot, still augments my concern. The remarkable contrast in these letters makes me unwilling to lay yours before the King, nor is it a pleasant task to be the bearer of disagreeable news. I must therefore beg you (if your decision is unalterably taken) either to acquaint the King of it yourself, or to convey it to his Majesty through the proper channel.

Townshend officially resigned on 8 December, but what mode he chose for conveying his resignation to the King does not appear, nor are his reasons anywhere stated: perhaps the events of the next few days so much overshadowed his decision — rendered meaningless by then — that none troubled to probe the motives of one whose actions were so often unaccountable. Men preferred to speculate on what he would do next.

(iv)

The House of Commons debate on the peace preliminaries opened on 9 December. A great deal depended on Pitt who, according to Lord Barrington, 'never made so long or so bad a speech';[4] and even those who praise certain passages, admit that it was not on his usual level — he was ill, and, in an agony of pain, left the House before the division. Moreover he disclaimed all connexion with other parts of the Opposition, which put a finishing blow to the anyhow disorganized following of Newcastle.

Fox spoke next, and was followed by Charles Townshend:

[1] Fox MSS.
[2] Add. MS. 36796.
[3] Add. MS. 36797, f. 25.
[4] Add. MS. 6834, ff. 41–2.

As he had the day before resigned his office of Secretary at War [writes James Harris], great expectations were raised as to the part he would take, but he spoke strongly and handsomely for the peace, and was deservedly applauded.

And here is Walpole's account:[1]

Charles Townshend, discontent, expecting much severe animadversion upon the treaty, and dreading to differ with Mr. Pitt when the latter was likely to exert all his powers, had come to the House prepared to arraign the preliminaries. Finding his mistake, and secure by the retreat of Pitt, he changed his battery, defended the peace as well as it could be defended, burned incense on the altar of prerogative, and sang almost hosannahs to the praise of the King.

Newdigate gives some of Townshend's arguments but in a manner difficult to follow.[2] His report contains, however, one striking sentence: 'The preliminaries adequate to your situation, not to your success.' Rigby wrote in high delight to Bedford, at 1 a.m. on 10 December:[3]

I never heard Pitt so dull in my life. . . . Charles Townshend replied to him *after he was gone*, and made the finest speech I ever heard in my life.

The division that followed was carried by the Court by 319 votes to 65. Harris states that 'the Townshends went away' before the division was taken — but as he speaks of Newcastle's friends, it is uncertain if he means Charles and George Townshend or the two Thomas Townshends (the fifth Townshend in the House — Charles Townshend of Honingham — voted in the minority). But Lady Temple wrote to her husband on 17 December:[4] 'There are people that think if Mr. Pitt had not said he was a single man, Charles Townshend, *cum multis aliis*, would never have voted for the peace.'

When after the deroute, the Opposition leaders were considering how to rally their forces in the Commons, Charles Townshend was often mentioned but always with doubt whether he would cooperate. Thus Newcastle to Devonshire, 12 December,[5] saying that Legge did not feel qualified to be sole leader, but would do his part, 'if Charles Townshend (of whose good intentions for us he

[1] *Memoirs of George III*, i. 183.
[2] Newdigate MS. B2542.
[3] Bedford MSS.
[4] *Grenville Papers*, ii. 22.
[5] Add. MS. 32945, ff. 280–1.

much doubts) and Mr. Attorney-General [Charles Yorke], would undertake it with him'. And to Thomas Walpole, the same day:[1]

> My nephew Charles Townshend (who never comes near me) may be at the head, if he pleases; and he will be sounded upon it.

Devonshire replied on 14 December, with more common sense:[2]

> Indeed, my dear Lord, I fear there is nothing to be done. I look upon Mr. Pitt as gone, Mr. Townshend very near the same.

On the other side Fox wrote on 11 December, when advising Bute to turn out 'conquered enemies':[3]

> Your Lordship will see that there is no malice in this by the advice I shall give with respect to Charles Townshend, whom I can have no personal reason to wish well to, many to do otherwise. It seems to me that he may be had. Get him with all his faults (I don't say trust him) and they won't be able even to make our attendance necessary.

And Rigby to Bedford, 16 December:[4]

> Charles Townshend declares in and out of the House that he will support the Administration out of employment. I suppose he will soon have what he wants. In good truth, he shines in Parliament more than ever. He captivated me so that I could not help making comparisons in the House between him and Pitt, rather injurious to the latter.

He was courted by both sides — Newcastle wrote to Devonshire on 23 December[5] that although Townshend had disappointed him several times, Lord Rockingham

> made me send, by Tommy Walpole, a note to let him know I should be at home as yesterday morning; to which Mr. Walpole had a very impertinent answer, that he could not possibly come that morning; that he had a great regard for the Duke of Newcastle; *though to engage* to it, he had received from me no one single act of kindness or I think civility. There is nothing to be done with him but to let him alone. He certainly now thinks Fox can't or won't hold out, and that he shall be the governor of the House of Commons for my Lord Bute.

At this time the Court seems again to have made him an offer of the Board of Trade, but the terms on which he was to take it had to be settled: how much executive power over the colonies was to be conceded to him, and was he to be in the Cabinet? Meanwhile

[1] Ibid., f. 285. [2] Ibid., f. 287. [3] Bute MSS.
[4] Bedford MSS. [5] Add. MS. 32945, ff. 342–3.

rumour assigned the prospect of even higher office to Townshend. Hardwicke told Newcastle on 5 January 1763[1] that he had heard Bute was trying to make Lord Egremont accept the Presidency of the Council in succession to Lord Granville (who had died on 2 January),

> with a view to giving the Southern Department to Charles Townshend, thinking that when he has attained the summit of his ambition, his Lordship may trust him with the conduct of the House of Commons. . . . I have been credibly informed that one of the principal arguments which my Lord Bute has urged to Townshend, when he has been pressing for the Board of Trade with the same powers Lord Halifax had, and that very lately — 'Why, my dear Charles, do you consider that you are only cutting the grass under your own feet, for you will certainly have the Southern Department sooner or later, and if you add these powers to the head of the Board of Trade now, you must leave them to your successor.'

And on 11 January:[2]

> It is now confidently reported that Charles Townshend has accepted head of the Board of Trade *without the additional powers*, but with the additional salary of £1000 per annum and being called to the Cabinet.

And Newcastle wrote to Devonshire on 15 January that the report

> which seems to prevail the most is that Charles Townshend is to be Secretary of State in the room of Lord Egremont, and Mr. Fox to be made a lord, and Lord Egremont to be President of the Council or Lord Lieutenant of Ireland, which he likes best.
>
> I own I can scarce think that my Lord Bute would place such a confidence in your Grace's friend and *my good nephew*.

Information from official sources about the negotiations with Charles Townshend is at that time scanty and fragmentary. Fox wrote to Bute on 29 December:[3]

> If, as I suppose, Charles Townshend is to be a Cabinet counsellor, might it not be right, my Lord, to summon him today? That the plan of reduction may be approved by him.

The plan here mentioned concerned reducing the strength of the Army, and although Welbore Ellis had on 16 December been appointed Townshend's successor at the War Office, during the next few months Townshend was consulted on Army matters.[4]

[1] Add. MS. 32946, f. 59. [2] Ibid., f. 90. [3] Bute MSS
[4] Fox to Bute, 30 December 1762, 6 January 1763.

With regard to his own re-employment there were barely traceable ups and downs. On 5 January 1763 Fox wrote to Bute: 'Charles Townshend seems in high good humour.' On 7 February, Fox, writing to Bute about Sir John Philipps's intention to move for a commission to examine the public accounts (very distasteful to Fox as Paymaster-General during the war), suggested that it might be put off for this session 'if proposed by a proper person. Lord Strange is the properest person, Charles Townshend extremely proper, and I think if you ask it will do it willingly and well.'

No such motion was made, and Townshend certainly did not stand up for Fox when the matter came before the House. On 10 February the King wrote to Bute:[1]

> Mr. Townshend's conduct surprizes me not the least. He ever will be so fickle that no man can depend on him. I think it a happy riddance.

Although the meaning of the last sentence is obscure, it seems to point to a hitch in the negotiations between Townshend and the Court.

Rigby wrote to Bedford on 16 February about differences in the Cabinet between Bute and Egremont, and added:[2]

> Charles Townshend will not be satisfied till he has wriggled him [Egremont] out of America first, and then out of the rest of the employment. He is impatient to be in place again, and one day the Board of Trade is fixed for him, the next they quarrel about the terms on which he is to take it, and so backwards and forwards it will be till he makes some furious speech, and then, if I guess right, Lord Egremont will be, as he deserves, a victim.

But on 23 February Rigby reported:[3]

> Charles Townshend kisses hands today for First Lord of Trade. He is to be of the Cabinet Council, and have the employment as Lord Halifax had it.

More accurate seems the account given by Horace Walpole in his *Memoirs*:[4]

> Charles Townshend . . . kissed hands for First Lord of Trade, with a nominal rank of Cabinet counsellor but without being permitted to go in to the King with state papers, except with those relating to the Board of Trade.

[1] Sedgwick, 189.
[2] Bedford MSS.
[3] *Bedford Correspondence*, iii. 210.
[4] Vol. i, p. 193.

No Cabinet minutes have been found for Townshend's period at the Board of Trade, but a letter from George III to Lord Egremont, docketed 30 March 1763, reads:[1] 'I desire Lord Egremont will also summon Mr. Charles Townshend to the Cabinet this morning.' Such an order would have been unnecessary had Townshend been a regular member of the Cabinet, and seems to refer to that particular meeting only. Nor does the relation in which Townshend as President of the Board was to stand toward Egremont as Secretary of State for the Southern Department, seem to have been clearly defined: Townshend, no doubt, tried 'to wriggle him out of America', and the matter was in dispute between them.[2]

There is in the Raynham MSS. a copy of a letter from Lord Townshend to Charles, dated 2 March 1763. It is in Lord Townshend's hand.

Dear Charles,

You may remember that about the beginning of last December, upon reading the paragraph in the *General Evening Post* which informed the public of your resignation of your former place, I immediately wrote you a letter from Balls[3] expressing my joy and congratulations to you on that wise guiding of yourself, as you by that act put yourself into that state of independency which was necessary to enable you to act that truly patriotic part which your country seemed more immediately to call for at this time. If I contradicted the general tenor of behaviour which prevails at this time in troubling you with a letter on that occasion, and it be not the mode now for a parent to show any concern for the welfare and happiness of his son, you acted like a man of fashion in taking no notice to me of that letter and in preserving that silence towards me which has been observed by you towards me for a considerable time before I wrote that letter, and which you have not broke through.

As I am too old to alter, and cannot easily extirpate that parental concern and affection which, by a long indulgence of them, are deeply rooted in my heart, you will I hope forgive me that I do now trouble you again though not with that joy which attended my other letter, with a transcript of a paragraph out of the *North Briton* of Saturday last, which is as follows, viz.

'That great reformer of abuses, the new Whig head of the Board of

[1] Wyndham MSS. at Petworth.

[2] Shelburne to Bute, 26 April 1763.

[3] Balls Park, near Hertford, which had come to Lord Townshend through his wife's family.

Trade, has just condescended to stipulate for an additional salary, without power, as the price of his support of this Tory government.'

I am,
dear Charles,
yours most affectionately.

(v)

There was another side to Townshend's character, little remarked upon by contemporaries, which indicates what he might have achieved in happier circumstances. James Harris notes in his parliamentary diary, under date of 22 February 1763:

> Mr. Charles Townshend made his report upon the state of private madhouses — 'twas ably drawn, and set forth a scene of great villainy. The report was ordered to be printed.

On 27 January a committee of the House of Commons had been appointed 'to consider the state of private madhouses', and Townshend seems to have taken the lead in the business. There is among the Buccleuch MSS a printed paper entitled 'A Case Humbly Offered to the Consideration of Parliament', which begins:

> The many unlawful, arbitrary, cruel, and oppressive acts which for some years past have been committed in places generally called private madhouses, of which the fullest and clearest proof can be given, call aloud, as is humbly submitted, for some speedy provision whereby his Majesty's subjects may be preserved against an evil that is daily increasing.

There follows a careful and sympathetic examination of a number of cases; and the paper concludes with a list of 23 regulations suggested for safeguarding persons to be admitted into any unlicensed madhouse.[1]

Horace Walpole describes the scheme as laudable, necessary, 'and founded on a crying evil'.[2] The House agreed to a resolution that 'the present state of private madhouses requires the interposition of the legislature', and leave was granted to bring in a Bill. But there the matter ended, and no Bill was introduced. Walpole writes: 'Charles Townshend took great pains in that business,

[1] See also *Parliamentary History*, xv. 1283–90.
[2] *Memoirs of George III*, i. 192.

distinguished himself, was content, and dropped it. The lawyers raised many objections, and removed none.' Should the disillusioned flippancy of this account be extended to Townshend? Nervously afflicted, he seems to have had real feeling for those worse stricken than he was, and he had 'taken great pains' to alleviate their suffering.

CHAPTER V

At the Board of Trade
March-September, 1763

(i)

On 2 March 1763 Bute wrote to Fox:[1] 'C. Townshend has given me a most unusual proof of the ungenerous turn of the present age'; and the King to Bute the next day:[2]

> Mr. Charles Townshend's conduct is what I should not have thought any other man capable of, but himself very much so, for I look on him as the worst man that lives. It was that made me tell my dear friend the other day I could never bear the thoughts of seeing him hold the seals. This confirms me in it, I would as soon employ a common thief as him.

What Townshend had done to provoke the violent anger of the King and Bute remains unascertained. George III was at no time fond of Townshend, but his language about him seldom reached this pitch; which goes far to destroy the picture of Townshend, painted by Bancroft in his *History of the United States*, as moulding and voicing the American policy of the Bute Government during his seven weeks as First Lord of Trade.

Bancroft states[3] that when Townshend's successor, Welbore Ellis, 'brought forward the Army estimates for the year, including . . . twenty regiments . . . for America' (this was on 25 February 1763), Townshend promptly 'explained the plan of the Ministry, that these regiments were, for the first year only, to be supported by England, and ever after by the colonies themselves', and thereby 'dazzled country gentlemen' who might otherwise have grudged the expense. The account of Townshend's intervention is taken from Burke's speech on American taxation (delivered eleven years later): but while Burke claimed that he well remembered Townshend's 'brilliant harangue on the subject', there is nothing to place it on that first day, and it seems doubtful whether there was any debate on the day the estimates were submitted to the House.

[1] Ilchester, *Letters to Henry Fox*, 172.
[2] Sedgwick, 195.
[3] *History of the United States*, v. 86–7.

The subject was opened by Ellis in a speech lasting an hour on Friday, 4 March, and of that debate there is a fairly full report by Harris, and another compiled for Bute by Charles Jenkinson.[1] In that opening speech Ellis is reported by Jenkinson to have stated 'that the American force was intended to be paid for a future year by America'; and George Townshend that he admired 'the plan of making the American army to be paid by the Americans'. About Charles Townshend, Jenkinson writes in a covering note to Bute:

> In the morning I was told that Mr. Charles Townshend was ill and that he would not come down to the House; he came however pretty late, but just before Mr. Pitt. Soon after he disappeared, and was not seen by anybody.

Similarly Walpole:[2] 'Charles Townshend, dreading the lash of Pitt on his late inconsistencies, retired early in the debate.' And there is a letter from Townshend to Pitt of 6 March on a different subject in which he mentions having been ill — 'a very severe attack upon my bowels'.[3] It was in this debate, and not on the report to the House on 7 March, as stated by Bancroft, that Pitt declared for an even stronger army.[4] Nor did Charles Townshend speak on 7 March, when the debate was resumed: there is a report of it by Jenkinson which names seventeen speakers, but Townshend is not among them.[5]

Bancroft further states that on 9 March Townshend 'came forward with part of the scheme for taxing America by Act of Parliament: duties on the trade between the continental colonies and the French and Spanish islands were prohibitive, and evaded with the connivance of custom house officers'. 'The Minister proposed to reduce the duty and enforce its collection; and he did it with such bold impetuosity that, "short as the term was, it seemed that he would carry it through before the rising of Parliament".' There follows a footnote referring to a letter from 'Jasper Mauduit [agent for Massachusetts in Great Britain] to Secretary Oliver, London, 23 March 1763', and quoting the following passage:

> Some days ago the first Lord of Trade proposed lowering the duties on French molasses from 6d. to 2d. per gallon, in order the more

[1] MS. North b. 5, ff. 87–8, 94–9, at the Bodleian.
[2] *Memoirs of George III*, i. 195.
[3] Chatham MSS.
[4] Had Bancroft examined more carefully Rigby's letter of 10 March which he quotes (*Bedford Correspondence*, iii. 218) he would have avoided the mistake.
[5] MS. North b. 5, ff. 89–91.

effectually to secure the payment; and, short as the term is, he will probably carry it through before the rising of Parliament.

The exact date of Townshend's proposal is difficult to determine: certainly there is nothing in the authorities quoted by Bancroft to prove that it took place on 9 March, and his account of the incident is muddled and inaccurate in its pre-suppositions. But so much is true that some time in March Charles Townshend brought up a proposal for taxing America, only he did it without any authority from the Government.

The King wrote to Bute in a letter marked merely 'one o'clock' and which can be dated with no greater precision than the middle of March:[1]

Mr. Jenkinson's account has much hurt me with regard to the part every branch of Government took of being silent on the proposal of Mr. Townshend for the American tax. Not only the Treasury, but Mr. Fox and Mr. Grenville ought to have spoke. This subject was new to none, having been thought of this whole winter. All ought to have declared that next session some tax will be laid before the House, but that it requires much information before a proper one can be stated, and thus have thrown out this insidious proposal. I think Mr. Townshend's conduct deserves the dismissing him, or the least the making him explain his intentions.

And next there is the following entry by Harris in his Parliamentary reports, which can hardly refer to the same debate since Grenville is seen disputing the matter with Townshend:

March 30, 1763. Dispute in the House betwixt Mr. George Grenville and Mr. Charles Townshend about American duties. The former against lowering them, the latter for doing it to a great degree, as the high duties produce nothing by driving all people to smuggle from the enormity of the gain. The matter adjourned to a long day.

So it was indeed — Jasper Mauduit wrote to the Speaker of the Massachusetts Assembly, 8 April 1763:[2] 'The bill for lowering the duty on French molasses is put off till another year.'

(ii)

About the middle of Townshend's short term at the Board of Trade the subject of the Government to be formed on Bute's

[1] Sedgwick, 201–2.

[2] *Jasper Mauduit*, ed. C. G. Washburne, *Mass. Hist. Soc. Collections*, vol. 74, p. 101.

impending retirement came under urgent consideration. Fox was consulted, and in a paper given to Bute on 11 March, he wrote:[1]

> I have said nothing of Charles Townshend. He must be left to that worst enemy, himself: care only being taken that no agreeableness, no wit, no zealous and clever behaviour, though on the right side, ever betray you into trusting him for half an hour.

But in fact what Fox had said previously implied the intention of leaving Townshend at the Board of Trade without any increase of powers; for when recommending Lord Gower for Secretary of State, Fox wrote:[2] 'If any man could do the office of Southern Secretary without either quarrelling with Charles Townshend, or letting down the dignity of his office, he would.'

In his next plan for the new Government, 17 March, Fox suggested Lord Shelburne for the Southern Department.[3]

> If, as I hope, that should drive Charles Townshend from the Board of Trade, let Oswald succeed him, and between Lord Shelburne and Oswald that greatest and most necessary of all schemes, the settlement of America, may be effected.

But Grenville, who after Fox's refusal of the Treasury was to be put at the head of the new Government, objected to Shelburne being made a Secretary of State;[4] argued that the sudden advancement of an inexperienced young man to that office would not be well received in either House; and added: 'As to Mr. Charles Townshend, it will certainly throw him into immediate opposition.' The King himself did not like the idea of Shelburne being made Secretary of State, possibly from the dislike he had for Shelburne's friend Fox. Writing to Bute on 24 March, he suggested that if Grenville was made First Lord of the Treasury, Townshend might succeed him at the Admiralty 'and Lord Shelburne be at the head of the Board of Trade'.[5] And the next day: 'Shelburne might either have the Board of Trade or Admiralty.' On 29 March Bute wrote to Fox about Shelburne:[6] 'His being in the Board of Trade . . . is a measure that I will not hear of being altered.' By 4 April it was settled that Shelburne was to have Townshend's office, and Townshend be removed to the Admiralty.

[1] Fitzmaurice, *Shelburne*, i. 146. [2] Ibid., 142.
[3] Ibid., 148. The paper is marked by Fitzmaurice 'Fox to Bute'; the original in the Lansdowne MSS. bears no superscription, and it seems more likely that it was addressed to Shelburne.
[4] *Grenville Papers*, ii. 33–40. [5] Sedgwick, 204–6. [6] Fox MSS.

The Board of Trade had now to be cleared for Shelburne, and Bute asked Townshend, who was at Adderbury, the Duchess of Argyll's house in Oxfordshire (which Townshend used as his country residence), to return to London. Apparently ignorant of what was happening there, Townshend sent on 5 April a note of excuses — 'for not returning to town at the time you desired and I fully intended to have done' — business on which he had gone to Adderbury obliged him to stay there a few days longer.[1] Now Bute informed him of the imminent changes and offered him the Admiralty.[2] Townshend replied on 7 April,[3] 'sensible of his Majesty's infinite goodness' and deeply grateful for 'this additional mark of . . . undeserved favour'.

> But, my Lord, I hope his Majesty will not impute it to any want of zeal for his service if, in the singular situation in which late circumstances have quit me, and upon a point so essential to me, I should with all humility entreat the permission of a few days before I give my answer.
>
> When I came into the department I have now the honour of presiding in, it was entirely at your Lordship's request; and I accepted it upon its present establishment, in some degree against my own judgment, merely from a persuasion that by such acceptance I should strengthen your Administration however I might lessen myself, but when your Lordship withdraws I can have no such motive nor am I now able to conjecture of whom the Ministry will consist.
>
> It would be painful to me to act a second time without my brother's concurrence, and these considerations, added to the importance of the thing, will I trust excuse the delay I require.

The same day Lady Dalkeith wrote to Bute as 'a sincere friend and near relation', and having expressed concern at his health making him resign office, reminded him of an offer he had made in the matter most interesting to her, of a peerage (the British peerage of her late father John, 2nd Duke of Argyll) being conferred on her and her children by Townshend. 'Mr. Townshend's delicacy has for a long time prevented my mentioning this subject to you' — but she now declared her 'great anxiety to receive this mark of his Majesty's goodness . . . through the protection of the person in the world we both most wish to receive it from'.[4]

[1] Bute MSS. The letter was brought to London on 6 April by Townshend's friend John Bindley; Bindley to Jenkinson, 7 April 1763, Bute MSS.

[2] Add. MS. 36797, ff. 39–40.

[3] Bute MSS. [4] Bute MSS.

Townshend was taking his time about the offer of the Admiralty, vacillating as he usually did on such occasions. The King wrote to Bute on Wednesday, 13 April:[1]

> As my dear friend has not heard from Charles Townshend, I will acquaint [him] with what George dropped to me, that his brother would support me strongly but wished to remain where he is. He said this he believed was the purport of what Charles had wrote to my dear friend, but that he did not tell me this as the fixed opinion of his brother, for that he would write confidentially to my dear friend from whom I should hear the whole. One word to George I believe will clinch the affair of his brother.

The same day, at nine o'clock, Charles Townshend wrote to Bute from Grosvenor Square: he had consulted his brother on Monday; called on Bute yesterday; and was desirous to wait on him in order to express his sentiments on the subject [opened to him a week ago] 'upon which, I imagine, it may be necessary on a public account, as well as proper for myself on many private ones, that I should not seem dilatory'. Bute saw Townshend the same day, and after the interview wrote to James Oswald:[2]

> I am under one of the greatest difficulties I ever was yet in. C. Townshend has been here, and all I could get from him was, that he earnestly besought the King to suffer him to remain where he was; that he would declare both to his Majesty and Mr. Grenville that he would give him and his ministry the fullest support, and carefully avoid all disputes with Lord Egremont; that if his Majesty would not permit this, he begged to remain a private man. This, without any variation, to the last, and I learn from the King that his brother George is of the same opinion. To turn him out on this is serious, and if not where is Shelburne? I protest I am bewildered, and wish to hear the cooler thoughts of a friend on this important matter.

Indeed, Bute suspected that were he to 'proceed to extremities with Townshend', Grenville, Egremont, and Halifax would join George Townshend and Lord Strange 'in deprecating' Bute's conduct.

Oswald replied:[3]

> Townshend can never be really serious in wishing to remain where he is. He has declared himself too explicitly, too warmly, and to too many persons, on that head. The original idea, therefore, of remaining where he is, must have been formed with a view to *embarrass*.

[1] Sedgwick, 219.
[2] *Memorials of James Oswald of Dunnikier*, 410–12.
[3] Ibid., 413–19.

He did not suspect the other Ministers of sharing that view; yet their jealousy against Shelburne would make them sympathize with Townshend:

> though nothing, surely, will embarrass the future Administration more than Mr. Townshend's continuing in the resolution of remaining where he is. The settlement of America must be the first and principal object. It will certainly be the chief point upon which all future opposition will attempt to throw its colours and raise its battery. It will prove, in a word, the chief engine of faction. Mr. Grenville is, I am sure, sensible of this. Can we imagine that either he, Lord Halifax, or Lord Egremont, or all these together, can manage Charles Townshend in that department? It may be possible, but surely the difficulties will be infinite.

It would moreover raise serious difficulties with Shelburne — 'you know the ardency of his temper: I'm afraid this department has been his favourite object.' It would therefore be in everybody's interest to alter Townshend's resolution.

> This . . . can only be done by your Lordship, his brother, and perhaps Strange. As to the others [Grenville, Egremont, and Halifax], I'm afraid he hates and despises them all three too much to be altered by anything they could say. . . . If this cannot be obtained, I am of opinion it will be found absolutely necessary that the two Secretaries should change departments. Townshend, I believe, is a little afraid of Halifax. He has served under him. The other he will try to embarrass, etc. But he is to be satisfied.

The King wrote the same night, 13 April, after having received Bute's report of his talk with Townshend:[1]

> I don't understand what Mr. Charles Townshend means by declaring he will support Government, and yet refuse to accept what is infinitely more honourable than the office he now holds, and what is necessary for the bringing Lord Shelburne in. The only manner I can think of not disobliging George Townshend is for my dear friend to send for him, and to acquaint him with what his brother has declared, and to tell him that my service requires his brother's changing his office, that if he does not I cannot look on him as one attached to me. This would carry George with us. If this is not agreeable to my dear friend, I should be for turning Charles Townshend out.

It was now decided that the King should send for Charles — he wrote to Bute on 14 April:[2] 'I . . . will not fail to speak strongly to

[1] Sedgwick, 220. [2] Ibid., 220–1.

him; if he acts as he ought, he must kiss hands tomorrow.' And then at 4 p.m.:

> Charles Townshend came here ten minutes ago, wishing to decline, without giving any one reason except that his support would then appear interested. With close pressing him I brought him round to accept. He will kiss hands tomorrow, and he understands that his peerage [Lady Dalkeith's peerage] hangs over his head as a future boon, though without any time fixed for his receiving it.

And next, on Friday, 15 April, 12.27 p.m.:

> Charles Townshend begged to see me before I dressed. It was to push in the strongest manner for Burrell[1] to be in the Admiralty; that he had no friend in that Board; that it lowered his character, which he knew I wished to support. I told him all the vacancies were filled up, that there was no room for his or any other man's friend. After a good deal of backwards and forwards, finding he gained no ground, he yielded, and kissed hands this moment. Then he wanted a promise, which I refused, and thus the thing stands at present. I write this lest my dear friend should see him, that he may be prepared for his visit.

How the King came to state that Townshend had kissed hands is somewhat difficult to understand — he in fact had not — and a further, greatly excited, letter followed at 1.15 p.m.:

> Since I sent to my dear friend, Charles Townshend has desired Lord Halifax to tell me he cannot kiss hands without Burrell. I have sent Lord Halifax out to tell him he yesterday accepted without conditions, and therefore expect he will kiss hands.

And the King remarked on the 'strange appearance of his holding back when called on by the Lord in Waiting'. But here is the third note, without mark of hour:

> Charles Townshend has refused because I won't promise him to vacate a seat in his board for Burrell. Lord Shelburne was present at the conversation with Grenville and Halifax. I have ordered all the rest to kiss. I will neither be trifled nor have exactions sat on me.

And a fourth, at 3.50 p.m.:[2]

> Charles Townshend is gone away, much hurt at Shelburne's having kissed hands, and seems inclining to eat up his words, for his demand was that on Monday either Lord Carysfort or some other Lord of the

[1] About Peter Burrell, see below, p. 105.
[2] For these four letters see Sedgwick, 223–4.

Admiralty should be removed for Mr. Burrell. Lord Halifax and Mr. Grenville promised him that any weight they could have should be used to gain the first vacancy in that Board for Mr. Burrell. That he refused, and returned to the first charge.

The following account of what took place at Court is taken from James Harris's memorandum on the formation of the Grenville Administration:[1]

April 15, 1763. Thursday. At the King's levee. Very full, but a long time before the King came out. Charles Townshend had informed Mr. Grenville that he would not accept the First Lord of the Admiralty yesterday. This morning he was with Secretary Clevland [John Clevland, M.P., Secretary of the Admiralty] at his lodgings conferring on Admiralty matters, and giving Clevland to understand he should accept the office and come immediately into the First Lord's house. When he came to court he took it into his head that he ought to have brought two at least of his friends into the Board with him. On that he takes his friend Peter Burrell (by virtue of his own right of entry) into the inner or second room, next the King's closet, that second room where his Majesty receives company and where no one ever goes before the doors are opened, except persons peculiarly privileged by their offices. Here he and Burrell opened the matter to Lord Halifax and Mr. Grenville. These gentlemen told him, Townshend, that a request at the first offer of the office to bring a friend with him might have been attended to, but that now through his own delay it was too late, the places were gone. Besides, that he himself had agreed the day before to accept without any mention of such conditions. This language did not avail; neither he nor Burrell were satisfied, and Burrell 'twas remarked took the lead in the remonstrance. Both at length came out to the company, apparently dissatisfied. The levee doors were then opened, and Lord Shelburne kissed hands for First Lord of Trade (Charles Townshend's present place).

. . . .

There appeared at court a general disapprobation of Charles Townshend's conduct.

(iii)

A month later, 18 May, Townshend wrote from Adderbury to his mother:[2]

I cannot pretend to you that my spirits are at present very good, for I am far from easy within myself. You know I love public business; I had a brilliant prospect as I was; my children are as yet not fully pro-

[1] Malmesbury MSS. [2] Townshend MSS. at Raynham.

vided for; I am too young for retirement; and I am separated from my brother. These considerations have perhaps too much influence over me, and, you will tell me, I ought not to be made uneasy by a conduct I approve. This is philosophically true, but the maxim is more just than practicable. However I will look forwards only, and wait with resignation the return of some of the means I have suffered to pass off unused, sometimes from neglect and sometimes from delicacy of making a better provision for myself and for what I love more than myself, my family.

The country is in beauty. Great and universal signs of plenty. The place itself much improved, and so much prettier than ever I saw it that I almost wonder I like it less.

Four weeks later, on 16 June, he wrote to his friend Chase Price apologising for not having done so earlier:[1]

It is not merely that I live at a distance from all interesting scenes of business or life . . . but I have been long very ill. . . . For some days I was doubtful if I should not be taken from the world . . . and though it is now six weeks since I was first seized by a cough which fell upon my lungs, I am at this instant hardly recovered. . . .

If you desire to know how I bear a solitude to which I have been so little accustomed, ask our friend Brocklesby[2] and learn from him, whether I sink under either treachery or oppression. Bid him tell you if I have the cold fit of despair or the hot fit of resentment, and whether I am not sincerely cheerful, self-pleased, resolute, and sanguine. Yes, my friend, I am true to myself and to the cause. I have not, in one word, *at any instant* lamented or departed from the part I lately took, but at the same time I am too determined not to be cool and too sincere not to be serious. . . . There is a dignity even in the manner of being displeased.

To that displeasure Townshend gave full expression in his criticisms of the Grenville Government: inactivity; 'proclamation of whim and firmness, internal jealousy and apprehension. No plan for our colonies.' 'In the meantime the cider counties confederate [against Bute's cider tax]; Wilkes's printers escape; and a universal, radical discontent sours the temper of all ranks of men in the kingdom.' The Government, wrote Townshend,

is a poor and baseless edifice; run up in haste; bad materials; designed rather as a show, than a building; and waiting only the first storm and the first burst of thunder and lightening to be levelled to the ground.

[1] Marquis of Salisbury's MSS. at Hatfield.
[2] Richard Brocklesby (1722–97), eminent physician; his dissertation at Leyden, June 1745, dealt with chest diseases. About him see *D.N.B.*

The storm broke in August 1763, and they weathered it. The King, advised by Bute, tried to rid himself of them by calling in Pitt; negotiations seemed at first to progress favourably, both at Pitt's preliminary interview with Bute on 25 August 1763, and with the King on Saturday, the 27th. The next audience with the King was fixed for Monday, the 29th, and on that day the negotiations unaccountably broke down. Pitt, wrote Hardwicke to his son Lord Royston on 4 September, 'affirms that if he was examined upon oath he could not pretend to say upon what this negotiation broke off'.[1] The King had to recall the Grenville Administration which, reinforced by the Bedfords, was now in a position to proscribe Bute and banish him from Court and even from London.

In Pitt's plan of Administration Charles Townshend was put down for Secretary of State, and, the King is reported to have told Grenville, was 'to carry on the King's business in the House of Commons when [Pitt] himself could not attend'.[2] In an undated letter to his mother, written some time in September, Townshend claimed to have kept at a distance during the crisis, 'avoiding all appearance of anxiety or solicitation'; and Pitt, 'without concert, the least communication, or any mutual intercourse, has given me the most public proof of his esteem and friendship in the most delicate and effectual manner'. The next sentence about 'how late the Ministry were in recollecting me, and what their friendly destination was', clearly refers to an offer after Grenville's recall on 29 August. Allegations made by the Ministers of Pitt having proscribed various people are denied by Townshend, and especially the report that Pitt had proposed to put the Army 'under the absolute command of a great person [the Duke of Cumberland]', annihilating the office of Secretary at War, which was spread 'to inflame the tempers of two young generals and secure them to the Ministry [Lord Granby and George Townshend]'.

> What happened to overturn everything between this time [Saturday] and Monday, I neither know nor care, for I know it was the dark work of some inauspicious hour, to which no person I respect contributed; grounded in no passage of the former proceedings. . . . Mr. Pitt delivered his advice, not any terms; that advice was adopted fully; and if in forming a sufficient Ministry he suggested too many alterations, he should have been checked at first; but he was not checked at first, because the Saturday night the alterations were

[1] P. C. Yorke, *Life of Hardwicke*, iii. 528.
[2] *Grenville Papers*, ii. 196–7.

thought necessary, the new system prudent, and the measure upon the whole reasonable. This is, as I am assured, the fair outline of this marvellous transaction: conceived in a panic, submitted to in despair, repented of as soon as resolved, and finally broken off in a manner so disgraceful to the Court and so ungratefully to the Crown, who has been made to confess the necessity of a change, and to stop equivocally at least in the execution of it, after so great progress and repeated approbation. As to myself, I am sorry to see a monarch whom I have served and whom I love thus successively sacrificed, at least in his quiet, to the arts of designing factions; passing from difficulty to distress; and opening his reign with repeated attempts to establish interested, incapable, and odious Ministers against the judgment of his people and contrary to the true honour of his Crown. I am sorry also to lose in leisure a part of my life that I could have diverted to the public service, but I had rather bear this or any reflection than be one either of those who insult, or of those who mislead, or of those who lessen, the Crown, or be a part of the present Ministry who have contrived to do all three: a cabal of desperate, exploded, detested characters, whom I have ever despised for their inability and abhorred for their conduct, and who, being recruited from all disbanded parties and tumbled from elevated stations by the justice of better times, seem rather to have been discharged by some general party jail delivery, than a phalanx or a chosen band, formed out of the able and independent of the age, to defend the Crown and sceptre from insolence.

The idea of offering Townshend the Board of Trade or the Admiralty was canvassed at the beginning of September, but whether it was ever made is uncertain. Welbore Ellis, in a letter to George Grenville on 2 September,[1] refers to an offer of the Admiralty to Townshend as a possibility apparently under consideration. In the Grenville diary for Monday, 5 September, occurs the following passage:[2]

Mr. [George] Townshend saw his brother Charles at Missenden on Sunday; he seems to determine to continue in opposition, did not wish for the Admiralty after being put in nomination by Mr. Pitt for Secretary of State. (N.B. The Admiralty was not offered to him.)

The curious thing is that in the original manuscript of the diary (which is in Mrs. Grenville's hand) the sentence first referred to the Board of Trade, which was next crossed out and 'Admiralty' substituted. And this is how the matter appears in a letter from

[1] Ibid., 103. [2] Ibid., 204.

Lord Sandwich to Lord Holland (the former Henry Fox), 26 September 1763:[1]

> Charles Townshend was to have had the seals with Mr. Pitt. Upon the change, his brother, who takes his part violently with us, went to sound him, not whether he would accept the same office which was already destined, but whether he would join with us in some other department. According to my information he showed a disposition to accept the seals, and said that as he had been placed there in the other plan he could not figure with us in a lower station. I believe he added that he did not intend to oppose, but I consider those as mere words, and it is taken for granted he will give us all the trouble he can.

(iv)

Townshend's marriage to Lady Dalkeith had made him financially independent of his father and their familiar correspondence naturally diminished a good deal over the following years. The dispute about Charles's marriage settlement had further embittered their relations, and during the next two years Lord Townshend is not mentioned in Charles's extant correspondence. The death of Charles's younger brother Roger, who was killed on 25 July 1759 at the capture of Fort Ticonderoga, seems to have had a softening influence on Lord Townshend which was reciprocated by Charles. 'Yesterday I heard from Lord Townshend', he wrote on 18 September 1759 to his sister-in-law Lady Ferrers (the wife of George Townshend), 'who suffers as we all do, and bears his part in our common calamity.' There is a letter of 15 December from Lord Townshend to Charles, written from Raynham, in an affectionate style rarely found in their correspondence. 'I have great joy in expectation of seeing you here at Christmas', writes Lord Townshend, 'and I thank you for the offer you make me of accommodating me with seeds and plants'; and the letter ends: 'My compliments to Lady Dalkeith and best wishes do always attend you and your's.' And on 6 April 1760 Charles wrote to his mother: 'I have a long letter from Raynham, but all wrote upon a breed of greyhounds. My Lord says he is well.'

By March 1763, when Lord Townshend wrote ironically to congratulate Charles on his appointment to the Board of Trade,[2] their relations had reverted to their old pattern, exacerbated apparently by political differences. Lord Townshend died on 12

[1] Ilchester, *Letters to Henry Fox*, 183.

[2] See above, pp. 87–8.

March 1764 and left Charles nothing: the bulk of his property went by entail or settlement to George and Lady Townshend; and all that Lord Townshend could dispose of himself was left, according to Horace Walpole,[1] to his mistress — 'a housemaid by whom he had three children'.

For most of his adult life Charles was closer to his brother George than to any man, and at all times he professed to entertain great regard for George's political opinions. Yet there were ups and downs in their relationship too, and on Charles's part a highly ambivalent attitude and at times a scarcely concealed jealousy of his brother. George was warm-hearted yet sensitive, quick to take offence and loath to give up his resentments. He hated Henry Fox, despised his uncle Newcastle, and never forgave Pitt for joining with Newcastle in July 1757. After the Duke of Cumberland resigned the command of the army in October 1757 George rejoined the service, was with Wolfe at Quebec (and took over the command after Wolfe's death), and afterwards served in Germany and Portugal. Politically he became connected with Bute and later was a strong supporter of the Grenville Administration. Charles's refusal to take the Admiralty when the Grenville Administration was being formed disconcerted George, and he took offence when Charles went into opposition with Pitt and Newcastle. Charles wrote to his mother about George in a letter of 17 July 1764:[2]

> Lady Dalkeith has told your Ladyship how frequently I have received letters from Raynham written in a temper not excuseable, in a language quite ill-bred, and continually alluding to circumstances and reports which have not the least foundation. At last, and after a long neglect, I answered the indifferent parts of one of these letters, and in a very plain and free manner gave my reasons for declining all correspondence upon other subjects. This resistance, not to say resentment, has produced by the last post a letter as remarkably affectionate, filled with apology, commendation, and confidence, with a very slight mixture of complaint, and even that rather meant to express concern than complaint.

The estrangement between the brothers was completely made up the following year when Charles took office in the Grenville Ministry, and henceforth they were politically inseparable.

Charles seems at all times to have found women more congenial than men and was more at ease in their company. He was little

[1] Walpole to Mann, 18 March 1764.

[2] Townshend MSS. at Raynham.

attracted toward them sexually, and there is no evidence of his ever having had a love affair. His marriage to a woman eight years his senior had more policy than passion in it, and seems to have been a comfortable rather than a happy marriage. He was not a man who could love deeply. Lady Dalkeith was of no great intellectual calibre and appears to have taken little interest in politics, yet she provided Charles with a haven where he could retreat from the disappointments of life and she exercised some stabilising influence upon him. Their first child was a daughter, born in 1756; then followed two sons in 1758 and 1761, both of whom died in early manhood, unmarried.

When Charles was dependent on his father he had spoken slightingly of his mother, and to please Lord Townshend had avoided close contact with her. After his marriage there was no longer any reason to restrain his feelings, and henceforth he was closer to Lady Townshend than to any one else. 'We converse upon all subjects without reserve or disguise', he wrote to her on 4 October 1757, and his letters to her are the truest and most outspoken expression of his hopes and desires. He could confide in her without fear of a rebuff or lack of sympathy, and they had many qualities in common. Both were intelligent, witty, and malicious; not burdened with a conscience or a faith; and both disliked Lord Townshend.

At no time in his life did Charles have any close or lasting loyalty to a political leader. Professions of political devotion were frequent on his part — to Newcastle in 1754, to Pitt in 1756, to Bute in 1761, to Newcastle again in 1763, to Grafton in 1767 — but the mere recital of them shows how little real devotion lay behind these professions. He swore loyalty to each successive Administration and kept faith with none — as promiscuous in his politics as his mother was in her love affairs. For Pitt, aloof and austere, he felt fear and also admiration — there must have been an unconscious identification of Pitt with his father; for the other Ministers, contempt and mockery, disguised by over-elaborate protestations of service. Nor could he, who felt loyalty to none, be expected to arouse loyalty in others; and there is hardly another man of his stature in Parliament during the period who had so few real followers. His closest associates in politics (apart from his brother) were all of a similar stamp: adventurers in the realms both of politics and finance to whom jobs, contracts, and profits were the natural prizes of the game. They saw in Townshend a patron who could be of service to them with Government, and he perhaps was not unwilling to join his interest with theirs.

John Huske, one of the oldest of Townshend's connexions, whose intervention at the general election of 1754 at Great Bedwyn on behalf of Roger Townshend has already been described,[1] was a North American who started as a merchant in Boston and came over to England in 1748. When Townshend became Treasurer of the Chamber in 1756, he appointed Huske his deputy. The office was concerned with the finance of the royal household and was practically a sinecure: the work was done by the deputy through whose hands passed considerable sums of money. Huske held this place until March 1761, when Townshend was appointed Secretary at War; and after Townshend's death, when Lady Dalkeith was clearing up her husband's accounts, Huske was found to have embezzled some £30,000 for which Townshend was nominally responsible. But Huske had fled beyond the reach of English justice to Paris, where he died in 1773; and it does not appear that Lady Dalkeith ever recovered the money.

Peter Burrell, whom Townshend tried to get appointed to the Admiralty Board in April 1763, was a London merchant, whose father, also a merchant, had held large Government contracts. Burrell entered Parliament in 1759 and his connexion with Townshend dates from about 1761. During the remaining few years of Townshend's life, Burrell followed faithfully all the twistings and windings of his friend's erratic political course, and one can only wonder why he attached himself to Townshend: he seems to have derived no benefits from the connexion in the shape of contracts or subscriptions to Government loans — the usual prizes of merchant M.P.'s. He was a touchy, irritable man, with a high notion of his own consequence, yet, apart from his friendship with Townshend, of little importance in politics.

Another who attached himself to Townshend and sought to profit from the connexion was John Bindley, a pushing, ambitious man, intelligent yet gullible and lacking foresight. Bindley began life in partnership with his father, a London distiller, but in 1761 he made over the business to his brother and became an official of the Board of Excise. His duties brought him into close contact with the Treasury and he became an authority on government finance,

[1] See above, p. 33.

ever ready to propound schemes of improvement in trade and revenue. His connexion with Townshend dates from 1762 when Bindley was anxious to leave the Board of Excise and enter Parliament. Townshend used him in political negotiations (where Bindley's zeal sometimes outran his discretion), and encouraged his parliamentary ambitions in language which is revealing of both men. He wrote to Bindley on 6 August 1765, shortly after the formation of the Rockingham Ministry:[1]

> It cannot be long before every impediment you have felt will be removed: you will *then* see your *fullest* wishes accomplished in the most pleasing manner, and in the meantime how large is your fortune and how great your prospect. As to me, you know I have been invariably your advocate and . . . friend . . . and if you choose to take your fate with me . . . I am ready to become one with you upon this plan of joint communication and common interest. . . .
>
> Be true to yourself; be sensible of your own consequence; be firm in your mind, and let not the minute darken the hour, nor the passing cloud of one hour give colour or gloom to so fair a day as you have before you. You will be great, if you will be explicit and patient. . . . Forgive this. It is from love for you.

Bindley had to wait until December 1766 when Townshend, then Chancellor of the Exchequer in the Chatham Administration, arranged for him to be brought in for Dover on the Government interest. After leaving the Excise he engaged in various business speculations with inadequate capital. His credit did not survive his patron's death, and in 1768 he fled to France and was declared bankrupt.

Perhaps the most interesting of all Townshend's connexions in the world of finance and business was Samuel Touchet, M.P. for Shaftesbury 1761–8. Touchet, the son of a Manchester linen and cotton manufacturer, set up for himself in London in the 1740's and by the end of George II's reign was one of the leading men in the City. Primarily an exporter of cotton and linen goods, he was also interested in shipping, insurance, the slave trade, and many other lines of business; he became a Government contractor and financier; and made a determined though unsuccessful bid to secure a monopoly of the African trade. He over-reached himself, and by 1761 was in financial difficulties. In 1763 his debts exceeded £300,000, and though his privilege as a Member of Parliament

[1] Buccleuch MSS.

prevented bankruptcy proceedings being taken against him, his business career was virtually over and that part of his life about to begin which was of importance to history. For in 1766 the ruined merchant became financial adviser to Charles Townshend at the Exchequer and helped to draft the ill-fated Townshend duties.

CHAPTER VI

In Opposition
1763-1765

Since his dismissal in April, and even before, Townshend had cultivated Pitt (in March 1763 he had gone to considerable trouble to obtain rank for an officer in whom Pitt interested himself).[1] Still more so after the August crisis. Edward Barnard, headmaster of Eton, who was connected with the Townshends, wrote to Lord Lincoln, 9 September:[2]

> I received yesterday a letter from Adderbury, which gives me the greatest pleasure, as I am assured that Mr. Townshend is properly affected with Mr. Pitt's great behaviour, and is resolved to support the same cause.

To Pitt himself Townshend wrote in effusive terms about 'the sincere and grateful sense I bear of your partiality, generosity, and friendship towards me upon a late occasion';[3] and in another letter of the same day about the satisfaction he received from Pitt's letter, 'which it is not in my power to describe, but, I thank God! it is in my nature to feel'.[4]

He cultivated Newcastle and Devonshire once more. Thus Newcastle wrote to Lord Cornwallis, 14 May:[5]

> Your cousin Charles, the late Secretary at War, was here yesterday with the Duke of Devonshire, and was determined to do as you and I wish.

But after Townshend had not been heard of for some time, Newcastle wrote to Devonshire, 20 July, having mentioned Townshend's illness:[6] 'I doubt my nephew Charles is not yet steady enough to be of this party [i.e. the Opposition], but I think he may at a proper time be sounded upon it.'

[1] See Townshend's letters to Pitt, 2, 6, 16 March 1763; Chatham MSS.
[2] Newcastle MSS., University of Nottingham library.
[3] 31 October; *Chatham Correspondence*, ii. 266.
[4] Chatham MSS.
[5] Add. MS. 32948, f. 289.
[6] See above, p. 99.

Some time in September Townshend was again ill — he wrote to Chase Price from Adderbury on 5 October:

> I have been to Oxford for two days . . . but I was so ill the whole time I kept my bed. . . . I could not visit the colleges . . .; the very first chapel and hall I entered dropped their pestilential, monkish dew upon my breast, and gave me an ague which I have never been able to remove till this day.

By the autumn he was on the whole counted as one of the inner circle of the Opposition. He planned in September to go to Chatsworth, but had to call off because of Lady Dalkeith's illness.[1] When Newcastle on 11 September discussed with Cumberland what to say in his forthcoming talk with Pitt, it was agreed that he should tell Pitt that while 'the whole machine must be directed by him', the subordinate parts could be taken with success by Townshend, Legge, James Grenville, and Charles Yorke.[2] On 9 October Devonshire took the same line at 'a tête à tête dinner' with Newcastle. Devonshire was

> determined to tell Mr. Pitt that if he will be at our head, we are ready to act with him and under him, and not to desire him to attend the Parliament when it is inconvenient with him, but he must give us his name, and let Charles Townshend (of whom he is sure), Mr. Legge, and Mr. Attorney-General [Charles Yorke] act under him and do the business.[3]

When a dinner of Opposition leaders was planned to be held before the opening of the session, Townshend was among the dozen to be invited.[4]

Considerable difficulty was caused to the leaders of the Opposition by the differences between Pitt and Charles Yorke on Parliamentary privilege, a point bound to come up as soon as the House re-assembled. Yorke, as Attorney-General, had advised that Wilkes's privilege as an M.P. did not protect him from arrest on a charge of seditious libel, while Pitt contended that it did, and the majority of the Opposition did not know which line to take. Townshend, in a talk with Newcastle on 3 November,[5] said he would not differ from Yorke and other legal authorities on such a question.

> He blames Mr. Pitt [wrote Newcastle] in the highest degree, is most zealous for beginning the first day, will never be with these Ministers,

[1] Townshend to Temple, 11 September 1763; *Grenville Papers* ii. 120–2.
[2] Add. MS. 32951, ff. 1–2.
[3] Add. MS. 33077, f. 95.
[4] Add. MS. 32951, ff. 350–1; 32952, f. 108.
[5] Ibid., ff. 184–203.

but as a prospect of stability must be his point *he will not engage without Mr. Pitt.*

But when the session opened on 15 November, although Pitt engaged from the very outset, Townshend remained silent;[1] still he voted with the Opposition, and was probably the 'Mr. Townshend' who acted as teller for them in the first division that day. When after a short delay caused by Wilkes having been wounded in his duel with Samuel Martin, the discussion on Parliamentary privilege was resumed on 23 and 24 November, Townshend again remained unusually silent — Horace Walpole wrote to Lord Hertford on the 25th:

> The best speech of all those that were *not* spoken was Charles Townshend's. He has for some time been informing the world that for the last three months he had constantly employed six clerks to search and transcribe records, journals, precedents, etc. The production of all this mountain of matter was a mouse, and that mouse was still-born; he has voted with us, but never uttered a word.

On 29 November he delivered 'an elegant speech' when congratulations were offered by the House on the marriage of Princess Augusta to the Hereditary Prince of Brunswick, and on 5 December spoke on naval and military matters. It was only on Friday, 16 December, when the House was about to adjourn for Christmas, that he entered the fray over Wilkes, who still pleaded inability to attend. Lord North, on behalf of Administration, moved that he be examined by a physician and a surgeon.

> This was warmly opposed [writes Walpole[2]]; and Charles Townshend, who knew that Pitt was provoked at his late silence, and who saw Grenville and North towering above him; and perhaps offended too that the Court seemed to despise him, broke out with much vehemence, turned Lord North into ridicule; and being told by Grenville that it would be wiser to submit to this motion, replied he should often differ with that gentleman, and hoped he should not have more wisdom to encounter than he had met with that day.

The Opposition leaders were delighted. Lord Rockingham wrote to Devonshire on 21 December:[3]

[1] See reports of the debate by Harris, Walpole, Newdigate, and William Strahan (in Peach, *Life of Ralph Allen*, 191–3); also Horace Walpole's letter to Lord Hertford, 17 November 1763. The only list in which his name occurs is that sent by Grenville to the King (Fortescue, *Correspondence of King George III*, i. no. 32, enclosure) which seems to register every interjection: it contains 127 names, Pitt's appearing 18 times.

[2] *Memoirs of George III*, i. 266.

[3] Devonshire MSS.

You must have heard of Charles Townshend's conduct on Friday last in the House of Commons. I am glad of it for the sake of his own character and I am so *willing* to think that he will be steady that I own I was thoroughly pleased. I have seen him since and he seems to be quite determined.

And to Newcastle on 20 December,[1] Rockingham wrote that he had congratulated Townshend upon his conduct; which was good for his character —

otherwise his behaviour after the holidays might have been assigned to some disappointment which he had met with during the holidays. I hope Charles Townshend will see the necessity of being steady and I do think he does.

Devonshire, though he thought Rockingham 'too sanguine' about Townshend, felt that his intentions, 'if it is possible to get at them,' were very material; and he sent word to Townshend 'that if he was disposed to come . . . I should be very ready to unite with him'.[2] George Onslow, having spent the morning of 29 December with Townshend, reported to Newcastle:[3]

If words and sentiments and engagements of the strongest sort are in any degree to be depended upon, we have all the reason in the world to be pleased with him.

But Horace Walpole, detached and perspicacious, perhaps best defined the position in his letter to Hertford of 29 December:

Mr. Charles Townshend . . . having sat silent through the question of privilege, found himself interested in the defence of Dr. Brocklesby![4] . . . I do not look upon this as productive of consequential speaking for the Opposition; on the contrary, I should expect him sooner in place, if the Ministry could be fools enough to restore weight to him, and could be ignorant that he can never hurt them so much as by being with them.

What was the reason for Townshend's long silence even if followed by a momentary outburst? Was he already thinking of how to work his way back into office? Entries in the Grenville diary for 10–11 January 1764,[5] though not based on impeccable evidence — the information about Townshend's views came from Bindley

[1] Add. MS. 32954, ff. 98–100.
[2] Devonshire to Newcastle, 26 December 1763; ibid. ff. 372–3.
[3] Ibid., f. 303.
[4] Wilkes's doctor and a friend of Townshend. See above, p. 99.
[5] *Grenville Papers*, ii. 482–3.

who could be trusted to lay it on thick — are probably not without substance:

> *Tuesday*, [*January*] *10th*. The King told Mr. Grenville that Mr. Charles Townshend had, by the means of Mr. Bindley, desired that Lord Halifax and Mr. Grenville might know that he respected their abilities and talents, and was desirous that he should know that he did so; that he saw there was nothing to be done in Opposition; that as to Mr. Pitt, he was a man nobody could act with; that he neither thought Lord Temple a good man, nor an agreeable man, and that as to such creatures as Tom Walpole and such as him, it was beneath him to act with them. Mr. Bindley said at the same time that he had no message to bring, but only that Mr. Townshend wished that Lord Halifax and Mr. Grenville should be acquainted with his sentiments concerning them.

The very next day Bindley came to Jenkinson 'with an express message' from Townshend, repeating phrases of regard and esteem for Grenville and Halifax,

> saying that he did not like the rest of the Administration, but these were the people he should like to act with; he enlarged upon his approbation of Mr. Grenville, and expressed great regret for the words of heat that had passed between them in the House of Commons just before the holidays. . . . To this message of Mr. Bindley's, Mr. Grenville only returned that he was obliged to Mr. Townshend for his good opinion, and should always be glad to see his talents employed in support of the King's measures.
>
> Mr. Townshend had been much offended at the King's not speaking to him when he carried the Duke of Buccleuch to Court, and tried to find out whether or no the King would speak to him when he went again. Mr. Grenville said, as to that he could say nothing.

The first debate on Wilkes after the recess was on 19 January, and that day, in a division on whether to adjourn, 'many of the minority left them', including, according to Harris, Charles Townshend and Burrell. But the next day, when Sir William Meredith moved for an inquiry into Wilkes's complaint of breach of privilege, Townshend, reports Harris,

> made a most vehement speech, with his usual flow of language and strong expression, in praise of Sir W. Meredith and his motion — that 'twas a motion that concerned the whole House — that 'twas particularly proper at this time, a time when those in power were pursuing such measures that no one could foresee any but the most fatal consequences from them etc. 'Twas finely turned, finely delivered, and embellished with all the topics of virtue, honour, etc.

When, however, Grenville called on him to produce instances on which he based his insinuations, 'Townshend heard all, took no notice, made no answer, named nothing.'

A similar report of the incident in the Grenville diary[1] concludes with a paragraph for which the authority is not named — possibly it was once more the bustling Bindley:

> Mr. Townshend sat silent, and that very evening repented of what he had done; went home in low spirits; said he had spoke very ill, and had given some offence in his speech to Mr. Grenville, for which he was very sorry.

Still, however serious the Government's position was over Wilkes and General Warrants, there was no response from Grenville to Townshend's alleged advances.

During the next few weeks Townshend was a frequent speaker, though by no means always on the Opposition side: on 31 January, when the Government narrowly escaped defeat on the repeal of the cider tax, Townshend 'laughed at the commonplace declamation about excise'; on 7 February he once more upheld 'the necessity of collecting inland duties by excise', and defended some of the measures taken by Government; and on the 10th absented himself from the division on the Cider Act.[2] Horace Walpole wrote that the Opposition had been at this time 'frequently obstructed and distressed' by Townshend, 'who oftener spoke against them than for them, and *that* generally when he had given the most solemn assurances of support'.[3] But over Wilkes and General Warrants he now spoke and voted against the Government: on 6 February he made, according to George Onslow, one of 'the finest speeches that ever were heard'; on the 12th was absent from the meeting of leading Members at Sir George Savile's 'where the motions were settled',[4] which, wrote Onslow to Newcastle,[5] 'surprised us all, and much alarms me'; but on the 13th did well on the examination of evidence and 'abused' Grenville.[6] He stayed for the debate of 14–15 February, and again voted against the Government —

> Charles, who, as he must be extraordinary [wrote Walpole to Hertford on the 15th] is now so in romantic nicety of honour. His father, who is dying or dead, at Bath, and from whom he hopes two thousand

[1] Ibid. 484–5. [2] Harris's parliamentary diary, Malmesbury MSS.
[3] Walpole, *Memoirs of George III*, i. 282.
[4] *History of the late minority* (1765), pp. 269–70.
[5] Add. MS. 32955, f. 449. [6] Ibid., ff. 366, 458.

a year, has sent for him. He has refused to go — lest his *steadiness* should be questioned.

He went in fact to Bath on the 15th but was back for the debate of the 17th;[1] and delivered a speech which Harris, though a strong Grenvillian, describes as 'a fine piece of enthusiasm, finely and forcibly delivered, and as well acted as ever Garrick did Othello'. Walpole, writing to Hertford on 19 February, calls it 'so fine that *it amazed even from him*'; and in a passage of his *Memoirs*, written about a year after Townshend's death[2] and therefore summarizing his view of Townshend's speeches:

> Charles Townshend made a most capital speech, replete with argument, history, and law, though severe on the lawyers: a speech, like most of his, easier to be described than detailed.

An echo of that speech still reverberates in Townshend's letter to Newcastle of 24 February[3] when he concludes

> with earnestly wishing you may see the constitution and welfare of this country restored . . . by the genuine descendants of those who . . . have been the constant guardians and Ministers of these kingdoms . . . animated by the example of our respective ancestors. . . . We will never desert the same principles and the same cause.

The next day, thinking of the forthcoming budget, Newcastle wrote to Townshend:[4]

> The next point of consequence . . . is their disposition of North America. The Duke of Devonshire has already talked to you upon it, and you must suggest to us what it may be proper to do there.

Thus, in spite of the line taken by Townshend over America on previous occasions, he still ranked as expert of the Newcastle Whigs on colonial problems; and this was a subject on which he rigidly adhered to the ideas he had formed more than ten years before.

On 7 March, writes Harris:

> Mr. Grenville gave notice that on Friday next [9 March] he would go at large into the ways and means (that is, in vulgar phrase, open the budget). Gave us some general idea of his plan, particularly as to the taxing America. Beckford rambled — hoped regard would be had to the American legislatures etc. Charles Townshend answered strongly

[1] Add. MS. 32956, f. 5.
[2] *Memoirs of George III*, i. 300.
[3] Add. MS. 32956, f. 95.
[4] Ibid., f. 104.

> for Government — that our plan of expenses being so great, America ought to share; wished everything at that time might be debated with temper; said of the Peace, that 'twas so good that for that very reason less likely to continue.

Here then was the first forecast of the Stamp Act and Townshend's reaction to it. But when on 9 March Grenville fully developed his scheme for taxing America, Townshend was not in the House; he had been sent off by Newcastle on a mission to which the Duke, somewhat shamefacedly, gave priority over the budget. When Lord Hardwicke was dying (he died on 6 March 1764), Lord Sandwich had put up his candidature for High Steward of Cambridge University in succession to Hardwicke and against Hardwicke's son and heir. The interest of the Yorke family, and Newcastle's own ease in managing the university of which he was Chancellor, were at stake, and seemed to the Duke to be of momentous consequence. He wrote to Townshend on 7 March:[1] 'The necessity of having a person of weight and consideration, and a particular friend and relation of my own, to go down to the university to direct and support our friends there appears most plainly to me'; but in an attempt to saddle Townshend with the responsibility, he added:

> On Friday is the budget. No man in England knows better than yourself what should be said or done upon it; and therefore I am sure that you will judge what it may be proper to do. Sir William Baker, I am sure, will act with you.

Townshend replied the same day 'at night'[2] that he was at Newcastle's service, and ready to go to Cambridge the next day. 'As to the budget Sir William Baker has my papers, it is not a day for division, and you are to judge how far the election should give way to it. I shall obey, not advise.' His sense of relative values was about as good as Newcastle's and, though the taxing of America was a pet scheme of his, he accepted William Baker, a leading pro-American, for his *locum tenens*. He started for Cambridge on 8 March: but he had placed the responsibility for the decision on Newcastle.

On Friday morning, 9 March, in a long and very zealous letter[3] he reported on his canvass of the university: 'I have assumed the honour of being employed by your Grace, with the approbation of Lord Hardwicke and his family and Lord Townshend.' And he

[1] Ibid., f. 250. [2] Ibid., f. 248. [3] Ibid., ff. 310–11.

concluded: 'My opinion is your Grace and the common cause of the university, Whiggism, and liberty will triumph here.' And on the 11th, in another long letter:[1] 'I could write for hours, but I have no hours, they are all devoted to you, to your Grace, and to the public, which is the same cause.' Walpole reported to Hertford on 11 March:

> The election at Cambridge is to be on Tuesday, 24th; Charles Townshend is gone thither, and I suppose, by this time, has ranted, and romanced, and turned every one of their ideas topsy-turvy.

It appears that Townshend was still at Cambridge when his father died on 12 March. Newcastle was highly pleased with him, addressed him as 'my dear friend and nephew', and ascribed Hardwicke's success to his exertions; while Townshend addressed Newcastle as 'my very dear lord' and was full of devotion to him.

Newcastle, in his letter to Townshend of 10 March, having dealt with Cambridge business, had added with somewhat forced cheerfulness:

> Now one word for G. Grenville: he *entertained* the House yesterday with a long speech of three hours and a quarter. Sir William Baker with a very short one, upon the plan you directed him.

But there was no denying that Grenville had carried the day. 'Mr. Grenville', writes Walpole,[2] 'opened the budget, fully, for brevity was not his failing; but he did it with art and ability too.' Of those best qualified to meet him in debate, Pitt and Legge were ill and Townshend and Charles Yorke absent. The Opposition failed to follow up its recent successes. Newcastle, conscious of his own responsibility in the matter, was now urging Townshend and Yorke to try to retrieve the position. Townshend, replying to a message from Newcastle on Wednesday, 14 March,[3] expressed 'great surprise at the precipitation' shown by the Government; he himself could not attend as his father was not to be buried till Monday (19 March); on Wednesday he had to go to Cambridge where the election would detain him; etc. He thought the House would not suffer the American Bill to come on 'in the absence of those who have such a right to be heard upon it'; and the rather, because the budget was opened in the absence of himself and many others![4] Newcastle replied with comprehensible exasperation:

[1] Ibid., ff. 358–9.
[2] *Memoirs of George III*, i. 309.
[3] Add. MS. 32957, f. 47.
[4] Ibid., f. 85.

I am extremely sorry that your necessary business prevents my having your advice and assistance in our Cambridge affair. I am obliged to attend it every hour in the day, and indeed have been reproached for preferring that consideration to the greater objects of the public; and particularly for sending Mr. Townshend to Cambridge the day that the budget was opened by Mr. Grenville; and that reproach will go still farther, for Mr. Grenville declared to the House yesterday that he intended that the American bill should be committed for Thursday next, the day of our election at Cambridge, and done on purpose to prevent Mr. Townshend's being in the House.

The next day, 16 March, Townshend heard that William Dowdeswell, his old fellow-student at Leyden, now M.P. for Worcestershire, was going to move for the repeal of the Militia Act and was to be supported by the Opposition. He wrote to Newcastle:[1]

I presume to control the sentiments of no set of men, but I maintain the government of my own; and . . . thus early apprise you, in self defence, that, such as I am, my conviction of the utility of the measure [the militia], my reverence for consistency in conduct, and my personal love for my brother (one of whose glories it is to have planned and executed this measure) must naturally and necessarily make me oppose Mr. Dowdeswell's motion with firmness and without distinction. Nothing can be so injurious or unreasonable as this intention: no man has sacrificed so much to those I act with, or received so little from their prosperity, as I have. . . .

Your Grace permits me to write to you as the thought occurs, or even as the maggot bites, and therefore your indulgence must be my apology.

Newcastle immediately replied with an assuaging letter. Thanking him for it, Townshend remarked:[2]

I am sorry you thought me *angry*. . . . Alarmed and mortified I certainly was, because I thought such a motion, made so lightly, and just as Lord Townshend withdrew from our House, would carry an ugly face, at the same time that I dreaded a difference of opinion among ourselves, upon a point not likely to be debated coolly, or forgot as soon as decided.

When the motion was made on 21 March, Townshend delivered a long and impassioned speech in defence of the militia; was supported by Newcastle's nephew George Onslow, while Thomas

[1] Ibid., ff. 119 and 120. [2] Ibid., f. 131.

Pelham and John Shelley, Newcastle's other relations in the House, were ready to assist him; which Townshend gratefully acknowledged in a letter to Newcastle on the 23rd.[1] 'No division', wrote Harris at the end of his notes of the debate, 'Opposition would have been divided, and Government had been unanimous.'

On 22 March the American Bill came up in committee; the Opposition was once more divided: North American mercantile interests clashed with those of the West Indians especially over the duty on molasses which now became the central subject of the Bill (especially as the discussion of stamp duties was left to the next year). Townshend was in the House, 'divided in civility to Sir W. Baker', but did not speak; similarly the next day he remained silent. On the 22nd he had a hasty consultation with Yorke who thought 'the questions of expediency and regulation arising out of the Bill now depending, too speculative and too nice to be much agitated', and declined to attend the Bill.[2] Townshend now felt that failing systematic and unanimous action, '*partial* opposition and *thin* attendance' tended only to

> spread the idea of disunion among the chiefs, and strengthen Ministry. I propose therefore, so far as relates to me, to attend merely as upon the molasses duty, because I saw the face of the House, the absence of our friends, an influence impressed on the former Friday too strong to be shaken, and resistance useless, if not imprudent.

On the whole Townshend would not engage without Yorke who, both from indolence and personal views of his own, was disinclined to action. Nevertheless Newcastle, clutching at Townshend's remark that he would still speak on the Sugar Bill, tried to encourage his friends by telling them that Townshend intended to deal in the House with Grenville's budget speech; which once more aroused Townshend's anger. Again Newcastle, hearing that Townshend was displeased with his having mentioned this intention to others, humbly apologised: he did not know that this was to be treated as confidential and did not understand 'that it depended on Mr. Yorke's attendance'.[3] Townshend answered politely — the matter had been exaggerated; but his moodiness again overclouded relations between them. Townshend spoke once more in the House before it adjourned on 19 April: on the 4th,

[1] Ibid., ff. 239–40.
[2] Townshend to Newcastle, 23 March 1764; ibid.
[3] Ibid., ff. 296–7.

Anthony Bacon, a merchant trading with North America, moved that its paper currency should not be legal tender. In the debate which ensued Townshend argued that although 'the colonies ought to have some currency that should be legal tender under proper regulations', the evils complained of called for the immediate interposition of Parliament. The matter was settled by a compromise which, though restraining the colonies from issuing more paper money with the clause of legal tender, did not affect any already issued.[1]

A few days after the House had risen, Conway was dismissed from the King's Bedchamber and from the command of his regiment for voting with the Opposition over Wilkes and General Warrants. It was hoped by some zealous members of the Opposition that this would rouse Townshend; but his letter to Newcastle of 28 April[2] harps on the hopeless state of the Opposition:

> I think the calm and submissive reception of such an outrage, done to our constitution in the person of such an officer, the deepest and most fatal symptom we have yet seen of general insensibility and incurable indifference. Around St. James's it is discussed and divided as interest directs the speaker, but in the City it is forgot, out of London it is not mentioned. . . .
>
> Lord Temple returned here yesterday: and Lord Lyttelton thinks him desponding. I am told his relation [Pitt] speaks the language of despair, and imputes freely the many ills, which he himself occasions, to our attention to Cambridge, of which, even this charge and his authority did not make me repent. Mr. Pitt has relinquished his house in town, and the furniture is removing.

In short, Townshend was preparing to relinquish Opposition, and, if possible, obtain reinstatement in office.

Two days later, 30 April, he sent Newcastle a further dissertation of about 2,000 words on 'the temper, character, and deadness of the time we live in'.[3] Ignoring the part which he himself had played, he wrote:

> Recollect, my Lord, the ingratitude you have yourself met with; the desertion of the majority of the Whigs; the many great names and

[1] See L. B. Namier, 'Charles Garth', *English Historical Review*, July 1939, p. 640.

[2] Add. MS. 32958, ff. 226–7.

[3] Ibid., ff. 248–53; printed from a copy in *H.M.C., Townshend MSS.*, pp. 398–401.

> families who have abandoned all union from obligation and consanguinity, upon the frivolous distinction of supporting the person of the King: the successful attack made upon the freedom of the press: the quiet reception of every act of violence offered to persons and to things: and the perfect state of tranquillity in the City and in the counties which now seemingly takes place under a ministry, lately so odious, and still so rash. Are not these proofs that the national temper is subdued? ... I agree with your Grace that the minority ... made the ministry and the Crown look pale upon their numbers in one part of the last session, and it is now said perseverance and activity would have given success. Perhaps this may be true; but, if it be, what was the sudden and secret cause which slackened their activity? Some impute it to jealousy; ... others to inattention. ... As to the visit to Cambridge, I know how loudly I have been condemned for that absence; but, my Lord! such loose censure does not even dwell upon me; especially when it comes from men with whom I have acted *voluntarily*, not by compact; ... in whose plans I had originally no participation, whose systems I am not bound to adopt, and to whom I stand, in no sense, nor any degree accountable. ... I shall ... unmortified by their harmless disapprobation, be ever pleased with having obeyed your commands, and endeavoured at least to assist my friend Lord Hardwicke and his family at Cambridge. I say this as often as I hear it, which is almost every day, from some of our most zealous friends who continually speak of this event, either in direct terms of blame, or by insinuations which are more offensive.

One can merely admire, or wonder at, the moral and intellectual acrobatics of Townshend's discourse: with what devotion to Newcastle he disclaimed all connexion with the Duke's party, and rubbed salt into the recent wound. With a strong unconscious guilt complex of his own, he knew how to play on the guilt feelings of others.

And next he proceeded to discuss positive plans of action, with a lack of understanding for the psychology and feelings of other men which was the bane of him as a politician:

> For myself, I am of opinion, my Lord, that the minority should be strengthened, if it can *be done upon proper terms*, by a connexion with Lord Bute, or with Lord Holland, or by the reconciling Lord Temple and Mr. Pitt with Mr. Grenville. Because I think the party in the House of Lords is weak, in the Court odious, and in itself not sufficient to success; at least with this Parliament, when there is only one Court, so young a King; at the close of an unpopular war, and in an age of extravagance, indigence, immorality, and indifference.

Could this be achieved, the state of the Opposition should be examined by allotting 'to particular men their separate departments in speaking to individuals', and a daily paper should be set up and circulated.

> Some leading men in each town through the several counties should be admitted to confidence, and be persuaded to give their clubs and districts the tone of conversation, recommended from hence.
>
> A committee should be appointed to consider and prepare heads of business for the next winter, and in one word the kingdom should be kept warm, and the chiefs attentive and laborious during the recess. Sir William Baker should be desired to put the City in motion, both as an example to other counties, and as an attack nearest home.

Having once more compared unfavourably the state and chances of the Opposition with those of the Government, and declared his preference for 'the characters, claims and interests' of those he had 'voluntarily supported', he reached the crucial point of his discourse: he would still wish to support them 'if any hope should remain of success'.

> But, my Lord, it must be [with] a reasonable hope of success, resulting from union, plan, activity, and strength. I am far from being in a condition to make even this prudent, after my family disappointments and the little favour I have ever met with from former Administrations. . . .

— meaning, of course, Newcastle himself, Devonshire, and Pitt.

On 5 May Newcastle reported to the Duke of Cumberland on a conference with Rockingham and Devonshire[1] — they

> entirely agreed in opinion upon the content of Mr. Townshend's letter and the cause of it, viz. to lay in a sort of deposit with us, as a justification of whatever part he should finally take.

And referring to this period, Horace Walpole wrote at the end of 1768 about Charles Townshend: 'unfortunately we could neither do with him, nor without him.'[2]

Townshend spent the summer of 1764 in writing Opposition propaganda and in sounding Grenville about his inclusion in the Government. In August he published anonymously a pamphlet, *A Defence of the Minority with regard to General Warrants*.[3] That

[1] Add. MS. 32958, ff. 307–11. [2] *Memoirs of George III*, i. 327.

[3] A truncated version of it was printed in *Gentleman's Magazine* for Augus 1764, pp. 354–9.

it was by him became soon known, and on 28 August was admitted by his friend Bindley to Charles Jenkinson.[1] George Selwyn wrote to Lord Holland on 9 September:[2]

> Charles's pamphlet I have read and did not like; it was so inferior to what we expected from him, and especially on that subject, that Mr. Elliot does not believe him to be the author of it.

Horace Walpole took a more favourable view:[3] 'It is well written, but does not sell much, as a notion prevails that it has been much altered and softened.' Style and matter are certainly good but not impressive, and there is something legalistically argumentative and over-elaborate about it — possibly the result of a divided purpose and divided feelings. But for its poor sale Townshend, hurt in his prodigious vanity, blamed the Opposition. In a letter to Thomas Walpole on 23 September 1764,[4] pretending that he did not know its author (he did not mind telling a lie even if known as such while he was telling it), he referred to

> the strange negligence in circulating this work, and from the objections peevishly made by the party it vindicates to the temper and tendency of this pamphlet . . . an indifference which resembles little the activity and union with which the majority espouse, maintain and circulate every weak word which interest or authority obtains in their favour.

Friends of his 'eagerly inquired' after it at Bristol, Bath, and Liverpool; he himself failed to get it at Oxford; Lord Townshend at Norwich, Lynn, or Yarmouth. If he were the author:

> No consideration should induce me to move one step further in the contest, but I would leave it to those who disapproved of his temper and found *his* argument imperfect, to merit more from the minority.

Newcastle, to whom Walpole had sent his correspondence with Townshend, replied on 30 September:[5]

> I own I think my nephew Charles has some reason to complain at the cool reception which his most excellent and most meritorious *Defence* has met with in some places; but he can never distinguish; and mixes everything and everybody together, in order to make that a measure with us all. . . .

[1] Jenkinson to Grenville, 28 August 1764; Grenville MSS in the possession of Sir John Murray.
[2] Lord Ilchester, *Letters to Henry Fox*, p. 201.
[3] Walpole to Lord Hertford, 27 August 1764.
[4] Thomas Walpole MSS. in the possession of Mr. David Holland.
[5] Add. MS. 32962, f. 179.

> We are, I think endeavouring to drive Charles Townshend and Charles Yorke from us,[1] whether they will or not. It is time never to be desperate with them, when they have done some overt act of being so with us.... Charles Townshend, I am persuaded, hardly wishes to be with us; but he must be encouraged and, in some measure, *courted*, or he is gone.

That this was to be Townshend's attitude, he showed even more clearly in his letter to Thomas Walpole of 9 October:

> I cannot refrain from saying that if men, either from dissipation, frivolity, singularity, or distrust will not consult, write, and cooperate, they must not be surprised to find both individuals and the public withdraw their affection and their hopes from what they will consider either as a whimsical or a scattered party.

But in fact by then two friends of his connected with the Government, Bindley and John Morton, had for some time been making overtures for his return to office.

[1] This may refer to Pitt's attitude, who was 'pretty bitter' against the two; see Add. MS. 32961, f. 42.

CHAPTER VII

Townshend in the Grenville and Rockingham Ministries 1765-1766

(i)

By the summer of 1764 Charles Townshend was thoroughly restless, and friends of his connected with the Government were making overtures for his return to office. John Bindley wrote about him to Charles Jenkinson on 15 June:[1]

> He is at Adderbury. His letter of today says *I am a free man, bound to no party or system*, etc. I hope therefore, dear sir, Government will find some means to engage and employ his talents. . . . I hear on all sides that minority is much displeased with its leaders. He is abused, Mr. Pitt is abused, C. Yorke is abused, and they tell me they all abuse one another.

And on 28 August Jenkinson wrote to George Grenville:[2] 'I have just seen Bindley. He gives the same account of Mr. Charles Townshend as those we have hitherto received.'

On his side Townshend heard and relished reports of forthcoming changes in Government. He wrote on 2 September to his friend Chase Price, then at Tonbridge:[3]

> I know not whether it be the same where you are, but here every post brings a new negotiation, some fresh alliance, and a new plan of Ministry. This day, the Duke of Bedford refuses to attend at council; the next, he is pacified; now Lord Bute and Mr. Pitt are in close concert; then the Duke of Bedford and Mr. Pitt agree to lay aside all their animosities; and in short each succeeding day confutes the former.

The intermediaries may have exaggerated to either side the eagerness of the other for an arrangement, and it is uncertain who took

[1] Jucker, *Jenkinson Papers*, 301.
[2] Grenville MSS., in the possession of Sir John Murray.
[3] Chase Price MSS., in the possession of the Marquis of Salisbury.

the first step. Townshend wrote to Lord Temple, Grenville's brother, on 6 October 1764:[1]

> Mr. Grenville has lately opened himself to a person, much my friend, upon the subject of my situation, and in a manner not a little singular and artful. He said, among other things, that he heard I am more warm than Mr. Pitt, who, it is said, was very moderate; that he adhered to his original resolution not to solicit any man to accept high office; that he now looked upon all accomodation as impossible, and that Government must be contended for. He assumed great cheerfulness and ease, and spoke of me very handsomely, though as the only individual supposed to be determined.

The person, much Townshend's friend, to whom Grenville opened himself was John Morton, M.P. for Abingdon, formerly a follower of Bute and now an adherent of the Grenville Ministry. On 15 October Morton writing to Grenville[2] refers to 'the business you did me the honour to entrust to my discretion in our last walk at Wotton [Grenville's house in Buckinghamshire]'; but he had only been able to see Townshend 'within these few days at my own house [at Tackley, in Oxfordshire]'.

> After repeated conversations on the subject, I have his leave to assure you that all reports of his engagements or inclinations to continue adverse measures are without foundation or truth.
>
> That he is most sincerely inclined to give all possible assistance to Government.

But the time and circumstances for it could not be discussed by letter, and Morton would not have written about it 'had it not been his [Townshend's] wish that you should know thus much as soon as possible'.

Grenville replied to Morton on 17 October by suggesting a meeting.[3] But more than a fortnight elapsed before they did meet. Meantime Townshend wrote to Morton on 28 October[4] (in reply to a letter so far untraced) with the obvious purpose of putting on record his own, gently twisted, version of what had so far passed between them:

> The letter informs me that Mr. Grenville had learnt from you what measures you had taken in consequence of his original conversation with you in London, and that, acquainted with the temper and purport of our conversation at Tackley, he wishes to hear the report of it

[1] *Grenville Papers*, ii. 443.
[2] Ibid., 448.
[3] Grenville's letter book, Huntington Library.
[4] Buccleuch MSS.

> more distinctly from you in person. You will on your arrival on Tuesday [30 October], be expected to make this second report, in which I conclude you will be much upon your guard, and think it prudent to keep strictly to that line which we have indeed observed ourselves.
>
> When you first called upon me at Adderbury I did not imagine you had any authority from Mr. Grenville, and therefore I touched upon all the topics which you had started cursorily and lightly, in the manner of common discourse. When I saw you next at your own house, and knew from yourself that you had been pressed to move these matters to me, I expressed to you without hesitation my impatience to see tranquillity restored. My earnest wishes to find a reconciliation accomplished as salutary to the public as honourable to the family I alluded to, my concern for the deplorable state of the kingdom, my willingness to concur in any reasonable plan for strengthening Government, and my principles of moderation and union. . . .

Further explanations, should there be any, would come best through his brother, Lord Townshend. And he concluded by recommending to Morton

> to restrain your conversation with Mr. Grenville to the professions I have made to you of personal respect for him, of duty to the Crown, of zeal for the public, and anxiety for union: adding, if you please, my declarations of my own freedom from all party engagements, my resolution to act a fair independent part, and my willingness to assist in any scheme for uniting men for the public good.

Morton replied on 29 October demurring against some of Townshend's assertions and injunctions —

> I thought I disclosed to you at our first meeting at Adderbury that I did not speak of such momentous matters without authority, and I believe when you reflect on some things that then passed you will be certain that you then understood I was not disclosing merely my own wishes.

And he added that in trying to gain Townshend's support for the Government, he had tried to serve the King rather than '*his present Minister*'.

Townshend replied the same day (Morton's letter having obviously been sent by messenger) with a disquisition such as he had long experienced and practised in correspondence with his family.

> There are some passages in your letter which seem to require an answer from me. . . . You have much mistaken the design of my

> letter . . . if you will read it again . . . it was not my intention to do you *imperfect* justice: far from it: my letter, taken entire, demonstrates. . . .

And with a touch of self-knowledge:

> As I have now replied to your letter, like a polemical controversist, paragraph by paragraph, I might fairly conclude here. . . .

Morton replied on 30 October, rather hurt — 'I am most unfortunate in my expression if by my last I gave you the least umbrage.' And next, on 3 November, he reported the talk he had had with Grenville. Morton had stated 'minutely and faithfully' what he thought himself authorised to say, Grenville responded with polite generalities but gave Morton to understand

> that the person who has repeatedly wrote to you on this subject [probably Bindley] never had any authority to disclose a syllable of any overture or proposal of any terms whatever. That in fact he never himself entertained such a design, or ever had in his opinion a proper authority [i.e. from the King] so to do.

Townshend, filled 'with astonishment', claimed to have come reluctantly into this transaction; asked Morton to compare 'my fears with your experience' —

> you have been treated with unexampled insincerity if you are not mistaken in every word which you have repeated from the person [Grenville] who at first proposed, then approved, and now disowns every step you have taken.

Morton replied on 8 November that he would satisfy Townshend 'under the gentleman's own hand, that I did not interfere without authority'. He expected a new approach from that quarter before very long — 'but be assured I am spoilt for any negotiation of this sort for the future.'

In a letter to Thomas Walpole on 9 October Townshend had threatened to dissociate himself from the Opposition:[1]

> If men, either from dissipation, frivolity, singularity, or distrust will not consult, write, and co-operate, they must not be surprised to find both individuals and the public withdraw their affection and their hopes from what they will consider either as a whimsical or a scattered party. . . . For myself, I . . . am truly satisfied to see every man preserving not only the freedom, but even the cast, of his own mind, as I find by two years experience that this is thought by great persons to be the most eligible plan.

[1] Thomas Walpole MSS., in the possession of Mr. David Holland.

On 8 November, the day the negotiations with Grenville broke down, Townshend wrote again to Walpole:

> Having acted on principle, in contempt of interest and ambition, I shall never be governed in any action by any authority but that of my own free judgement, independent equally of the favour of Court and the censure of an Opposition. It is my *remaining* peculiar advantage to have no *obligations* to any party; to have no family or party leagues or stipulated confederacy; and to be at full liberty to act, without breach of *any one* engagement, with either *individuals* or *bodies of men* as I shall think most for my own honour and the public good.

Having thus proclaimed his full independence Townshend made a new approach to Grenville, more direct and concrete than any in the tentative soundings of the preceding months. Jenkinson wrote to Grenville on 20 November 1764:[1]

> Bindley has just been with me. He has been with C. Townshend for six hours.
>
> He found him in the best humour imaginable both with respect to himself and to Government.

Townshend fully approved of Bindley supporting Administration and believed every sensible man would now do the same.

> With respect to himself, Mr. Townshend said that the Pay Office and being a Cabinet councillor (which he was, he said, before)[2] would satisfy him.
>
> I rather understood that he would be content to wait for Lord Holland's death.... He said he desired only to be second in the House of Commons. You will judge how far all this is to be relied on, and what use should be made of it, but Bindley will call on you tomorrow.

Grenville's reply is not recorded, but Townshend seems to have talked freely about his plans — Gilly Williams wrote to George Selwyn on 4 January 1765:[3]

> We dine tomorrow at Charles Townshend's. What he is now I know not, but the last time we saw him he had no acrimony in him, but seemed rather looking towards the Pay Office, which, I suppose, Lord Holland will soon quit, either by a natural or political death.

[1] *Grenville Papers*, ii. 465.

[2] If he claimed merely a place in the Nominal Cabinet, the statement referring to February–April 1763 was probably correct; but Jenkinson, who at that time had been secretary to Bute, significantly adds 'he said'.

[3] Jesse, *George Selwyn and his Contemporaries*, i. 342; see also pp. 368 and 373.

The House re-assembled on 10 January; and on the 20th there was a debate on the Naval Estimates. Horace Walpole wrote to Hertford the same day:

> Dowdeswell, in a long and very sensible speech, proposed to reduce the number of sailors to ten thousand. He was answered by — Charles Townshend — oh yes! — are you surprised? nobody here was: no, not even at his assertion that he had always applauded the Peace. . . . Well, you want to know what place he is to have — so does he too.

Harris's report of Townshend's speech touches on another point: 'Townshend . . . asserts *the supremacy of this country* over the colonies — would not have them emancipated.'[1] And on 6 February, when Grenville introduced the American Stamp Bill, Harris describes Townshend's speech in support of the Bill as 'lively and eloquent'. Similarly, Onslow wrote to Newcastle:[2] 'Charles Townshend and Barré spoke well' — he bracketed them together although they spoke on opposite sides, and, writes Walpole,[3] Townshend received 'a pretty heavy thump from Barré'. But no one in the House as yet appreciated even remotely the importance the Stamp Act was to assume shortly, and for fuller reports of the speeches it is necessary to turn to the correspondence of colonial agents, especially the report sent to Connecticut on 11 February by Jared Ingersoll.[4] According to this, Townshend concluded his speech in favour of the Stamp Bill with a peroration which recalls the style of letters from his father to him:

> And now will these Americans, children planted by our care, nourished up by our indulgence until they are grown to a degree of strength and opulence, and protected by our arms, will they grudge to contribute their mite to relieve us from the heavy weight of that burden which we lie under?

In reply Barré delivered his much-quoted indictment of the mother country: 'They planted by your care? No! your oppressions planted them in America. . . . They nourished by your indulgence? They grew by your neglect of them', etc.

Townshend spoke during that session on a great variety of more

[1] The point was taken up the next day by Beckford; see Walpole, *Memoirs of George III*, ii. 34.

[2] Add. MS. 32965, f. 346.

[3] To Hertford, 12 February 1765.

[4] *Collections of Connecticut Historical Society, Fitch Papers*, ii. 317–26. It was first published in 1766 in *Mr. Ingersoll's Letters relating to the Stamp Act*, and some extracts from it appear in *Parliamentary History*, xvi. 38.

or less innocuous subjects: in support of Meredith's renewed motion on General Warrants (by now a worn out theme); on the African trade in which his friend Samuel Touchet was greatly interested; on the East India Company Bill; three times on duties on silk (a subject which a month later was to produce serious riots in London: on 24 April, according to Harris, Townshend was 'very abusive on the mercers, and seemed by a well-acted zeal for the manufacturers, to speak to the gallery, rather than to the House'); for the Masters in Chancery Bill; and, 'with his usual vivacity', for the Broad Wheel Carriage Bill. He voted with the Government on the motion to limit the power of the Attorney-General to issue informations for libel; and kept silent when the dismissal of service officers for votes in the House of Commons came up in debate on 23 January.

All that time he was trying to make his way back into office. On 23 February George Townshend told Grenville[1] that Charles 'had made a very explicit declaration to him of his firm resolution to take a firm and cordial part with Mr. Grenville'; that 'he had withdrawn himself from the Opposition'; and 'wished to have a conversation with Mr. Grenville, in which he would explain himself in the fullest manner'. Grenville, obviously suspecting that Charles might try to secure a return to office through Bute, replied:

> That he should be glad to see Mr. Charles Townshend taking a part that became him in support of Government, but . . . that if he wished to attain any situation in the King's service through any channel but Mr. Grenville's, whilst he held the high rank he does in the King's service, Mr. Grenville would quit that moment.

On the 26th Lord Granby pressed Grenville to see Charles, and said that Lord Townshend and himself would answer for the sincerity of Charles's professions. Grenville met Charles at Lord Townshend's on 3 March:[2]

> Mr. Charles Townshend made the fullest declaration imaginable of his intentions to unite cordially with Mr. Grenville, assuring him that he was under no engagements whatsoever with the Opposition. . . . He gave the most cordial assurances to Mr. Grenville of his firmness, and readiness to assist him in everything in his power.

He asked for no office, and reserved for himself entire liberty should the question of Conway's dismissal come before the House.

[1] Grenville diary, *Grenville Papers*, iii. 118–19. [2] Ibid., 120–1.

He assured Grenville that he was not in communication with Bute, and had not seen him 'these four months'. Asked by Grenville, he said he preferred that their interview should be kept a secret.

On 23 April, when Grenville convened at his house thirty-four leading Government supporters in the Commons to read out to them the King's speech on the Regency Bill, Townshend was among them — besides Charles Yorke the only one who held no office. But while questions about the Bill were being discussed over which the Grenville Administration differed from the King and incurred his displeasure — the right to be reserved to him of appointing the Regent, and the question of including the dowager Princess of Wales among those capable of being Regent — Townshend preserved discreet silence. He only spoke in the House after these questions had been settled, when on 11 May, George Onslow, one of the most zealous on the Opposition side, tried to delay matters by moving the adjournment. 'Charles Townshend, they say, surpassed all he had ever done in a wrangle with Onslow', wrote Walpole to Hertford, 12 May. And Harris records how that day

> the two Onslows . . . fell on Charles Townshend . . . lamenting the loss of their old friend, and commenting in particular on his late silence, for he spoke but little for some time past. This fired him, he rose and with the greatest vivacity and wit vindicated himself, and chastised his antagonists, to the no small entertainment, I may say relish, of the House.[1]

Townshend afterwards told Harris that Onslow had been sent to him five times by Newcastle 'to persuade him . . . to oppose the Regency Bill, and that he had always refused it'.

Even before the Regency Bill had widened the breach between the King and the Grenville Administration, George III had applied for the Duke of Cumberland's assistance in forming a new Government. The matter was in abeyance while the Regency Bill was passing through Parliament, but on 13 May the King once more entrusted the Duke with the task. The next day Cumberland acquainted Newcastle and Rockingham with it and with the outline of the new Administration chalked out by the King 'for all our joint considerations': in this Pitt and Townshend

[1] For the names of speakers in this debate, see also Grenville's report to the King, Fortescue, *Correspondence of King George III*, i. p. 90.

were named for Secretaries of State.[1] The suggestion was repeated in a message sent by Cumberland to Pitt: 'that his Majesty had chalked out the above-mentioned arrangement, thinking Mr. Charles Townshend might be the properest person to execute, whenever Mr. Pitt's health should incapacitate him from either Court or Parliament attendance.'[2] The choice hardly sprang from a preference of the King's, but, remembering Pitt's proposals of August 1763, he presumably thought that the selection would be acceptable to Pitt; the latter's reaction, however, is not recorded. After the negotiation with Pitt had failed, Townshend was once more named for Secretary of State in an Administration to be formed from Newcastle's friends: Lord Lyttelton was suggested for the Treasury, and Lord Egmont and Townshend were to be Secretaries of State. Lyttelton and Townshend both refused.[3]

The King had consequently to recall the Grenville-Bedford Administration who were now in a position to impose terms on him: one of these was that Lord Holland (whom they suspected of a share in the attempt to displace them) should be removed from the Pay Office, which was to be given to Townshend. Of all the conditions, that was the least repugnant to the King, who had an old dislike of Holland; and on 24 May Townshend kissed hands for the office. But it required Townshend's peculiar lack of psychological insight not to perceive that the manner and circumstances in which he was brought in were bound to extend to him the King's resentment; of how George III had even previously felt toward him he was probably unaware. Newcastle wrote to the Bishop of Oxford on 1 June:[4]

> His Majesty shows great distinction to every one of *our friends* preferably to his Ministers, or any of their supporters. Charles Townshend, the Paymaster, is very much hurt at it; and outrageous that George Onslow, the greatest opposer, and particularly of the Regency bill, should be so much distinguished at Court, when he, *the new Paymaster*, was taken very little notice of.

[1] See Cumberland's 'Statement', published in Albemarle, *Rockingham Memoirs*, i. 185–203, where from 16 April onwards events are antedated by a week.

[2] Newcastle's *Narrative of the Changes in the Ministry*, edited by M. Bateson, p. 6, mentions 'some loose conversations about employments' already in the April talks: 'Mr. Pitt to be Secretary of State, I think, with Charles Townshend'; there is nothing to that effect in Cumberland's 'Statement'.

[3] Newcastle's *Narrative*, 15.

[4] Add. MS. 32967, ff. 1–7.

And Townshend wrote to his brother on 3 July, having noted the King's resolve to dismiss the Grenville Administration:[1]

> I have been assured, upon expressing my surprise at the change we both experienced so lately in the behaviour to us at St. James's, that my acceptance had been unpleasing to the King, from the manner in which it had been *forced* upon him, at *such* a *time*, and with other *similar* affronts to him; upon which I have ventured to deny the fact, and to recapitulate the circumstances of that long-depending promotion, and the explanation which accompanied the offer and appointment; to which I was answered, Lord Townshend and you, believe me, have been deceived, and if ever you should return to the Closet this *very* matter will be the *first* to be *cleared up*.

Toward Lord Holland Townshend behaved in a most considerate manner. According to John Powell, Holland's right hand man at the Pay Office who was now to fill the same place under Townshend, the latter had refused to accept the office till convinced that Holland's dismissal was inevitable;[2] and having taken it over, behaved with the greatest kindness and civility to Holland and all his friends.[3] When Holland wrote to thank him, Townshend replied with a panegyric on Holland.[4] And George Selwyn wrote to Holland on 13 June:[5]

> I find there are those who think Charles's behaviour to you political. I don't like to hear people take away the merit of good-natured actions, but in whatever light this can be seen, it cannot be a disadvantageous one to him.

The King, having accepted Grenville's conditions under duress, could not be reconciled to the reinstatement of the Administration; continued contacts with Cumberland and the Opposition; and on 12 June asked the Duke to make a new approach to Pitt, and to Newcastle and his friends. In the negotiations with Pitt, which broke down over Lord Temple's refusal of the Treasury, measures rather than men were discussed.[6] Still, a fairly full list of those

[1] Original in Add. MS. 34713, ff. 253–6; printed from copy, now in the possesion of Sir John Murray, in *Grenville Papers*, iii. 65–6.

[2] Lord Ilchester, *Henry Fox*, ii. 302.

[3] Ilchester, *Letters to Henry Fox*, 219, 221.

[4] It is described as such by Ilchester who prints a long excerpt from it in *Henry Fox*, ii. 302–3.

[5] *Letters to Henry Fox*, 224.

[6] Newcastle's *Narrative*, 23; the information given there is based on a letter from Lord Albemarle, Cumberland's political agent, of 19 June 1765, Add. MS. 32967, f. 79.

thought of for the chief offices appears in the Grenville diary for 25 June,[1] no doubt communicated to Grenville by Temple; Charles Townshend is not mentioned. But when Cumberland turned to Newcastle and Rockingham (or even earlier — as soon as they expected to be asked), Townshend from the very outset appears in their lists for Secretary of State for the Northern Department or for Chancellor of the Exchequer.[2] He was not, however, at the meeting of Newcastle's friends at Claremont on 30 June summoned to consider whether to undertake forming a Government.[3]

The decision having been taken in favour of such an attempt, Newcastle saw Cumberland the next morning and persuaded him to make another effort — 'His Royal Highness . . . will send the Duke of Grafton or my Lord Rockingham to Charles Townshend tomorrow', wrote Newcastle to the Duke of Portland on 1 July.[4] And Lord Albemarle wrote to Newcastle on 2 July, at 5 p.m., after Cumberland's return from Windsor:[5]

> The King directed His Royal Highness to thank your Grace, and to assure you . . . that though his present situation was very unpleasant and uneasy to him, he would wait patiently till Mr. Townshend's and Mr. Yorke's opinions were asked. . . .
>
> The Marquis [of Rockingham] goes today or tomorrow to Mr. C. Townshend's.

On that day, Townshend, before Rockingham's visit, wrote to his brother, and having examined their own position at Court, and discoursed on the distressed position of the King, Government, and country, added:[6]

> As to me, I am sincerely sorry to see the confusion. . . . I desire not to make any advantage of it to myself, for late experience had deadened my ambition by lessening my confidence. I only wish to have misconceptions unjustly entertained of us fully removed. I seek no

[1] *Grenville Papers*, iii. 201.

[2] See lists of 26 and 27 June, Add. MS. 32967, ff. 114–15 and 128–33, and a series of later lists, ff. 161–4, 240–4, etc., some of them printed from copies in the Windsor Archives in Fortescue, i. nos. 101, 104, 111, 117.

[3] In the list as preserved in Add. MS. 33003, f. 30, and printed in *Rockingham Memoirs*, i. 218–20, there appears 'Mr. C.T. of Honingham' followed by 'Mr. C.T. junior' — which is obviously a mistake for Thomas Townshend junior. Charles Townshend, the subject of this biography, was senior in years to his cousin Charles Townshend of Honingham and is never described as 'junior'. If a distinguishing mark were required, he would appear as 'Rt. Hon.' or merely 'Hon.'.

[4] Add. MS. 32967, f. 186. [5] Ibid., f. 193. [6] *Grenville Papers*, iii. 66.

power; and I mean, if the tide brings to me any communication or overture, to decline any answer until I have seen you, that *we who* acted so honourably in the last instance may be the *same* men in the same *union* upon every future occasion.

Rockingham was with Charles Townshend on 4 July, and seems to have left in a rather hopeful mood — Newcastle wrote to him on 5 July:[1]

I . . . rejoice to see the good situation that you represent things in, and particularly at Adderbury. . . . I wish you had mentioned what the previous steps were that were proposed at Adderbury.

But in reality there was no basis for such optimism: Charles was now closely joined to his brother who was actuated by an old and passionate hostility to Cumberland. Charles wrote to him on 4 July, relating how Rockingham had come to Adderbury and opened to him 'the situation of public affairs' and the arrangement of offices under consideration.[2]

He then suggested a wish to me that I would be Chancellor of the Exchequer, and upon my saying I would not be to any man living, he threw out the seals to me. As soon as he had finished this map of the Court, and the etching of a new Ministry, I began with lamenting the wretched state of the King and kingdom from frequent, injudicious, and momentary changes in Administration. I then lamented the little kindness I had found at Court upon my late acceptance, which I said had made me seek the country and deadened my ambition; and I added how much I was surprised to find myself *now* so necessary, who, in the last week was not, to my knowledge at least, in the least regarded, perhaps intended to have been forgot.

I desired leave to decline any conversation until these two extraordinary circumstances, so very expressive of indifference and of censure, were clearly explained, and repeated my resolution to enter upon no confidential conversation until I had seen you, with whom I should act entirely. I then asked his Lordship why no express had been sent to you. . . .

Lord Rockingham . . . confirmed the suspicion which I before had of the cause of the King's coldness to us both. . . .

To this I said . . . that . . . these points must be fully cleared up.

Charles concluded with the following review of the situation, perspicacious in parts, but revealing in its last sentence a hitherto suppressed desire to 'embark in the system', which leads him into discussing once more the circumstances of his recent appointment.

[1] Add. MS. 32967, ff. 253–4. [2] *Grenville Papers*, iii. 67–9.

The plan opened to me has not the show of much stability nor of necessary strength in it. The Treasury, where Mr. Dowdeswell would be Chancellor of the Exchequer, would be unequal, at least in common estimation; the Duke of Grafton, though sensible, is very inexperienced in business; Mr. Pitt's *private* approbation would not bring weight with it, and would be for ever disputed; and most men would think the offices of trust and difficulty too generally filled with persons very respectable for their birth and characters, but not enough in the habit of business. On the other hand, it is delicate to disobey the Crown in such a minute of distraction, especially after Mr. Pitt's forgetfulness of us both, in consequence of the last step which he has heard represented falsely, and as a condition imposed upon the King upon the return of the Ministry, which you know it was not, and Mr. Grenville, I dare say, will testify to others willingly.

Charles came to London on 5 July at night, and saw his brother the next morning.[1] Lord Townshend saw Grenville on the 6th; said he did not mean to resign his appointment at the Ordnance, but would not engage to support the new Administration; and represented Charles's refusal of the Exchequer 'as a sacrifice to Mr. Grenville', which Grenville would not accept as such — 'he called upon no man to resign'.[2] On the 7th the King pressed Lord Townshend to persuade Charles to take the Exchequer, which Charles 'continued to refuse both on his brother's account and his own, declaring strongly his disapprobation of the new Ministry'.[3] On the 9th the King again saw Lord Townshend and urged him to persuade Charles 'to take the office of Secretary of State, which they now offered him' but Charles persisted in his refusal. 'The King afterwards saw Mr. Charles Townshend, who, in conformity to his brother, still refused to accept the seals.'[4] About this interview, Chase Price wrote to Portland on 18 July 1765,[5] that while Townshend's refusal is public, 'the mode of that refusal is unpublished':

When he was in the Closet with the King he gave him in writing an account of the circumstances and situation of this nation, that if his words were not sufficient he might [be] tied by his opinion upon paper, that his behaviour next sessions might be weighed accordingly, and that no ill impression or animadversion upon his conduct might

[1] Grenville diary, ibid. 207; and George Selwyn to Lord Holland, 6 July, Ilchester, *Letters to Henry Fox*, 226–7.
[2] Grenville diary, 6 July; *Grenville Papers*, iii. 207.
[3] Ibid., 209. [4] Ibid., 211. [5] Portland MSS.

be received by his Majesty to his disadvantage uncontradictory to this essay or memorial.

No confirmation of this account has been found but the action is so much in Townshend's style, and Chase Price on the whole so good a source, that it seems worth recording.

That Lord Townshend was moved by his dislike of Cumberland and by pique at being himself neglected, was widely asserted at the time[1] and was probably correct. Charles retained the Pay Office, and his brother the lieutenant-generalship of the Ordnance, without committing themselves to the Rockingham Government, an arrangement which shows the importance which Rockingham attached to not having them in declared opposition. A correspondent wrote to Lord Holland on 16 July:

> Charles seems extremely well pleased with himself for his manner of acting on this occasion. He told Lord Rockingham that he neither desired nor would know any of their transactions, that he might be able to declare in the *House* that he knew nothing of the plan nor ever had the least hand in it.

This at least seems to have been his own version; and to Charles James Fox he gave as reason for declining office that 'he did not choose to be responsible for measures which he supposed would be whatever Mr. Pitt *should graciously please to command*'. 'Those were his words', added Fox.[2]

Once more, as in 1756–61, but this time by his own choice, Townshend was on the periphery of Government, in it but not of it: in a post lucrative and dignified but not politically effective; uneasily balanced between support of Government and opposition to it.

(ii)

On the formation of the Rockingham Government, Lord Digby wrote to his uncle Lord Holland:[3]

> You think this Ministry will last, and I agree with you . . . but I think Mr. Conway so unable, so weak and indecisive for a Minister in the House of Commons, that I think they must call upon Charles Townshend, and have him at any rate.

[1] See e.g. letter from Charles Fox to his father after a talk with Lady Townshend, 13 July, *Letters to Henry Fox*, 233; from Upton to Holland, 16 July, ibid., 236; from Chase Price to Portland, quoted above; etc.

[2] *Letters to Henry Fox*, 242.

[3] Ibid., 238.

Even before the Duke of Cumberland died on 30 October 1765 there were rumours that Townshend was 'likely to be made part of the system before the Parliament meets'.[1] After the Duke's death, when the need for additional strength was acutely felt, Townshend was among those approached. Rockingham wrote to Newcastle on 1 December:[2] 'Charles Townshend continues professing the most favourable intentions, but does not seem to choose to be now called to the Cabinet.'

Throughout the autumn of 1765 news kept reaching England of the riots and disturbances caused in America by the attempt to enforce Grenville's Stamp Act, and as the meeting of Parliament drew nearer the Opposition to the Rockingham Ministry began to line up in defence of Grenville's American policy. When Parliament met on 17 December 1765, Grenville moved an amendment to the Address declaring the colonies in a state of rebellion. That same night Conway, leader in the Commons, wrote to the King about the debate:[3] 'Mr. Charles Townshend . . . spoke exceeding well; and in the fullest, handsomest, and strongest manner against the amendment.' A fuller report, which accords with Townshend's basic conceptions but shows him opposing Grenville on purely practical grounds, is given by James Harris:

> Charles Townshend owns his difficulties — tells us he has no share in the Cabinet — would wait for farther information from America — disapproves of Mr. Grenville's addition — strong for the supremacy of Parliament — yet we and the colonies mutually dependent — if you have done anything to stop or injure their trade, relieve them and they will submit.

Still, the differences in interpretation to which Townshend's ambivalent speech gave rise, are shown by the report sent to Pitt by George Cooke:[4]

> Mr. Charles Townshend asserted with vehemence his approbation of the Stamp Act and for enforcing it, leant much to Mr. George Grenville's opinion, soothed him, and sat down — determined to vote against his amendment!

Anyhow he voted with the Government. During January Townshend was again unusually silent: he did not speak in the

[1] Rigby to Bedford, 26 October, Bedford MSS. For other rumours about Townshend in October 1765 see *Grenville Papers*, iii. 87, 90, 101.
[2] Add. MS. 32972, f. 93.
[3] Fortescue, i. 202.
[4] *Chatham Correspondence*, ii. 351; corrected from the original in the P.R.O.

vital debate on the Address, 14 January 1766; nor in the debate on the American papers, 17 January; nor on the petition from the Stamp Act Congress, 27 January; and, though present, did not vote on the Anstruther Burghs election petition, 31 January. When on 15 January Rockingham pressed the King for a new approach to Pitt, and declared that the Government could hardly carry on without him, the King tried to explore the possibility of a new Administration composed of men unconnected with any party: the two Townshends were included in a plan outlined on 16 January, Charles being put down for Secretary of State.[1] The one coherent account of this transaction appears in a memorandum by the Duke of Grafton, incorporated in his *Autobiography*;[2] with regard to Charles Townshend he writes that on 16 January, at 9 p.m., he was with the King,

> who could not persuade that gentleman to take a leading part in the forming a new Administration. On the contrary, Mr. Townshend endeavoured to prove to the King that Mr. Pitt alone was the minister who could put his Majesty's affairs into an easy and solid state.

As others also refused, the idea was dropped.

In spite of Townshend's ambiguous attitude, Rockingham summoned him to his most intimate and vital deliberations on the policy to be adopted towards America; and the solution, a repeal of the Stamp Act accompanied by the Declaratory Act asserting Great Britain's sovereign rights over the colonies, was very much along the lines of Townshend's speech of 17 December 1765 as reported by Harris. Rockingham wrote to Charles Yorke in a letter dated 'Sunday night, near 1 o'clock, January 17th 1766' (which is wrong: the Sunday was on 19 January, and the letter was presumably written in the early hours of Monday, the 20th):[3]

> The Duke of Grafton, General Conway, Charles Townshend, Mr. Dowdeswell are to dine with me on Tuesday next. I have sent to Mr. Hussey and to Lord Dartmouth to desire them to come, and I much wish that you would, that we may converse upon the mode and manner and matter of the proceedings relative to the affairs which

[1] Fortescue, i. nos. 178, 198, 201 and 324, where the relevant documents are jumbled up and misdated and rendered meaningless — see my *Additions and Corrections to Sir John Fortescue*.

[2] Pp. 64–6; see also Grafton's two letters to Pitt of 16 and 17 January 1766, misdated in *Chatham Correspondence*, and misplaced accordingly in vol. II, 317–18.

[3] Add. MS. 35430, f. 31.

come on on Tuesday sennight [28 January]. If you can not dine with me I wish you could come in the evening.

Charles Townshend and General Conway, Dowdeswell and the Duke of Grafton were here this evening. The ideas we joined in are nearly what I talked of to you this morning.

That is, a *Declaratory Act* in general terms, afterwards to proceed to *considerations of trade*, and final determination on *the Stamp Act*, a *repeal* of which its own demerits and inconveniences *felt here* will justify.

That Charles Townshend dined with them on the 21st is confirmed by a letter written by Lady Rockingham at night 'past 11 o'clock' to Newcastle who was not invited:[1]

My Lord ... has seen tonight a pretty mixed set of company and bids me say that the conversation he has had with them, promises to be productive of events going well; and his Lordship seems in admirable spirits.... My Lord is now at supper in the next room with part of those I mentioned, which are Lord Egmont, Charles Yorke, and Charles Townshend, and who else I know not.

During the debates on the resolutions on American policy, 3 to 6 February, Townshend still preserved silence, and only broke it on 7 February, over Grenville's motion to address the King to enforce the laws in the colonies. The fullest account of Townshend's speech is by Nathaniel Ryder:[2]

Does not rise to differ from the spirit and the temper expressed by the honourable gentleman who proposed this address. He feels for the situation of North America as much as Grenville. He thinks if some proper plan is not formed for governing as well as quieting them, at present and for the future, it will be extremely dangerous.

The magistrates at present in many colonies elective, the judges dependent on the assemblies for their salaries.

He thinks the address carries strongly an opinion in favour of enforcing the Stamp Act. He has expressed no opinion upon that subject, and therefore hopes for the favour and judgment of the committee when he opposes this address as being very preclusive and tending directly to the enforcing the Stamp Act. This is a sufficient reason for us to reject.

But how will this be felt in America? When they see our resolution wound up with this address, they will think us determined upon the repeal.

We are now without forts or troops. Our magistrates without

[1] Add. MS. 32973, f. 224. [2] Harrowby MSS.

inclinations and without power. Would you raise this temper while you are the most unable to resist it? And perhaps drive them to such extremities that if you should [words obscure] by a resolution to repeal, it may be then too late to go back. And we shall accelerate the mischief we would wish to retard.

A picture of America. No commerce, no trade, no legislature. [Words obscure] The West Indies feeling their share of the common calamity.

If a delay is necessary, do not let us lose the fruits of this delay by this hasty, this preclusive measure, and by this untimely and unseasonable signification to them of a resolution which we have not yet taken and which we perhaps may not take at all.

Here then is another speech on the crucial problem of the session so ambivalent as to lend itself to various interpretations. James West thus reported it to Newcastle:[1]

> Mr. Charles Townshend opposed it [Grenville's motion] strongly as premature and prejudging and serving only to enrage a people too much inflamed, without having proper strength to enforce obedience.

On the other hand, this is how Sir Roger Newdigate, a strong supporter of Grenville's American policy, minuted the speech in his notes:[2]

> Unless the plan of government in North America be altered — the governors — judges for their salaries — unless that spirit be — magistrates that have no inclination if they had power, and no power if they had inclination — your admirals are engaged in blocking up the port of New York — contra.

And there is no real contradiction between the three reports.

On 11 February, in connexion with the question of examining witnesses on the state of the colonies, Townshend, according to West,[3] declared that

> he could not repeal the Act on account of the right whereby it was imposed, nor on account of the violence that had been used against it, but only, if at all, on the impracticability or inexpediency of it, or the inability of the colonies to pay the tax.

The next day he seemed to Harris 'rather to favour non-repeal'. He did not speak in the chief debate on the repeal, 21–22 February; stayed to the end; and presumably voted for the repeal —

[1] Add. MS. 32973, f. 373.
[2] Newdigate MSS., Warwickshire Record Office.
[3] Add. MS. 32973, f. 411.

his name does not appear in any of the lists of those voting against the Government in this division. Newcastle wrote to Rockingham in the morning of the 22nd, after the debate had ended: 'Charles Townshend and poor Sir William Meredith have great merit, as I suppose they were both very ill.' Why exactly Townshend voted as he did is difficult to gauge: in his feelings he obviously agreed with Grenville, adhering to his basic tenets with regard to America.

On 30 April William Dowdeswell, Chancellor of the Exchequer, moved a series of commercial regulations concerning America and the West Indies, lowering the duty on molasses, giving some privileges to the Santa Cruz planters, and establishing a free port in Dominica. Harris reports:

> Charles Townshend defended the regulations and the free port in particular, in framing which I should imagine he had a principal hand; defended the Santa Cruz measure, whose planters had consulted him.

Much more reliable on this occasion appears West's report to Newcastle:[1]

> Mr. Charles Townshend spoke . . . elegantly and masterly on the whole state of America, the immensity of the questions, the tendency of them, the vague determination of a free port not known to any part of the globe in its full extent, improper to the highest degree unless Great Britain was sure that every article of import and export was in her favour, which in fact is directly otherwise, and therefore left the whole in the same uncertainty as he found it.

This was frequently the case with Townshend's speeches. After his death, William Burke, quoting a saying by Edmund about its being dangerous for a man 'to accustom himself to a display of parts in saying the best things he could on both sides of a question', added that 'through a vanity of shewing his parts' Townshend had acquired an incapacity of examining a subject on its merits: had he been able 'to form real opinions of his own he would probably have adhered to them, and certainly they would have had a weight which nothing that came from him ever had'.[2] But can a man form stable opinions without real political convictions?

(iii)

The Duke of Grafton's resignation of the Secretaryship of State at the end of April 1766 opened up once more the question of a

[1] Add. MS. 32975, f. 58.
[2] *Correspondence of Edmund Burke* (1958 edition), i. 326–7.

reconstruction of the Government. A 'plan of Administration' in Newcastle's hand, 30 April,[1] proposed moving Conway to the Northern Department, giving the Southern to Hardwicke, and making Charles Townshend Secretary for America. The next night the future of the Government was discussed by the Cabinet, and Lord Egmont, First Lord of the Admiralty, thus concluded his report to the King of the discussion:[2]

> There was also some talk upon the subject of filling up the Duke of Grafton's place, by which it appeared that the Duke of Newcastle has proposed, and General Conway has adopted, the idea of bringing Charles Townshend into the House of Lords as Secretary of State.[3] But no person entered so far into this matter as to propose advising your Majesty one way or other upon it.

Newcastle, writing to Rockingham on 6 May about the proposed appointments, thus enlarged on his idea of making Townshend Secretary of State for America:[4]

> No man in England understands it so well, and consequently nobody would be so agreeable to those who are particularly interested in what relates either to the West Indies or North America.

And on 7 May, when sending a copy of that letter to Conway,[5] he expressed joy on 'the arrangement approved by my Lord Rockingham and made this day at Court', boasted of his having been the first to suggest Townshend for this appointment, and spoke of

> that attention to the settlement and government of our colonies which in their present situation they will require. Charles Townshend knows more of the matter than anybody; and when his pride and reputation depend upon it, I don't doubt but he will acquit himself to his own honour and the satisfaction of his friends.

Conway replied the same day:[6] 'I think there is much good in the idea of Charles Townshend.'

In a 'plan taken down by my Lord Rockingham', and dated 'Lord Rockingham's house, May 12, 1766',[7] there is still the entry: 'Townshend — Secretary of State for America; Mr. Charles

[1] Add. MS. 33001, f. 206.
[2] Fortescue, i. 301.
[3] The holder of a third Secretaryship of State, a newly created office, would be precluded from sitting in the House of Commons.
[4] Add. MS. 32975, f. 89.
[5] Ibid., f. 104.
[6] Ibid., f. 102.
[7] Add. MS. 33001, f. 225.

Townshend — a peer.' And during the night of the 13th–14th Rockingham wrote to Newcastle:[1]

> I did not see Charles Townshend this morning nor evening, and don't propose speaking to him till I have had another conversation with your Grace and our friends.

Next, Rockingham thus concluded a letter to Newcastle dated 'Wednesday afternoon, 4 o'clock, May 14th 1766':[2] 'I have just thought of the enclosed arrangement which I would suggest.' Townshend no longer appears in this new list, and Lord Dartmouth, First Lord of Trade, was suggested for the American Secretaryship. And on 18 May the King wrote to Egmont about the arrangements to which he had consented:[3] 'Lord Dartmouth is to remain head of the Board of Trade with the tour de baton in America.' Was the offer ever made to Townshend, and was it refused by him? The answer is not in the papers of the King at Windsor, nor in the Newcastle or Rockingham papers. But on 23 May Thomas Whately gave George Grenville 'Charles Townshend's account of his transaction about the Seals'[4] — whether he had it from Townshend direct or at second hand is not stated; it is richly embellished probably both at the source and in transmission. When offered Grafton's office, the story goes, he refused 'because the system would never do'. Next a peerage was offered, 'which he said was worse and worse' — he could not afford it and was 'too young to retire into a hospital'. Then he was offered the post of Secretary of State for America. On his declining,

> the conversation growing warm, he was desired to explain himself, to which he answered that he meant to keep his place, and that they durst not take it from him if they could, and could not if they durst, which he hoped was sufficiently explicit.

The offer in three instalments is obviously an invention; and so is the language which he is alleged to have used to the Ministers; still, the story suggests that an offer was made and declined. There is a paper of 17 May 1766, marked 'plan proposed this day by my Lord Rockingham to the King and agreed to by his Majesty',[5] which contains the following entry:

> Peerage for Lady Dalkeith settled on Mr. Townshend's son, agreed to by his Majesty.

[1] Add. MS. 32975, f. 164, incorrectly dated.
[2] Ibid., ff. 178–80.
[3] Fortescue, i. no. 311.
[4] *Grenville Papers*, iii. 234–7.
[5] Add. MS. 33001, f. 227.

This transaction is referred to in a letter from Townshend to Grafton of 9 October 1766;[1] why it was not carried through at the time is not clear, but the fact of Rockingham making the proposal points to his having continued on friendly terms with Townshend.

[1] Grafton MSS.

CHAPTER VIII

Chancellor of the Exchequer and Cabinet Minister 1766-1767

(i)

After the resignation of Grafton, the Rockingham Ministry began to disintegrate; Pitt openly turned against them; and on 7 July 1766 the King sent for him to form a new Administration. Grafton was induced to accept the Treasury, although he knew himself to be unfitted for the office; Conway remained as leader of the House of Commons; while Pitt took the Privy Seal and was created Earl of Chatham. It was his plan to form an Administration which should transcend and obliterate party divisions, and to direct it by remote control from the House of Lords. Part of the blame for his failure must be laid on his own impracticable and arrogant temper, part on the illness which began to afflict him in December 1766; but for the most ill-omened act of the Chatham Administration — the decision to raise a revenue from America by import duties — the main responsibility must be assigned to Charles Townshend.

Three factors combined to make the first year of the Chatham Administration an opportune time to renew the attempt to tax America. In the first place, it was the general feeling in the House of Commons that the colonies should make some contribution toward their own defence. The Stamp Act had been repealed on grounds of expediency, but those who had advised the Declaratory Act had never intended that it should remain the empty declaration of an abstract right. Pitt, alone of the leading men in the House of Commons, had declared that the British Parliament had no right to impose a tax on the colonies; most Members of Parliament believed that they did have the right and should exercise it, but in a manner that could not be represented as oppressive or an innovation conflicting with established custom.

When Pitt went into the House of Lords he withdrew from a strong position whence he could dominate the political battlefield to one where his peculiar gifts and weapons were of little use. Grenville, author of the Stamp Act and foremost advocate of the taxation of America, was now the strongest man in the House of Commons. Moreover, Chatham never welded his Cabinet together into a team, nor were they meant to act without his direction. His illness in December 1766 left them at sixes and sevens, and on his virtual retirement from business the following March his Olympian authority devolved upon subordinates incapable of exercising it. Grafton and Conway, his vicegerents, professed Chatham's political convictions without his faith; and Shelburne, who alone seems to have understood the implications of Townshend's American policy, was distrusted by his colleagues.

Of the Cabinet only Charles Townshend had deep-rooted ideas on American policy. In the personalised terms in which the American problem was usually discussed, he, who had been the oppressed son, now became the heavy father. There was interaction between his emotional life and his political ideas, and the confusion of the times enabled him to force his fantasies on to reality. These took shape not only as an attempt to raise a revenue from America but as a re-modelling of the colonial governments and a re-assertion of British authority. It was the policy he had steadily pursued since he first applied himself to colonial affairs during his apprenticeship at the Board of Trade; its implementation was his only effective political legacy; but he died before its consequences became apparent. These led inescapably to one of two alternatives: either to the extinction of representative institutions in the colonies, or independence from the mother country.

(ii)

Lord Temple having on 17 July definitely refused to come into Pitt's scheme for a new Government, Pitt sent for the Duke of Grafton, and in a two hours' talk on Saturday the 19th urged him to accept the Treasury. About their next interview Grafton writes in his *Autobiography*:[1]

> I do not recollect whether it was the next or the following day that I returned to North End [Pitt's house at Hampstead], when the

[1] P. 92.

conversation chiefly turned on the particulars of the intended arrangement.... I much pressed Mr. Pitt that Mr. Townshend might be the Chancellor of the Exchequer. Mr. Pitt... said everything to dissuade me from taking as a second one from whom I should possibly meet with many unexpected disappointments. I had seen Mr. Townshend and was weak enough to persist in my desire, as I had found him eager to give up the Paymaster's place for this office. Mr. Townshend might possibly view this situation as the readiest road to the upper seat, and his professions had gained me over to expect every assistance from him.... Mr. Pitt at last gave way, though much against his inclination as well as his opinion. Mr. Townshend, however, was not to be called to the Cabinet.

20 July is the correct date of this second talk, as on Monday morning, 21 July, Grafton was at his country house, Wakefield Lodge near Stony Stratford, some 55 miles from London, having presumably returned there the previous night. From there he wrote to Pitt:[1]

Lest you should imagine that I have met with Mr. Charles Townshend, I thought it proper to acquaint you that he was set out from Adderbury for London before my message got there. Give me leave only to add that if that gentleman makes difficulties of accepting the post you propose for him, that in my opinion I see no way that it will answer the expectation of the public but by your undertaking that office which you have allotted me.

In the case of anyone but Townshend it might seem impossible to square such anticipation of difficulties about a post with the previous application for it. But it may also well be that Grafton, writing nearly 40 years after the events, confused or telescoped them in his account; which can be accepted in broad outline, though not in detail where contradicted by documentary evidence. The broad outline in this case is that to begin with Grafton felt unable to take the Treasury unless he had Townshend for Chancellor of the Exchequer.

Pitt saw Townshend on Monday, 21 July — that day Lord Northington wrote to the King at 10 p.m.[2] that Pitt's scheme seemed to stand as previously outlined,

only that I find he has had an interview with Charles Townshend to be Chancellor of the Exchequer, but I believe without success or an absolute negative.

[1] *Chatham Correspondence*, ii. 452. [2] Fortescue, i. no. 357.

On the morning of the 22nd Townshend received through Dingley, Pitt's landlord at North End, a message from Pitt[1] which he understood 'to contract the time' allowed him for an answer; he regretted having to give it 'without any communication with Lord Townshend and others with whom I act in friendship'. And Charles proceeded with a turgid discourse of half-hearted acceptance fit to serve as basis for subsequent claims:

> When I had the honour of being appointed to the office which I now hold, I refused acceptance until I had first obtained from the best authority the fullest assurance that it had been proposed to me with his Majesty's entire approbation: upon the same principle I am now ready to change it if it be his Majesty's pleasure, and I should think myself both an ungrateful servant and a bad citizen if in such an hour as this I should decline from motives of interest or love of ease, resulting from the most lucrative office, to take whatever station his Majesty shall command me in an administration formed with his perfect approbation.

Pitt replied the same night, 'past nine',[2] that in Townshend's letter he found

> some misapprehension of the intention of my wishes expressed by Mr. Dingley. It was simply this: that if you could without inconvenience come to a resolution ... before I am to attend the King tomorrow morning, I should take it as a favour.

But in view of Lord Townshend's absence,

> a circumstance I was ignorant of ... give me leave, Sir, to waive for the present the answer you have been so good to make, and to leave to your maturest consideration the part you shall judge proper to take.

The next meeting with Townshend on Thursday, 24 July, left Pitt convinced that things were settled between them, and at 6 p.m. he wrote to the King asking permission to attend him the next day, 'as the final arrangement of the Treasury is a matter too highly importing your Majesty's service to admit delay.' The King fixed an appointment for the next morning, Friday 25th, at 11,[3] and after it Pitt wrote to Townshend (at 4 p.m.) with unusual cordiality:[4]

[1] Townshend to Pitt, 22 July; *Chatham Correspondence*, ii. 456–7.
[2] Buccleuch MSS.
[3] Fortescue, i. nos. 361–2.
[4] Buccleuch MSS.

I am but just able in this hasty line to assure you that I have with a sincere pleasure done justice to your zeal for the King's service, as well as to your handsome and obliging proceedings towards the Duke of Grafton and myself. His Majesty has most graciously received my humble advice to make the man of England, whose talents can best serve him, Chancellor of the Exchequer. I am to add, which I do with particular satisfaction, that the King will see you on Sunday next, if you will be at Court. Accept my warm congratulations on these marks of his Majesty's favour, and believe me with affectionate esteem and consideration, etc.

Meantime Townshend had been passing through ranges of indecision to a negative conclusion. The first extant document of that morning is a note from him to Grafton (they both lived in Grosvenor Square), undated but presumably written about 11 a.m.[1] It starts by referring to a 'friendly message' from Grafton (of which the contents are unknown); and next to a note which, in spite of the confusion of pronouns, seems to be from Townshend to Grafton — possibly this very note. Then Townshend goes on to argue the correct construction of Pitt's, by now irrelevant, message sent through Dingley three days earlier (the urge to prove himself right was irresistible with Townshend); incidentally represents Pitt's telling Dingley (of all men!) about his forthcoming translation to the House of Lords;[2] and then comes the sting in the tail: Pitt spoke 'as if everything was settled' between him and Townshend — but Townshend obviously thought differently about it.

Here is the text of Townshend's note:

Mr. Townshend's compliments wait upon the Duke of Grafton. He is obliged to his Grace for the honour of his friendly message, and begs that he will not be anxious about the point alluded to in his note. Mr. Pitt is now with the King. Mr. Dingley has been with Mr. T. and acknowledged the message sent by Mr. Pitt to Mr. T. in the sense and positive construction which Mr. T. put upon it in his answer to Mr. Pitt, and at the same time has given Mr. T. to understand that Mr. Pitt this morning signified that he should be a peer, and spoke of me to him this day in the highest terms, but as if everything was settled.

[1] Grafton MSS.

[2] Again there is confusion of pronouns; 'that he should be a peer' cannot, however, refer to Townshend: it would have been incompatible with the Exchequer. If it refers to Pitt, Grafton was told at third hand what, according to his *Autobiography*, p. 97, he, Camden, and Northington, to their dismay, first learnt at the Queen's House on the 28th. But more probably Townshend is referring in a loose manner to the promise of a peerage for Lady Dalkeith.

An hour later Townshend wrote a further letter to Grafton, dated 'Friday noon', obscure in its contradictory allusions which can be read both as a farewell letter and as an acceptance:[1]

I mean to desire an audience this morning of the King. If any [thing][2] should pass, you will give me leave to transmit it to you. I cannot conclude without repeating my assurances of inseparable attachment to your Grace and Mr. Pitt, and my satisfaction to recollect that the late transaction has had one good effect, that of bringing me to be known with more exactness both by your Grace and Mr. Pitt. Upon the whole, it is possibly as well for the public that things are finally settled as they are, and I agree with Mr. Pitt in his ideas of the dangers arising from sudden variations in matters once communicated. An union with you is a great object with me, but that may be formed as we are.

Before receiving this second letter, Grafton had started one to Pitt, dated 'Grosvenor Square, Friday morning', which apparently summarises a talk he had with Townshend on the previous night:[3]

Thinking it very possible that I may not find you at home, as Mr. Townshend has just informed me that you was with the King, I sit down to write these few lines. First, to acquaint you that Mr. Townshend was last night so thoroughly convinced of your firmness in adhering to the determination concerning him, that he seemed to have laid aside all hopes of any change in his favour: he approved and admired the motive from which it came, and was sensible that as you had thought first of him, you had still the same opinion, notwithstanding the untoward circumstance that might render it difficult or perhaps wrong for you to revert again to him for the post that had been mentioned to him.

His wish was as strong that it might take place but as he intimated that he did not desire that he should appear to solicit it too violently, I could not propose to him to see you again upon it and to talk the point once more over, lest he should change his idea again and look upon himself as recherché. On the contrary, I told him that I left you in the same way of thinking; which, perhaps, made him still more look upon it as a desperate case. Thus, sir, the matter stands. On the other hand, every dissatisfied person is endeavouring to persuade the Duke of Portland, Dowdeswell, etc., that they are slighted by being left without any notice whether they are to be in or out. The consequences of all these points considered, and the declarations that have been spread

[1] *Chatham Correspondence*, ii. 462.
[2] The word is omitted in the original but inserted in the printed text.
[3] *Chatham Correspondence*, ii. 459–61.

by Mr. Townshend's friends that he is not to be the man, joined to the enclosed note I have received from him since I have begun this letter, convince me that I must and do readily waive my own feelings, readily embrace the proposition of leaving Mr. Dowdeswell where he is, as I plainly perceive that it is for the general good and very likely for my own private ease of mind.

Thus Grafton himself began to perceive the danger of having Townshend at the Exchequer — but neither the vital importance of the impending decision nor the tangled situation stopped him from going that night to Wakefield Lodge: he would return to London on Sunday evening, and offered to call on Pitt at Hampstead on his way back.

Townshend, by the time he saw the King, had reached his negative conclusion — the King wrote to Pitt that same day, 25 July, at 4.15 p.m., i.e. a quarter of an hour after Pitt had penned his cordial note to Townshend:[1]

I think it necessary to acquaint you with my having seen Mr. Townshend, who expressed to me his reasons for having determined to stay in the Pay Office. I told him there must be some misunderstanding, for that you had this morning acquainted me with his desire of being Chancellor of the Exchequer. He left me uncertain what he should do, but that if he took it, he must say it was by my express commands not his choice, that what he held was more honourable and worth £7000 per annum, whilst the other was but £2500; that if he accepted, he hoped he should have some indemnification; that Lord Rockingham being quiet would much depend on Mr. Dowdeswell's remaining Chancellor of the Exchequer. In short, he left me in a state of great uncertainty, and means to talk again with you.

Pitt replied at 6.30 p.m.:[2]

I most humbly beg leave to submit to your Majesty's wisdom that, after the earnest and dutiful zeal towards your Majesty's service so fully expressed by Mr. C. Townshend yesterday, and his full declarations that *now* or whenever it could be judged proper he wished and asked as a favour to have the honour to serve your Majesty as Chancellor of the Exchequer under the Duke of Grafton, any more fluctuation or variation from what your Majesty has been most graciously pleased to fix in my audience of this day with regard to Chancellor of the Exchequer would be totally destructive of all steadiness and dignity in Administration. Mr. C. Townshend is engaged to serve in that office

[1] Fortescue, i. no. 363; *Chatham Correspondence*, ii. 463.
[2] Fortescue, i. no. 364.

and I am persuaded will not retract his declarations. Permit me, sir, most humbly to add that if Lord Rockingham's being *quiet*, as Mr. C. Townshend informs your Majesty, depends on no other motive than Mr. Dowdeswell continuing Chancellor of the Exchequer, I most humbly advise that a resolution be finally taken that Mr. Dowdeswell be immediately acquainted by your Majesty's command that he is not to remain in that office.

But apparently before Pitt could act, he received Townshend's reply to his own letter of 4 p.m.[1] which repeats his *leitmotif* of cheerful and disinterested submission to commands put on him (with about as little sincerity as he had felt on such occasions toward his father):

I have the honour of your friendly letter, in which you are so kind as to relate to me the manner in which you have this day represented to his Majesty the conversations which have passed between us upon the subject of the Chancellorship of the Exchequer. Your recommendation to any office of rank and trust is in itself the highest satisfaction to me, and would be thought by the world to be the greatest honour to any man. The personal love I have for the Duke of Grafton is with me another very strong motive for accepting the post you wish in a ministry formed under your sanction, and when these motives are confirmed by the express commands of my Sovereign, whose will in the disposal of any consequence or talents I have is to me a law, I hesitate not from motives of interest or love of ease to take that part which conforms to your wishes, my plan of union with the Duke of Grafton, and the commands of my Sovereign. It is my earnest wish to cultivate and merit in every measure of business and act of my life your confidence and esteem, and I shall be happy indeed if in the pressing and critical circumstances of this kingdom I should be acknowledged by posterity to have in any degree contributed under your protection to facilitate the re-establishment of general confidence, real government, and a permanent system of measures.

In consequence Pitt wrote to the King on 26 July, 9 p.m.,[2] that Townshend

has accepted the office of Chancellor of the Exchequer, clearly and directly, in a letter to me last night, full of the properest expressions of duty and zeal for your Majesty's service.

Still, on the previous night Townshend had sent Grafton his own version of what had happened, differing in some essentials

[1] *Chatham Correspondence*, ii. 464–5. It is dated 'July 26', but was obviously written and received on the 25th.

[2] Fortescue, i. no. 366.

from that of the King (see above p. 152); and emphasising, much more than he had dared to in his letter to Pitt, the sacrifices he was making in accepting the office:[1]

> In performance of my promise, I report to your Grace the result of the audience which I had this day; in which I found that Mr. Pitt had renewed the subject of our last conversation, and informed his Majesty that he earnestly wished that I might be the Chancellor of the Exchequer. I then stated the difference of the offices in real income and supposed rank: I frankly declared my resolution to act as the King should command; and professed my ambition to prefer the honour (for such I think it is) of contributing with Mr. Pitt and your Grace to the stability of government, to any emolument or any ease. The King in the kindest manner left me to consider and decide, only adding that my manner of acting was too liberal to permit him to press me as he would do other men. I have since received the most friendly and honourable letter from Mr. Pitt, and on Sunday I shall again see the King. In the meantime, your Grace may be assured that I shall accept; still desiring to be understood that I relinquish my own natural inclination and evident interest, upon the hope of being known by you, Mr. Pitt, and the Crown, to sacrifice with cheerfulness and from principle all that men usually pursue to the veneration I bear Mr. Pitt, my plan of union with your Grace, and my gratitude to my Sovereign.
>
> Here let this anxious matter rest. If you feel it as I do, words are useless. God prosper our joint labours, and may our mutual trust, affection, and friendship grow from every act of our lives.

But Townshend's real feelings were known even at the time — Robert Wilmot, secretary to the Lord Chamberlain, wrote on 2 August 1766 to his brother, Sir John Eardley Wilmot, who had succeeded Lord Camden (now Lord Chancellor) as Lord Chief Justice of the Common Pleas:[2] 'Charles Townshend thinks himself injured by having the Chancellorship of the Exchequer crammed down his throat.' And while Horace Walpole's account of how Townshend was made to accept the Exchequer is inaccurate in its factual statements,[3] it is true in a surrealist way and the remark that the 'method of imposing an office of such confidence' was 'unprecedented', seems justified.

[1] Grafton, *Autobiography*, 96–7; the original in the Grafton MSS. is docketed: 'Rx 26th'.

[2] *Memoirs of the Life of Sir J. E. Wilmot*, by John Wilmot, p. 45.

[3] *Memoirs of King George III*, ii. 246.

(iii)

'Charles Townshend has a fine game to play', wrote Lord Albemarle to Rockingham on 1 August.[1] 'If I am not mistaken he will soon take the lead in the House of Commons.' Townshend was now nearer the centre of power than he had ever been. Though Chatham distrusted him and had no intention of taking him into his confidence, Townshend's support in the House of Commons was essential to the new Ministry — and could not be relied upon. Conway, leader of the House, was no match for Grenville: Minister *malgré lui*, uneasy in his conscience because his friends the Rockinghams were excluded from the Cabinet, it seemed that he must soon make way for Townshend. Had Townshend possessed, in Horace Walpole's words,[2] 'common truth, common sincerity, common honesty, common modesty, common steadiness, common courage, and common sense', he must have become effective First Minister. But he had not the qualities for political leadership, neither the faith nor the courage, and his role under the Chatham Administration was to make confusion worse confounded.

Grafton, unsure of himself, and fearful of failing Chatham in his office, had obviously planned to rely a good deal on Townshend, his deputy at the Board of Treasury. On 28 August he invited Townshend, together with Conway, Shelburne, and Lord Chancellor Camden, to meet the chairman and deputy-chairman of the East India Company at dinner, where the forthcoming Parliamentary inquiry into the Company's affairs was to be discussed.[3] But Townshend did not wish to assume responsibility outside his department while not as yet admitted to the Cabinet. Without openly parading his grievance, he sulked and refused his co-operation, even on matters in which he was specially interested and informed. When consulted by Grafton on the affairs of Canada, he replied, 4 September:[4]

> I did imagine that the servants of the Crown did intend to have *a Cabinet* upon the *general* state of that province. . . . In Cabinet, your Grace knows, I could be of no service, because I am not in the course of that attendance, nor should I choose to be called upon extraordinary occasions out of the natural channel of my office.

[1] Rockingham MSS., Sheffield City Library.
[2] *Memoirs*, iii. 72.
[3] *Chatham Correspondence*, iii. 59.
[4] Buccleuch MSS.

He was admitted to the Cabinet, presumably at Grafton's persuasion, at the beginning of October — the first Chancellor of the Exchequer to sit in Cabinet alongside the First Lord of the Treasury. Grafton writes in his *Autobiography*:[1]

> On the night preceding Lord Chatham's first journey to Bath, Mr. Charles Townshend was for the first time summoned to the Cabinet. The business was on a general view and statement of the actual situation and interests of the various powers in Europe: Lord Chatham had certainly taken the lead in this consideration in so masterly a manner as to raise the admiration and desire of us all to co-operate with him in forwarding these views. Mr. Townshend was particularly astonished, and owned to me, as I was carrying him in my carriage home, that Lord Chatham had just shown to us what inferior animals we were, and that, as much as he had seen of him before, he did not conceive till that night his superiority to be so very transcendant. Mr. Townshend, however, soon forgot the great and extensive mind of the minister; and I had daily to hear or to read his train of grievances, among which the disappointment he had met with in his application for a peerage for Lady Dalkeith was not the least.

A few days later, on a rumour that Sir William Maynard was to be created a peer, Townshend put in his claim for Lady Dalkeith's peerage. He told Grafton that it had been promised by George III (which was true) and also by George II (which seems highly unlikely).[2] To Grafton's reply, that for the time being the King did not propose to create any new peers, Townshend countered with a letter which shows how well he could project on to reality his own version of events:[3]

> I had fondly conceived hopes that I should not have found unwillingness after so many proofs of my conformity to meet the commands of the Crown and the plan of the servants of it, yet, if this must be, if no concurrence on my part, against my own interest and to oblige others, can beget confidence, nor confidence, in my instance and person, produce favour, I wish to know this. I have acted an open, disinterested, friendly part, if something invisible and incurable renders that useless I had better learn this, rather than pursue a vexatious plan of labour and a sterile cultivation of those who can not desire what they do not value.

[1] P. 105.
[2] Townshend to Grafton, 9 October 1766, Grafton MSS.
[3] Townshend to Grafton, 10 October 1766, Grafton MSS.

He ended this part of his letter by describing himself as the only man in Administration who had 'submitted in everything and asked for nothing'.

Five days later, on 16 October, Townshend wrote to his step-son, the Duke of Buccleuch, then in Paris:[1]

> We have as usual a very unsettled state of men and things. Lord Chatham is minister in the most absolute sense of the word; yet, by being ill or absent [at Bath] business moves slowly and incertainly. As for me, I obeyed the Crown and left a quiet and lucrative office of great rank to come into a scene of hurry and anxiety, with less profit. In this I thought I acted honourably: I find Lord Chatham so incurably jealous of me, so open to idle reports and so reserved, that I have little satisfaction in my situation. When he comes to London this ambiguity must have its settlement, and some final explanation follow. In the mean time I labour, prepare for the session, and am resigned to the issue.

When, however, Chatham returned to London for the meeting of Parliament, Townshend suppressed his grievances — at least for the time being. 'Charles Townshend, I hear, is now in good humour', wrote George Onslow to Newcastle on 7 November, 'his plans he still keeps to himself.'[2] What these were is not known, nor even if he had any, but Onslow's remark indicates that it was expected that Townshend would follow a line of his own — which is not surprising in view of his record. Yet when Chatham's dismissal of Lord Edgcumbe provoked a breach with the Rockingham party, Townshend tried to play a conciliatory part. To Grafton he expressed his wish 'that disunion may be prevented among men who cannot separate without weakness to the public', and declared 'against the propriety of the removal [of Lord Edgcumbe] as a piece of political management'.[3] The break with the Rockinghams resulted in an estrangement between Conway and Chatham, which, according to Horace Walpole (from his intimacy with Conway and Grafton, the best authority on this period), Townshend tried to use to his own advantage:[4]

> Charles Townshend, restless in any situation, fond of mischief, and not without envy of the lead allotted to Conway, was incessant in inciting him to retire, by painting to him the pride and folly of Lord

[1] Buccleuch MSS. [2] Rockingham MSS.
[3] Dowdeswell to Rockingham, 20 November 1766, Rockingham MSS.
[4] *Memoirs*, ii. 285.

Chatham, the improbability of his maintaining such shattered power, and alarming him with threats of resigning and leaving him alone in the House of Commons.

When on 25 November William Beckford proposed the Government motion for an inquiry into the affairs of the East India Company, Townshend made a much-admired speech. 'Charles Townshend stated the matter quite new,' wrote Henry Flood, 'disclaimed all the offensive parts, and made a very artful, conciliating, able, and eloquent speech.'[1] On 5 December, on the Bill to indemnify those who had advised the recent embargo on corn, he had a 'sharp altercation' with Grenville and 'both ridiculed and flattered him'.[2] By then Grenville, Bedford, and Rockingham were all in declared opposition to the Chatham Administration, while Conway and Townshend were beginning to assume the roles of rebels within the Cabinet.

(iv)

The Chatham Administration had to deal with the stupendous problems of India and America, fit to test the wisest statesmanship and demanding a high degree of union in the Cabinet. But Chatham was ill, Grafton incapable, Conway irresolute, and Townshend irresponsible — hardly any Government in modern British history has faced issues of comparable magnitude with such a feeble equipment of faith and courage. The story of the Chatham Administration is both comic and tragic: a comedy for contemporaries, a tragedy for later generations; and its course was determined to a large extent by the conduct of two mentally unbalanced men — Chatham himself and Charles Townshend.[3]

The Seven Years War had left Great Britain the dominant European power in India. But British authority was not that of the State but of the East India Company, a joint-stock company primarily interested in commerce and enjoying a monopoly of trade between Britain and India. Clive's assumption in 1765 of control over the finances of Bengal had virtually given the Company territorial responsibilities in India — which it was ill-equipped to exercise — and hopes of a vastly increased revenue had led to an outburst of activity in East India stock. In September

[1] *Chatham Correspondence*, iii. 144. [2] *Memoirs*, ii. 286.

[3] The best accounts of the Chatham Administration are in Walpole, *Memoirs*, and Brooke, *The Chatham Administration*. For East Indian affairs, see L. S. Sutherland, *The East India Company in Eighteenth-Century Politics*.

1766 the court of proprietors had overruled the directors and increased the dividend from 6% to 10%, thus giving a new impetus to speculation, based not on any solid improvement in the Company's position and prospects but on exaggerated ideas of the amount of the territorial revenues which would be available for distribution as dividend.

At this stage Chatham announced that he proposed to hold a Parliamentary inquiry into the affairs of the Company. The full extent of his plan for the future of the Company he never revealed, not even to the Cabinet, and all he seemed to expect from the inquiry was a declaration that the right to the territorial revenues lay in the Crown, not the Company. Once that had been determined, he wrote, 'the ways to ulterior and final proceedings upon this transcendent object' would 'open themselves naturally and clearly enough'.[1] Only later did he give any indication of what concrete proposals he had had in mind in 1766. Writing in 1773, he declared that he had never intended to refuse the Company a share in the territorial revenues, but that this was not to be considered as 'private property . . . to be portioned out in dividends' but as 'in trust for the public purposes of defence of India and the extension of trade'.[2]

The vague and sometimes menacing language in which Chatham spoke of the Company, and his selection of William Beckford, M.P. for London, an avowed enemy of monopoly, to make the motion for an inquiry, spread uneasiness among East India proprietors. A declaration of the Crown's right to the territorial revenues could be held to be an infringement of the Company's charter, and was certainly a restraint on the activities of speculators. And among these speculators was Charles Townshend. There is a letter to him,[3] dated 2 September 1766, from John Powell, an official of the Pay Office, who had long handled Lord Holland's financial affairs and was now acting in a similar capacity for Townshend. Powell writes, in reply to a message which Townshend had sent him through Touchet:

> I have ordered £7000 four per cents more to be sold to make good the purchase of India stock. I shall transfer the four per cents out of my name and put the India stock into my name. Therefore no opinion

[1] Fitzmaurice, *Life of Shelburne*, i. 298.
[2] *Chatham Correspondence*, iv. 264–5.
[3] Buccleuch MSS.

can possibly arise that this business is done for your account, it will be set down in opinion for the account of Lord H[olland].

And Townshend wrote to his brother on 1 October about another transaction:[1] 'I this day paid the £1500 to Mr. Lee, and could have made 15% at the very moment. Such is the price paid for money by those who adventure in the East India funds.'

Townshend had thus a direct pecuniary interest in forestalling Chatham's plan for an inquiry. And, as was usual with him, there was the urge to oppose the Government of which he was a member. On this measure, he was supported by Conway, who had conscientious scruples about Chatham's policy; both would have preferred a settlement with the Company, which did not raise the question of the right to the territorial revenues. Informed observers believed they could discern an undertone of hostility to Chatham's plan in Townshend's speech on Beckford's motion for the inquiry (25 November): Rockingham described it as 'languid', and according to Grenville, Townshend 'leaned much' towards the Opposition.[2] Burke, writing on 2 December, reported a rumour that Chatham had sent for Townshend and 'read him a severe lecture on his conduct, and told him he expected not an official, but a determined, manly, and earnest support'.[3]

Still, even if this rumour be correct, Chatham's rebuke had little effect on Townshend's conduct. On 6 December, at a meeting of Government men of business to consider the next stage of the East India inquiry, Townshend came out into open opposition. What took place can be gathered from Chatham's letter to Grafton of 7 December:[4]

I grieve most heartily at the report of the meeting last night. If the inquiry is to be contracted within the ideas of Mr. Chancellor of the Exchequer . . . the whole becomes a *farce*, and the *Ministry a ridiculous phantom*. . . . Mr. C. Townshend's fluctuations and incurable weaknesses cannot comport with his remaining in that critical office.

'Lord Chatham flamed at the notice of Townshend's adverse conduct', wrote Walpole,[5] 'and vowed himself would resign, or Townshend should be turned out.' But on 8 December, the evening before Beckford was to make his motion for papers, Grafton saw

[1] Townshend MSS. at Raynham.
[2] Add. MS. 32980, ff. 74–5; *Grenville Papers*, iii. 389.
[3] *Burke Correspondence* (1958 edition), i. 284.
[4] Grafton, *Autobiography*, 110.
[5] *Memoirs*, ii. 279.

Townshend and reported to the King that he was 'not without hopes that Mr. Townshend will at least sit quiet, if he does not support the measure'.[1] The following day Townshend spoke for Beckford's motion and dropped no hint of his disagreement with Chatham.

Next, Townshend made approaches to the directors of the Company, to try and induce them to formulate proposals which would serve as a basis for negotiations with the Government. If a financial settlement could be reached, satisfactory to both sides, the inquiry might be by-passed and the question of right shelved. On 17 December, at a meeting of the general court of proprietors of East India stock, the question of opening negotiations with the Government was considered but adjourned until 31 December. In a letter to Grafton, undated but apparently written the following day,[2] Townshend gave an account of this meeting and outlined the terms (presumably drawn up after consultation with the directors) on which it would be to the interest of the Company to treat.

> The proprietors at large [Townshend wrote] and the directors are certainly disposed to negotiate; the sense of the public may be clearly collected from the great rise of the stock upon an expectation of some agreement and from the equal fall in the evening upon finding their error; and I am prepared that a negotiation will now open in despite of all the . . . apprehensions of unreasonableness in the ideas of Government. I will go further and venture to say I have as little doubt of a proposition being carried in the general court, if it be well considered, if it be suited to the nature of the case and the state of the times, and if it be afterwards supported by the concurrent strength of the Administration and the directors.

There is in the Buccleuch MSS. the copy of a letter to Chatham, almost identical with the one Townshend sent to Grafton. Both letters conclude with the following paragraph:

> Perhaps I may seem too moderate, but your Grace [your Lordship] will recollect that I have held this language from the very beginning, wishing to avoid the necessity of a parliamentary decision upon so very new, mixed, and judicial a question, affecting so large a body of men; and thinking that, from all the circumstances attending the rights claimed, from the nature of the acquisitions themselves, from the impracticability of substituting the public in the place of the Company in the collecting, investing, conducting, and remitting the revenue, and from the inability of the Company to uphold such an

[1] Fortescue, i. no. 438. [2] Grafton MSS.

empire by their own power, that it were to be wished it could be determined upon the ground of reciprocal advantage.

After writing this, Townshend seems to have got cold feet. Such positively expressed opposition to Chatham's policy must have led to a show-down, which could end only in Townshend's dismissal or resignation. So he contented himself with protesting to Grafton and did not send the letter to Chatham.

When Parliament rose for the Christmas recess, Chatham went to Bath but Townshend remained in London to concert matters with the East India Company. That he was authorised to open discussions with the directors seems clear from his letter to Grafton of 1 January 1767,[1] in which he takes pains to point out that he had not departed from the line laid down for his guidance. The result of his efforts was that on 31 December the General Court empowered the directors to open negotiations with Government. 'This important matter seems to me to be now taken out of the light of hostile contest', Townshend wrote to Grafton on 1 January, 'and put into a train of amicable negotiation.' And to Chatham he stressed the importance of 'an amicable and happy conclusion of this vast subject'.[2]

Chatham, however, did not see the matter quite in the same light. The motion empowering the directors to negotiate, he wrote to Townshend on 2 January, 'is so worded that it may contain all that is right and desirable: it may also conceal with a specious generality certain narrow notions that would frustrate national justice and public prosperity';[3] and he emphasised the need for an 'adequate' as well as an 'amicable and happy' conclusion. Then followed a verbal sparring match of a kind to which Townshend was well accustomed. 'The only way of making the issue adequate was to make it amicable', he replied on 4 January; which provoked a re-affirmation of Chatham's policy:

> I can venture upon no method of defining the idea of *adequate* [Chatham wrote to Townshend on 6 January] but by assuming or deciding the question of right; and by considering consequently whatever portion of the revenue shall be left by Parliament to the Company as indulgence and matter of discretion.

And there, for the time being, the matter was allowed to rest.

[1] Grafton MSS.

[2] *Chatham Correspondence*, iii. 152.

[3] Ibid., 153, 156, 158.

On 6 January the directors formally communicated to the Treasury the resolutions of the General Court of 31 December, which Grafton duly forwarded to Chatham at Bath. Chatham described them as 'preposterous' and refused to admit them as a basis for negotiations because they entirely ignored 'the great objects of Parliamentary inquiry and national justice'.[1] The inquiry was due to open on 22 January, and on the 11th Chatham set out for London but was forced to return to Bath with an attack of gout. Without him the Administration was in confusion, and the lead in the Cabinet was taken by the only man who had a policy and was prepared to force it through.

On 8 January Townshend had written to Conway about East Indian affairs:[2]

> I cannot withdraw from my settled judgement, formed upon a very accurate survey of things and mature consideration of general principles, and therefore I much fear the issue, not on the part of the general court, but on the part of Administration. Should I be a prophet in this, I have only to wish it may be soon decided, that I may speak my sense and retire from a laborious station, accompanied with no power, no influence nor weight, but oppressed with responsibility, and from which I shall recede with infinite pleasure.

But there was no need to talk of resignation: with Chatham absent and disabled by the gout, Townshend was master. When on 20 January Beckford proposed that the papers which had been presented to the House should be printed, Townshend requested him to defer the motion 'as he hoped to settle all matters with the East India Company to the satisfaction of the public'.[3] 'Mr. Townshend from his late conversations with the directors is very sanguine', wrote Conway to Chatham on 24 January.[4] 'They are preparing immediately to come to Administration, with even very advantageous proposals.' And Townshend himself told George Onslow 'that all was done and in a better way than could have been expected'.[5]

Townshend's speech of 22 January, the day the East India inquiry came on in the Commons, was thus reported by Beckford to Chatham:[6]

[1] Grafton, *Autobiography*, 112.
[2] Buccleuch MSS.
[3] *Chatham Correspondence*, iii. 176.
[4] Ibid., 175.
[5] Add. MS. 32980, f. 159.
[6] *Chatham Correspondence*, iii. 177.

> Mr. Charles Townshend talked a great deal on the occasion in answer to what Mr. George Grenville had thrown out: namely that he thought the East India Company had a right to their territorial revenues. At the same time [he] declared he had no idea of their private bargains, that Parliament was the proper judge, and that it was the duty of every Member to make as good a bargain as possible for the public. Charles seemed to put the whole stress of the negotiation on the *quantum* to be given by the Company for the prolongation of the term of their charter, and regulations and concessions to be made by the legislature which would amazingly increase the trade and profit of the Company: in short, he uttered so many kind and comfortable words for their consolation that the stock rose the next and the succeeding day six per centum.

He talked Chatham's language to counter Chatham's policy and further his own profit. The inquiry was postponed for another month, and then again until 6 March.

On 6 February the directors presented proposals to the Administration. In return for an extension of their charter, the guarantee of their territorial revenues, and reductions of the import duties on some of their products, they offered the sum of £500,000 and a proportion of their future profits.[1] Whether, or to what extent, Townshend had any share in framing these proposals does not appear from his papers, nor exactly what line he took towards them when they were considered in Cabinet. According to Grafton, the Cabinet were agreed in thinking the proposals 'unintelligible' — 'no one would venture to pronounce even an opinion on what they protested they did not understand' — and they were referred back to the directors for further explanation.[2] Meanwhile Grafton pressed Chatham to come to London where his direction was sorely needed on both Indian and American affairs. Chatham left Bath on 16 February but was taken ill at Marlborough, and did not reach London until 2 March. Then, crippled with gout, his mind almost paralysed by mental illness, he made one last effort to rally his divided Cabinet, before sinking into a torpor which was to last for over two years.

The Company's answers to the Government's queries had been in Grafton's hands since 21 February, and he had delayed putting them before the Cabinet till Chatham's arrival. Chatham had now

[1] For a summary of the Company's proposals, see Sutherland, *The East India Company in Eighteenth-Century Politics*, pp. 159–60.

[2] *Chatham Correspondence*, iii. 204.

arrived, but in no state to attend to business; yet a decision could no longer be postponed, for the inquiry was due to open on 6 March. The proposals were considered by the Cabinet at two meetings, on 2 and 3 March, and a complete deadlock resulted. Charles Jenkinson wrote to Lord Bute on the evening of 3 March:[1]

> I saw C.T. this morning; he told me there was a Cabinet last night in which there were warm contests, particularly between C.T. on [the] one hand, and the Chancellor [Camden] on the other. The Chancellor was for deciding the question of right as it relates to the East India Company in the House of Commons on Friday [6 March], and after that to negotiate with the Company for the collection of the revenues. Charles and Conway were against this, and they broke up without coming to any resolution. They meet again tonight at the President's; I don't hear that there was the least mention last night of Lord Chatham's name or of his opinions, nor do they expect that he will be at the Cabinet tonight. The Duke of Grafton was all this morning with Lord Chatham. He sent his excuses on that account to the Treasury. I wait with impatience for the decision of the Cabinet of this evening; the continuance of this Administration in its present state depends upon it.

This second Cabinet meeting was as fruitless as the previous one, and ended with Townshend and Conway refusing to conduct the East India inquiry in the House of Commons. The next day (4 March) Chatham offered Townshend's office to Lord North, who declined it. The confusion in the Ministry was complete.

It was not only to Jenkinson that Townshend had talked. On 5 March, the evening before the inquiry was due to open, Lord Rockingham wrote to the Duke of Newcastle:[2]

> Your Grace may rely on this — that Charles Townshend and Mr. Conway are of one opinion, the rest of the Cabinet of another. I hope and believe it will appear *openly* tomorrow as neither of them will take the conduct of the East India affair in the House of Commons. . . . It is even not impossible that Charles Townshend may not be Chancellor of the Exchequer by the House of Commons hour.

Rockingham claimed to have received this information from 'such indisputable authority as leaves it beyond doubt'. Whose was that authority? Only Conway and Townshend would have any interest in betraying the secret of the Cabinet's divisions to the leader of the principal Opposition party, and Conway was much

[1] Bute MSS. [2] Add. MS. 32980, ff. 207–8.

too discreet and honourable. But it was characteristic of Townshend when in office to cultivate the Opposition, and he would hardly be restrained by considerations of loyalty to Chatham. The conclusion seems inescapable that he deliberately leaked Cabinet secrets to the Opposition.

What followed in the House on 6 March was farcical. Beckford moved that the Company's papers be printed and their proposals laid before the House. Townshend and Conway objected on the ground that the proposals were incomplete, but said nothing of their disagreement with the rest of the Cabinet. Then, in Horace Walpole's words:[1]

> In the midst of the debate, the military and naval chiefs, by their posts members of the Cabinet, but with all their merits very incompetent judges of state affairs, and still worse qualified to engage in the subtleties of a parliamentary discussion — both, I say, Lord Granby and Sir Edward Hawke, blabbed out the secret which the ministers were veiling, and which even the treachery and loquacity of Townshend had not dared openly to disclose. Lord Granby told the House that the offers had been found inadmissible; and Sir Edward . . . declared that the majority of the council had rejected it.

Upon this Townshend made a second speech, 'said his situation had put him under difficulties before, but that now he thought himself at liberty . . . reserved himself on the question of right and jurisdiction, but asserted strongly the preference of treaty to force'.[2] 'Townshend has acted in his usual wild, romancing, indiscreet manner', wrote Walpole, 'and has told everybody he is turned out.'[3] Whether or not he knew of Chatham's attempt to replace him (and according to Shelburne he did),[4] he now felt pretty safe and could afford to laugh at the Opposition for their failure to divide the House and thus expose the differences in the Cabinet. Newcastle wrote to Rockingham on 8 March, reporting a conversation with George Onslow (who Townshend knew could be trusted to pass on this sort of news to Newcastle):[5]

> He [Onslow] tells me everything will be made up between the ministry and Charles Townshend. The Duke of Grafton is very sanguine in it; and that Charles Townshend told him, he did not see why it might not be so. . . .

[1] *Memoirs*, ii. 305. [2] *Burke Correspondence* (1958 edition), i. 298.
[3] Walpole to Mann, 8 March 1767.
[4] *Chatham Correspondence*, iii. 235. [5] Add. MS. 32980 f. 228.

Charles Townshend told him . . . that never any people lost such an opportunity as we did the other day, that after what he and Mr. Conway had declared, we should have amended or turned Beckford's question so as to have got himself and Conway with us upon a division.

This is a strong argument for our pursuing it tomorrow, though I doubt we shall have but little chance of having them with us.

When the Opposition motion against printing the papers was made on 9 March Townshend was not in the House, and the Government motion to adjourn was carried by only 180 to 147.

It was about this time that Townshend's speculations in East India stock became known. Horace Walpole wrote to Mann on 19 March:

Charles Townshend's tergiversations appear to have been the result of private jobbing. He had dealt largely in India stock, cried up the Company's right to raise that stock, has sold out most advantageously, and now cries it down. What! and can a Chancellor of the Exchequer stand such an aspersion Oh! my dear sir, his character cannot be lowered.

Much of the stock was undoubtedly purchased in the names of other men and it is hardly possible to ascertain the extent of Townshend's speculations. Nor is it of consequence compared with the fact of his having speculated at a time when as Chancellor of the Exchequer and member of the Cabinet he was politically concerned with the affairs of the Company. Still, it is possible to obtain some figures from an examination of his accounts as Paymaster-general, for much of his speculation was carried on with Government money issued to him when he held the Pay Office, and which in accordance with eighteenth-century practice he continued to hold after he had resigned that office.[1] In June 1766, shortly before he went to the Exchequer, he held in East India stock £5,500 (valued at £9,900). At Christmas 1766 his holding had increased to £17,000 (worth £37,400), but at the time of his death he held nothing but £500 needed to qualify for a vote in the General Court. Because of the imperfectly kept accounts, it is not possible to say when he began to sell out nor to calculate his total profits, but it is known that by April 1767 he had made over £7000 by speculation in India stock.

[1] For these figures, and the practice of the Pay Office during this period, see L. S. Sutherland and J. Binney, 'Henry Fox as Paymaster-General of the Forces', *English Historical Review*, 1955.

(v)

Chatham's illness led to the abandonment of his plan for the East India Company. True, the inquiry took place, but not with the result Chatham had intended: the House of Commons heard evidence on the state of the Company's affairs and on events in India, but came to no conclusions and the inquiry had no share in the determination of Government policy. That policy now developed along the lines laid down by Townshend, and the question of the right to the territorial revenues was shelved. Instead, negotiations were begun for an agreement under which the Company would make an annual payment to the Crown in return for the extension of its charter and the de facto possession of its territorial revenues.

Townshend set to work with Sir George Colebrooke and other directors of the Company to drawn up a further set of proposals for the consideration of the Government. But at the General Court of 12 March there was opposition from a group of proprietors led by Laurence Sulivan, a friend of Lord Shelburne, and one of the ablest men concerned in the Company's affairs. Sulivan succeeded in getting a decision on the directors' plan postponed and offered to draw up one of his own, based on the principle that the territorial and trading revenues were to be kept separate. The initiative thus passed from Townshend, and the fruits of his victory over Chatham were reaped by Shelburne and Sulivan. Townshend had no close allies in high positions in the Company and had hitherto played little part in its internal politics. As Chancellor of the Exchequer he was concerned now to get the best terms he could for the Crown, and to extract the utmost political credit from the transaction. The game was being played the way he had always wanted it, and until events took a fresh turn he held aloof from the manœuvres within the Company.

On 27 March the Cabinet commissioned Conway, Grafton, and Townshend to negotiate an agreement with the Company. Townshend, pushing aside his nominal superior, Grafton, seems to have taken the lead on behalf of the Cabinet in these negotiations, but their exact course is difficult to trace from his extant correspondence. On 1 May, when the inquiry was to be resumed, Henry Crabb Boulton, a director of the Company, told the House that the negotiations were almost complete, which Townshend himself confirmed later in the debate. Then on 6 May there came a new turn in East Indian affairs when a group of speculators, against the advice of the directors, carried a motion in the General Court to raise the dividend from 10% to 12½%. The agreement which had been so long under discussion and was almost on the point of conclusion was now in jeopardy, and East Indian affairs again became a matter of contention within the Cabinet and of party divisions in the House of Commons.

It is improbable that Townshend had any share in this move to increase the dividend, and it is not certain that he was still engaged in East India speculation at that time. The Cabinet's reply was a Bill to prohibit the Company from increasing its dividend for a period of twelve months without consent of Parliament. The decision to introduce the Bill must have been taken on 7 May (it was brought into the House on the 8th), but no reports are known of the Cabinet's discussions or what line Townshend took. Despite his subsequent attitude, he must presumably have made no serious opposition to the principle of the Bill; and according to Walpole, he helped to draw up the motion of 8 May.

Still, it is surprising that the motion for leave to bring in the Dividend Bill was made not by Conway, the leader of the House, nor by Townshend, in whose department it fell, but by Jeremiah Dyson, a junior Minister and the foremost expert of his time on Parliamentary procedure. In the earlier part of the day Townshend made, according to Walpole, 'a very cool, sensible speech', and, with reference to East Indian affairs, told the House 'that he hoped he had atoned for the inconsideration of his past life by the care he had taken in that business'. When the Dividend Bill came on Townshend had gone to dinner, and was recalled to the House by a message from Conway. He then made a second speech, almost unique in Parliamentary annals, unique even for him.

Walpole in his first account of what became known as Townshend's 'champagne speech' (in a letter to Mann of 12 May) describes Townshend as 'half drunk when he made it'. In his *Memoirs of King George III*[1] however, he writes that Townshend was 'more intoxicated with spirits'. Sir George Colebrooke, who dined with Townshend that evening, denies that he was drunk or that the speech was unpremeditated — 'it was a speech he had meditated a great while upon, and it was only by accident that it

[1] *Memoirs*, iii. 17.

found utterance that day'. The need to explain it by intoxication shows how extraordinary Townshend's conduct appeared. Yet he never made a speech more in character — it was extraordinary only for a member of the Cabinet and a Chancellor of the Exchequer.

> The first thing he did [writes Walpole] was to call God to witness that he had not been consulted on the motion — a confession implying that he was not consulted on a business in his own department, and the more marvellous as the disgrace of which he seemed to complain or boast of was absolutely false. There were sitting round him twelve persons who had been in consultation with him that very morning and with his assistance had drawn up the motion on his own table, and who were petrified at his most unparalleled effrontery and causeless want of truth. When he sat down again, Conway asked him softly how he could affirm so gross a falsehood. He replied carelessly, 'I thought it would be better to say so.'

No detailed report of the champagne speech exists and probably none was ever made. But there is an account by Horace Walpole, written shortly after it was delivered, which not only gives the substance of the speech but also the impression it made on the House:[1]

> It lasted an hour, with torrents of wit, ridicule, vanity, lies, and beautiful language . . . every sentence teemed with various allusions and metaphors, and every period was complete, correct, and harmonious. His variety of tones and gesticulations surpassed the best actor in comedy, yet the faltering of his pronunciation from liquor, and the buffoonery of his humour and mimicry, would not have been suffered in high comedy. Nothing had given occasion to his speech, and there was no occasion on which it would not have been as proper, or to say truth, as improper, for if anything could exceed his parts it was his indiscretion . . . it was impertinent and offensive to all it described or seemed to compliment, and it was most painful to those who had any love for him. The purport seemed to be an intention of recommending Lord Rockingham's party for ministers, with himself as the lead of them; complimenting but sneering at Grenville; and slightly noting Conway. But lest the great families whom he adopted should assume too much, he ridiculed the incompetence of birth and high blood, cried up the sole advantage of ability and experience, and informed those he protected their rank was not talents, and that they must wait till ripened and not come to government as if forced in a hotbed. The most injurious part fell on the Crown, he stating the mischiefs of the late so frequent changes, calling for restitution of the

[1] *Letters of Horace Walpole*, ed. Mrs. Paget Toynbee, vii. 105–6.

first post in Administration to the House of Commons, and treating the actual ministry as no longer existent. Government, he said, must not continue to be what he himself was always called, a weathercock.

Nobody but he could have made that speech, and nobody but he would have made [it] if they could. It was at once a proof that his abilities were superior to those of all men, and his judgment below that of any man. It showed him capable of being, and unfit to be, First Minister. . . .

The House was in a roar of rapture, and some clapped their hands with ecstasy, like audience in a theatre. . . .

In this speech he beat Lord Chatham in language, Burke in metaphors, Grenville in presumption, Rigby in impudence, himself in folly, and everybody in good humour . . . and if his speech was received with delight, it was only remembered with pity.

In vino veritas: there was much in this speech that Townshend had long felt and never dared to say. And Walpole writes further, in his *Memoirs of King George III*:[1]

He went to supper with us at Mr. Conway's, where, the flood of his gaiety not being exhausted, he kept the table in a roar till two in the morning, by various sallies and pictures, the last of which was a scene in which he mimicked inimitably his own wife and another great lady with whom he fancied himself in love, and both whose foibles and manner he counterfeited to the life.

The General Court's decision to increase the dividend, and the Cabinet's reply in the form of the Dividend Bill, had thrown the negotiations into the melting-pot again; and new alignments took place within the Company. Laurence Sulivan came forward with a fresh set of proposals, more favourable to the Ministry, and in return Townshend undertook to do all he could to oppose the Dividend Bill. At the General Court of 18 May Sulivan carried his proposals in substance, and a petition to the House of Commons against the Dividend Bill was voted. John Huske, one of Townshend's observers in the Company, concluded his report, written at 4 a.m. the following morning, shortly after the Court broke up:[2]

I am so fatigued I can say no more than that I heartily congratulate you on this happy issue of the contest; provided you give us this $12\frac{1}{2}\%$ contended for, though we have expressed nothing to the House in the petition on this head but our desire to defend and support the legality, equity, and propriety of the increase.

[1] *Memoirs*, iii. 19. [2] Buccleuch MSS.

Townshend's volte-face on the Dividend Bill excited little comment — perhaps after his 'champagne speech' no behaviour of his was considered too bizarre. On 26 May he voted against the Government on an Opposition amendment that the permitted dividend should be 12½%, but according to Charles Jenkinson he carried only one Government supporter (Samuel Touchet) with him into the Opposition lobby.[1] The Bill passed the Commons with a comfortable majority but the Lords only after a hard fight; yet to the agreement with the Company there was no serious opposition in either House.

To sum up Townshend's part in the East India politics of this session: he was able, through Chatham's illness and the weakness of his Cabinet colleagues, to nullify Chatham's policy; at no time did he show statemanship or an appreciation of the Company's problems; and his conduct may have been guided by no more rational motive than his own pecuniary interest. The net result of his intervention in East Indian affairs was totally to discredit him as a politician.

(vi)

Though East Indian affairs absorbed the attention of Chatham's Cabinet, it was in the field of North American policy that the most momentous decisions were taken and here that Charles Townshend achieved his greatest triumph — the only accomplishment of his life which renders his biography of historical significance. If ever there was a case of men making history by chance, without being aware of the implications of their policy, it was the enactment of the Townshend duties. For the key posts in Chatham's Cabinet were held by men who professed friendship for America and who were opposed to the taxation of the colonies by the British Parliament. Chatham himself, Lord Chancellor Camden, and Shelburne, who was primarily responsible for the administration of the colonies, had all voted against the Declaratory Act; while Grafton, head of the Treasury, and Conway, Minister in the House of Commons, had taken the lead in the repeal of the Stamp Act. The Cabinet was overwhelmingly pro-American; and Townshend's plan to raise a revenue in America was countenanced and abetted by men who were publicly pledged to oppose that policy.

[1] Add. MS. 38205, f. 174.

At first sight it appears that the decision to introduce the Townshend duties was taken almost by sheer chance, the result of a foolish boast made in the heat of debate. On 26 January 1767, during the debate on the Army estimates, Grenville moved an amendment that the expense of the troops stationed in America should be met by the colonies themselves. This was defeated by 106 votes to 35, but Townshend, replying for the Government, accepted Grenville's principle while opposing his amendment, and 'pledged himself that something should be done this sessions towards creating a revenue [in America]'.[1] When challenged by Lord George Sackville, he added that he did not mean to imply that the American revenue would be sufficient to cover all the expenses of the troops: it would at first be only a contribution, which he hoped would later be increased.

Grafton in his *Autobiography*,[2] written forty years later, gives the following account of this incident, which is substantially correct. After explaining that the Cabinet's policy towards America was to avoid 'harsh and positive' measures, Grafton continues:

> Such were the genuine sentiments of the King's servants, when, in an ill-fated hour, Mr. Townshend chose to boast in Parliament that he knew the mode by which a revenue might be drawn from America *without offence*. Mr. Grenville fixed him down directly to pledge himself on the declaration, which was received with such welcome by the bulk of the House as dismayed Mr. Conway, who stood astonished at the unauthorized proceeding of his vain and imprudent colleague. On being questioned by the Cabinet on the evening following, how he had ventured to depart on so essential a point from the profession of the whole ministry, Mr. C. Townshend turned to Mr. Conway, appealing to him whether the House was not bent on obtaining a revenue of some sort from the colonies.

Even more amazing in a way than Townshend's pledging the Cabinet to a policy they disapproved, is the lack of notice taken of it by contemporaries. Few seemed to have realized that this was a return to Grenville's American policy, which had been in effect abandoned when the Rockingham Administration repealed the Stamp Act. Perhaps contemporaries were misled by the distinction between internal taxes and import duties, on which the colonists themselves seemed to lay so much stress, and failed to see that the

[1] Newdigate MS. B2548, Warws. Record Office. [2] Pp. 126–7.

real difference was between taxation for revenue and taxation for the regulation of commerce. Conway's report to the King mentions Townshend among the speakers but gives no report of what he said;[1] Horace Walpole's account in his *Memoirs*,[2] written in October 1769, says nothing of Townshend's pledge; Beckford, who had opposed the Stamp Act, wrote to Chatham the following day, but was so pre-occupied with Indian affairs that in a short paragraph on America he does not mention Townshend's performance.[3] Dowdeswell, leader of the Rockingham group in the Commons, was in the House when Townshend spoke, but said nothing; and Townshend's speech is not mentioned in the correspondence of Burke, Newcastle, or Rockingham. Even Chatham himself, when informed by Shelburne of Townshend's pledge, took no notice of it.[4]

Townshend's speech had been in his most flippant style, but his pledge was not entirely improvised: he was self-willed and irresponsible rather than spontaneous. He had for some time been formulating plans for America and had taken no trouble to keep them secret. Shelburne writes in his letter to Chatham of 1 February:[5]

> I have heard indeed from general conversation that Mr. Townshend has a plan for establishing a board of customs in America, and by a new regulation of the tea duty here, and some other alterations, to produce a revenue on imports there. I am myself in no respect able or sufficiently informed to form a judgment how far this may be likely to answer the end or no; but in many views it appears a matter that will require the deepest consideration, at this time especially. Besides, I believe your Lordship will think the speech I have just mentioned to you is not the way to make any thing go down well in North America.

The financial regulations were worked out by Townshend and his unofficial advisers, John Huske and Samuel Touchet. In the Townshend MSS. of the Duke of Buccleuch there is what may well be the first draft of the Townshend duties, in Touchet's hand;[6] and Townshend wrote in June to Grafton about Touchet, when recommending him for a reward:[7] 'He and he alone has the merit of whatever has been honourably done in this winter for the public and the Treasury in the choice of taxes.'

[1] Fortescue, i. no. 469.
[2] Vol. ii, p. 293.
[3] *Chatham Correspondence*, iii. 176–8.
[4] Ibid., 188–90.
[5] Ibid., 185.
[6] For this, and a letter from Huske about the duties, see appendices.
[7] Grafton MSS.

It is sometimes said (even by Horace Walpole) that the Government's defeat on 27 February on an Opposition motion to reduce the Land Tax from 4s. to 3s. in the pound was a further reason for the imposition of the Townshend duties. But Townshend's pledge to raise a revenue in America was given a month before the Government defeat on the land tax; moreover, the produce of his duties was to be used entirely in America, and in any case was too small to cover the loss of revenue suffered by the reduction of the Land Tax. Nor was Townshend's plan merely a fiscal measure: it was part of a grand design to strengthen British authority in the colonies, and to make the royal officials independent of the colonial Assemblies. This was Townshend's real end, to which the raising a revenue was merely a means.

Though the repeal of the Stamp Act had removed the Americans' major grievance, the aftermath of the attempt to enforce it was by no means over. The Assembly of Massachusetts Bay had passed an Act pardoning the rioters in the Stamp Act disturbances, and New York had refused to comply with the Mutiny Act and make provision for British troops stationed in the colony. These acts of defiance of the home Government could not be condoned by the Chatham Administration, and Chatham himself seems to have felt that sufficient lenity had been shown to the colonies.[1] Here, then, is another reason why Townshend's plan excited so little opposition: the climate of Parliamentary opinion was in its favour.

Chatham had suggested that the conduct of New York should be laid before Parliament, but gave no indication of what concrete steps he wished to see taken. The matter fell properly within Shelburne's department and its introduction into the House of Commons was Conway's responsibility, but Townshend seems from the beginning to have taken the lead — once again, he was the only Minister with a policy and with sufficient drive to force it on the Cabinet. Grafton wrote to Chatham on 13 March, describing the Cabinet meeting of the previous night:[2]

> The American, or rather New York, point was settled, and that it should be by Act of Parliament. . . . The vote of supply for the American extraordinaries was then considered, when Mr. Townshend declared that if the reduction of them was not determined before the

[1] *Chatham Correspondence*, iii, 188–9, 193–4; Grafton, *Autobiography*, 119.
[2] *Chatham Correspondence*, iii. 231–2.

closing of the committee of supply, by drawing the troops nearer the great towns, laying the Indian charges upon the provinces, and by laying a tax upon the American ports, he would not remain Chancellor of the Exchequer. His behaviour on the whole was such as no Cabinet will I am confident ever submit to.

And Shelburne to Chatham, the same day:[1]

Mr. Townshend . . . mentioned the extraordinaries of America, and the necessity of voting a particular sum, which he said he neither could nor would move unless the cabinet previously took the whole state of America into consideration and enabled him to declare to the House the opinion of Administration as to the forts, the Indian trade, the disposition of the troops, in short the whole arrangements, considered with a view to a general reduction of expense, and a duty which he undertook should be laid to defray what remained: that he had promised this to the House, and upon the authority of what passed in the cabinet, and if he could not make it good he should be obliged to consider the best means, by what he should say or by his conduct, to make it appear that it was not his fault and against his opinion.

The plan of moving the troops in America nearer the large towns had been originally put forward by Grenville, not by Townshend;[2] while perhaps only Townshend would have had the effrontery to tell the Cabinet, what each member knew to be false, that it was on their authority that he had given his pledge to raise a revenue from America. Shelburne ended his letter as did Grafton: 'It appears to me quite impossible that Mr. Townshend can mean to go on in the King's service.' But Grafton writes lamely in his *Autobiography*:[3] 'No one of the ministry had authority sufficient to advise the dismission of Mr. Charles Townshend, and nothing less could have stopped the measure, Lord Chatham's absence being in this instance, as well as others, much to be lamented.'

There is a note from Townshend to Grafton, docketed 'April 1767', and probably written shortly before 30 April (when the House was due to go into committee on the American papers), in which Townshend clearly appears as the originator of the Government's policy towards New York:[4]

Mr. Townshend certainly suggested originally in conversation the mode of proceeding towards New York since considered in cabinet

[1] Ibid., 232–6.
[2] In the debate of 18 February 1767 on the American extraordinaries. See Walpole, *Memoirs*, ii, 296.
[3] P. 127.
[4] Grafton MSS.

> and he is sensible that the Duke of Grafton, understanding the first discussion of it in council to have ended in a final resolution, did soon after assure the House of Lords that a bill would be prepared to enforce the Mutiny Act.

There is also a draft in the Buccleuch MSS. of the resolutions on New York which were to be put before the House, with additions and corrections in Townshend's hand. These resolutions stated in substance that the province had failed to make adequate provision for the troops stationed there, and that the Governor should be prohibited from giving his assent to any Act of the Assembly until it had complied with the provisions of the Mutiny Act.

Conway, apparently alone in the Cabinet, thought these resolutions too severe, and refused to be responsible for them in the House. Townshend, therefore, undertook to introduce them on 5 May. 'That very morning', writes Walpole, 'he pretended to have fallen down-stairs and cut his eye dangerously.'[1] Three days later, during his 'champagne speech',

> In the fervour of speaking Townshend rubbed off the patch from his eye, which he had represented as grievously cut three days before: no mark was discernible, but to the nearest spectators a scratch so slight that he might have made, and perhaps did make it himself, with a pin.

And this was Walpole's comment: 'His strange irresolution and versatility could not conceal itself even on so public an occasion.'

There seems to have been more behind this incident than even the well-informed Walpole was aware of. There is in the Grafton MSS. a letter from Townshend to Grafton, undated, but which seems to have been written on 5 May:

> Mr. Townshend presents his compliments to the Duke of Grafton.
>
> He sincerely laments that the opportunity has not been taken of soliciting his Majesty's assent to the proposition of independent salaries for the civil officers of North America, especially as he had pledged himself to the House for some measure of this sort, and had the assurances of Lord Shelburne in the last cabinet for the whole extent of the establishment, and the Duke of Grafton on Saturday adopted the idea at least as far as New York. In this distress Mr. Townshend does not think he can with honour move the resolutions this day, and therefore hopes either to have the authority or that some means may be found of postponing the matter for a day or two till he can receive it. He feels his honour absolutely at stake. He did not

[1] *Memoirs*, iii. 15, 19.

> suggest the matter to the King, because as the Duke of Grafton knows, he has *never* presumed to move in such high matters alone or originally.

Grafton must have read the last sentence with a wry smile. His first reaction was to stand up to Townshend, and he asked Lord North to open the resolutions. But in the Commons on 5 May Rigby proposed that the American business should be postponed until Townshend had recovered, which was agreed to by the House. What happened during the next few days cannot be accurately traced from either the Townshend or Grafton MSS., but so much is clear: that Townshend talked of resignation (according to Walpole, 'not only threatened to resign, but falsely affirmed that he had offered his resignation to the King');[1] and that on 13 May, when he at last proposed the American resolutions, he had authority to make the declaration he wished.

Walpole describes Townshend's speech of that day as 'consonant to the character of a man of business, and so unlike the wanton sallies of the man of parts and pleasure';[2] it must indeed have been a contrast to the 'champagne speech' delivered only five days earlier. Townshend did not confine himself to the resolutions against New York, and his speech contains the fullest exposé he ever gave to the House of his American policy.[3] 'Mr. Townshend', wrote Thomas Bradshaw, Secretary to the Treasury, in his report to Grafton, 'opened the business of the day with a declaration that he was not at council when it was resolved to lay the American papers before the House' — a disingenuous declaration which probably deceived no one. He then mentioned the duties he proposed to lay on America and his plan to establish a board of customs at New York. ('I was not aware of the mistrust and jealousy which this appointment would bring on', writes Grafton in his *Autobiography*, '. . . otherwise it should never have had my assent.'[4]) He dealt with the delinquent colonies, Massachusetts Bay and New York, and then said:

[1] For Townshend's threat of resignation, see Walpole, *Memoirs*, iii. 29, and Grafton, *Autobiography*, 178.

[2] Walpole, *Memoirs*, iii. 24.

[3] Three reports of this speech, from which the following quotations are taken, are known to exist: Walpole, *Memoirs*, iii. 21–5; a report drawn up for Grafton by Thomas Bradshaw, *Autobiography*, 176–8; and one by Charles Garth, agent for South Carolina, *South Carolina Historical and Genealogical Magazine*, xxix, 227–30. There is substantial agreement between these reports.

[4] P. 127.

> In general it did not become Parliament to engage in controversy with its colonies, but by one act to assert its sovereignty. He warned the House to beware lest the provinces engaged in a common cause. Our right of taxation was indubitable, yet himself had been for repealing the Stamp Act to prevent mischief. Should their disobedience return, the authority of Parliament had been weakened; and unless supported with spirit and dignity, must be destroyed.

Next, he outlined his plan 'for improving the system of government in the colonies': he proposed 'that out of the fund arising from the American duties ... his Majesty should be enabled to establish salaries ... better suited to support the dignity of the respective officers, and for which to be no longer dependent upon the pleasure of any Assembly'. This provision, commented Charles Garth, agent for South Carolina, when the Bill received the royal assent, 'must operate to render the Assembly ... rather insignificant'. That was its purpose.

The New York resolutions were carried in committee by 180 votes to 98. The Townshend duties (on glass, lead, painters' colours, paper, and tea) passed through the Committee of Ways and Means without opposition and almost without discussion — no reports are extant of any debate on them. The sixteenth resolution of the Committee of Ways and Means laid down that the duties were to be applied to make provision for the administration of justice and the support of the civil government 'where it should be found necessary'. The preamble of the Act of Parliament (7 George III, c. 46) which authorised the duties repeats the same statement in almost the same words.

Thus after fourteen years, towards the end of his career and life, Charles Townshend, the reputed weathercock, carried into effect the scheme which he had put forward as a very junior Minister in 1753–4: a steadiness of purpose with which he has not been credited.

(vii)

Chatham's withdrawal in March 1767 elevated the Duke of Grafton to the position of de facto head of Administration, and allowed Charles Townshend plenty of scope to display his wonted versatility. His antics during the next few months, when Grafton's Ministry was struggling against a union of all three Opposition parties, supply a comic element to the tragic last year of Townshend's life. He made up to each of the political leaders in turn, ridiculed them behind their backs, and ended by being distrusted by all.

Rockingham was the first victim of Townshend's political confidence trick, and he seems to have been taken in completely. About the second week of March 1767, after Chatham had abdicated as head of Administration and the East India inquiry had been deprived of its sting, Townshend began to give Rockingham hopes that he would soon resign. The following extracts from Rockingham's letters to Newcastle trace the gradual decline of these hopes:[1]

17 March 'Charles was in high spirits and his conversation both in *public* and *private* last night very agreeable. Nothing quite decisive but not far from it.'

19 March 'I had a moment's conversation with Charles Townshend — all well.'

24 March 'My two supper visitors [Townshend and Conway] are gone. We must still have three or four days patience — or rather suspense. I am still of opinion that good may ensue — whether in *both* or in one I cannot ascertain, but I continue to like the appearances.'

29 March 'I saw Charles Townshend last night. No actual decision, much talk of probability of its soon happening, but upon the whole not ground sufficient for our sanguine expectations.'

In April Townshend was entertaining Grenville with gibes at his Cabinet colleagues. The entry in the Grenville diary for 1 April reads:[2]

Mr. Charles Townshend comes every day in the House to talk with Mr. Grenville, and to abuse Lord Chatham, and laugh at the Administration; and speaking in relation to what would be proper to be done in America, he said Mr. Conway was upon that subject below low-water mark.

On 23 May:

In the House of Commons there is greater confusion than ever, Mr. Charles Townshend thwarting and abusing the Administration on all occasions, and declaring that he shall be out of employment shortly.

On 5 June Townshend asked to see Grenville, who gave to James Harris the following account of their conversation:[3]

[1] Add. MS. 32980, ff. 333–4, 343–4, 372, 418–19.
[2] *Grenville Papers*, iv. 222, 225.
[3] Malmesbury MSS.

> Townshend expressed the impossibility of his going on with the present set of people — his wish to be detached from them — said that he chose rather to be dismissed than to withdraw himself — that he expected in the ensuing holidays to be dismissed — if not, that then he should soon after resign himself. That he could not think of acting under the Duke of Grafton, much less Lord Rockingham. Allowed Mr. Grenville to be the properest person to manage the finances . . . thought that they two together might lead the House of Commons.

It is unlikely that Grenville took this seriously — he knew well there could be no such thing as joint leadership of the House of Commons — or Townshend either: he was simply putting out his tongue at Grafton and Rockingham.

He alternately sulked to Grafton and then courted him. When in April Lady Dalkeith, by the death of her mother the Duchess of Argyll, succeeded to a fortune said to be £4000 per annum, Townshend flaunted his independence at Grafton:[1]

> Your Grace's regard for me [he wrote on 24 April] will incline you to be pleased with hearing that my late accession of fortune has placed me and what I love more than myself, my children, in great affluence and ample station. The relish for this is heightened in me by the recollection of former uncertainties, the neglect of my family, and the delay of every favour I have ever had reason to expect from the Crown. I am now out of the reach of fortune, and can act without anxiety.

The failure to obtain a peerage for Lady Dalkeith, which he seems to have blamed on Grafton, rankled sorely. But on 12 June the Duke of Richmond reported Townshend and Grafton to be again on amicable terms,[2] and there is a very friendly letter from Townshend to Grafton of 25 June which concludes:[3]

> I never wish to have any mark of approbation separate from your Grace, and even in censure I should have thought it an honour to have been of late attacked in the same manner and in the same papers with the Duke of Grafton.

This, it should be remembered, was written less than three weeks after he had told Grenville 'that he could not think of acting under the Duke of Grafton', and at a time when the Rockinghams were

[1] Grafton MSS.
[2] Richmond to Rockingham, 12 June 1767, Rockingham MSS.
[3] Grafton MSS.

almost daily expecting him to resign and come over to their side.[1]

Detached observers were able to assess correctly the effect of Townshend's conduct. Thus Lady Mary Coke, his sister-in-law, records a conversation of 1 June with Lady Dalkeith, when Lady Dalkeith 'seemed to think Mr. Townshend had been very ill treated'.[2]

> I heard all she had a mind to say, and then told her that I had as high an opinion of Mr. Townshend's abilities as she could possibly have, and most sincerely wished him well, but that I was sorry to say his want of steadiness, and his abusing and ridiculing every mortal in different companies, had created him so many enemies that there was nobody that thought they could depend upon him. I next told her that I had been informed by one who wished him well that he had on all occasions this winter paid compliments to Mr. Grenville and Mr. Dowdeswell in the House of Commons, which was very particular, as they were engaged in a party against the Court, and it was observed he as constantly passed over in silence the merits of those that acted with him, all which was thought extraordinary conduct.

Lady Mary also reports Sir Gilbert Elliot (probably her informant of the above paragraph) as 'much concerned at Mr. Townshend's conduct, which he fears will make his great abilities useless to the country and of little service to himself'. Indeed, by this time most people had seen through Townshend. During the negotiations of July for a reconstruction of the Ministry, he was not a principal, and the question of his participation in a new Government was not crucial. He resented his exclusion, without understanding why it had come about; and wrote to Grafton on 14 July:[3]

> Lord Rockingham has not spoke one word to me; the King did not yesterday recollect Lady Dalkeith's peerage; and I find so little real kindness that I earnestly desire to mix in nothing.

The nemesis of character had overtaken him.

And he was intriguing to the last. There is a memorandum by Lord Townshend of 17 September, a fortnight after Charles's death, reporting a conversation with Theobald Taaffe, a notorious swindler and professional gambler:[4]

[1] See Hardwicke's letters to Rockingham of 22 and 25 June, Rockingham MSS.

[2] *Journal of Lady Mary Coke*, ii. 9, 13.

[3] Grafton MSS.

[4] The whereabouts of this memorandum is unknown. The extract quoted was printed in a catalogue issued by Francis Edwards, bookseller, of 83 High Street Marylebone, London, W.1, circa 1925.

> He acquainted me [writes Lord Townshend] that my brother Charles had carried on just before his death a negotiation through him to Mr. Rigby and thence to the Duke of Bedford, Lord Temple, and Mr. Grenville, by which the second was to have been First Lord of the Treasury, my brother Secretary of State and direction of the House of Commons, Duke of Bedford and Mr. Grenville would support but no places.

How much belief should be attached to this story is difficult to say: there is no evidence for it in the papers of those concerned. Told of anyone but Townshend it would be ridiculous, and told by such a man as Taaffe invites suspicion. Yet there is no doubt that Townshend did have dealings with Taaffe. After Townshend's death Taaffe offered Lord Clive for £7000 the nomination to three seats in Cornwall at the forthcoming General Election which he claimed he had secured for Townshend; but Clive, distrusting Taaffe's ability to fulfil his engagements, turned down the offer.[1] And Lady Greenwich (as Lady Dalkeith had by then become) wrote to Lord Townshend on 21 October 1768:[2]

> 'Tis too true that for the three last years of our dead friend's life, this Taaffe was often with him, and very wretched it made me, as I knew he was a man of very bad character. I expressed my uneasiness at it, and my dear Mr. Townshend's answer was that he was not the bad man I thought him and begged I would not make myself uneasy for he never placed confidence in these sort of people. For some time after he did not dine at our house, which gave me comfort, till I found that he frequently came of evenings after I was gone out.

And later in the same letter there is another passage which throws considerable light on Townshend's choice of associates:

> 'Tis most true, my dear Lord, what you say, that there are ever such wretches as these hovering about considerable men and doing infinite mischief. I well remember a conversation you and I had in Audley Square, at the time our dear friend took the office of Chancellor of the Exchequer. That you expressed with great affection your wishes that so many of these sort of men that you saw at our house was banished from it. Alas, my dear Lord, if it had not been for these low meddlers and advisers, how many most unpleasant things would have been prevented.

[1] See letters to Lord Clive from George Clive, 1 October 1767, and from Chase Price, 21 October 1767, in the MSS. of Lord Powis.

[2] Townshend MSS. at Raynham.

What she does not seem to have realized was that Townshend preferred to confide in such men as Touchet, Bindley, and Taaffe — plungers and gamblers that they were.

(viii)

In August 1767 Lord Townshend, largely through Charles's influence, was appointed Lord Lieutenant of Ireland, and Lady Dalkeith at last received her peerage. They were Charles Townshend's last triumphs. His death on 4 September was sudden. Horace Walpole wrote:[1]

> Charles Townshend is dead. All those parts and fire are extinguished; those volatile salts are evaporated; that first eloquence of the world is dumb; that duplicity is fixed; that cowardice terminated heroically. He joked on death as naturally as he used to do on the living. . . . With a robust person he had always a menacing constitution. He had a fever the whole summer, recovered as it was thought, relapsed, was neglected, and it turned to an incurable putrid fever.

He died intestate, with his affairs in great confusion.[2] Lady Mary Coke wrote on 15 September:[3]

> By all I can find out, he trusted so many different people with his money that I fear there will be losses, as it was very frequent with him to order his money to be placed out in other people's names.

'Never was there a man who left his affairs in such disorder' — or those of the State encumbered with a more fatal inheritance.

It is easier for a biographer to analyse the shortcomings and mistakes of a man than to convey an idea of his genius, charm, or eloquence, unless they are transmitted in his writings, which is not the case with Charles Townshend. For us 'that first eloquence of the world' remains 'dumb'. The record we have is of a man of quite exceptional ability, unhappy and self-frustrated, and now best remembered for the disastrous part he played in the prelude to the American Revolution.

*

But our disabilities devolving from the flow of time may be, up to a point, compensated by it. The mass of recorded impressions can now be examined alongside other contemporaneous material, and

[1] Walpole to Mann, 27 September 1767.
[2] See letters from Lady Greenwich to Lord Townshend, 16 January, 26 July 1768; Townshend MSS. at Raynham.
[3] *Journal of Lady Mary Coke*, ii. 126, 130.

considered in the light of recent discoveries on the promptings of human actions, the probable links between action and character, and the effect on a man of the lingering hopes and disabling fears of the child he once was. With such aids a more coherent estimate may perhaps be hazarded of the parliamentarian who ardently and steadfastly wished to play a conspicuous part in the affairs of the state, but lacked a true sense of responsibility. Even some unifying factor may perhaps be found to draw together the disjointed personality of this elusive man.

Charles Townshend started life endowed and disabled in about equal measure. Having grown up into a tall, well-built man with an engaging manner, he was acclaimed a wit with a pretty gift for mimicry. His voice was loud and he had a talent for putting other men's thoughts into better shape than they felt able to do. Given 'the art of shining', he trained himself to be a brilliant orator and no mean actor. (There was that speech in the House, applauded long and loud as for an *encore*.) His abilities were deemed wonderful and he was said to have art enough to disguise anything except his prodigious vanity. But what was he disguising?

Grievous ill-health he bore manfully, could allude to lightly, and was glad to cash in on. Purposeful and flippant, he handled with dexterity incidents arising out of his 'inveterate disorder'; and by often putting to good use the tragic element in his life, managed to give that element a farcical appearance. Beside being purposeful, he possessed the great driving power of a basically robust man; was secretly tenacious; worked quick and hard, even with 'exceeding application'; was at times the only minister with a definite policy and, naturally enough, was able more than once to force his will on a languid Cabinet. For all that, subject to his 'menacing constitution', he was distracted by a deeply ingrained restlessness. It irked him to be closely associated for any length of time with the same set of men; yet men significantly employed in the 'public business' which he loved were few. A way out of the recurring impasse was to get himself dismissed, rather than overtly to withdraw from this or that working group. Such tactics made easier his foreseen attempts to resume a little later an association broken through no fault of his as it were. The forward glance, necessary to a politician, he did have but also a disastrous inability properly to use it. Erratic behaviour ensued at the decisive moment; accompanied by histrionics, antics of staggering effrontery, and much lying — the better to wriggle out of a situation largely engineered by him in the first instance. Early in life he had acquired an addiction to posturing, attitudinising, putting on an act — with an immediate practical end in view. Become a public figure, he lost himself in quick successions of turns. Like so much accumulated dust they settled on his image, to obliterate the genuine Charles Townshend. And, the better to cover up some inadmissible flaw, the farce was debased to ludicrous clowning.

It was Charles Townshend's character damaged beyond repair by early associates that, above all, deprived him of success. He grew up into a self-damaging type, and was from then on predestined to remain a brilliant failure. Edginess, incalculability, and a confusion of facts and detail accompanied his epileptic fits. Lord Townshend — no fool either — had early on noted and genuinely sympathised with the obvious temporary deterioration. But, true to himself, had sorely aggravated his son's moments of acute strain: truculent, hortatory, self-righteous, reproachful, ironical, he had as good as forced the youth — uncharitable and treated without charity — to despise his bullying tormentor who held him trapped; and who instructed him to deride his mother — at least a supplementary source of authority and comfort to most people when young. Intelligent but confused, resourceful but alarmed, the young Charles had sought relief in all-embracing derision. It included even himself. The product was a curiously antisocial man — one who needed the society of well-endowed people to keep his spirits buoyant, his abilities in trim; but despised all and sundry as mere tools to further his intentions; homunculi to be used, amused, and pandered to, for the coming hour of exploitation, itself treated as a game. Protective poverty of heart was the contrived shield of his stricken, vulnerable self; gifted enough to be aware, however dimly, of its ugliness and purpose, he consistently disguised or veiled it.

Two faint exceptions suggest that extreme poverty of heart need not have been his. He showed a proper concern for the children of the family, his own and Lady Dalkeith's; and his desire to ease the hideous lot of the insane seems to have been sincere. From the children he could expect nothing immediately and little of value to him in the long run; from the insane he could exact nothing at all. Rudiments of the warmer feelings seem to have been there. But early associates in adverse circumstances had unwittingly blighted them.

APPENDIX A

Letter from John Huske to Charles Townshend, 9 April 1767

Sir,

The duty I proposed to lay upon wine from Spain, Portugal, and Italy *directly* to America was £7 per ton, which is the same as Mr. Grenville imposed upon wine from Madeira and the Azores to America in 1763. But if any wine of the produce of those countries should be re-exported from Great Britain to her colonies, then the drawback and duty was to be the same as the Act of 1763 specifies, which to the best of my memory was to leave no more than £4 per ton in England and to pay ten shillings per ton upon importation into America. This alteration of the duty was made with a view to encourage re-exportation from hence in preference to taking from foreign countries direct, if practicable, or more advantageous to the adventurer in any case that might possibly arise. I also proposed *double* said duties upon the wines of France, or any other country besides Spain, Portugal, and Italy.

I also proposed three pence per gallon on olive oil, 2s. 6d. per cwt. on dried or preserved fruit, and 2/6 for every 100 of lemons or oranges from Europe, Madeira, the Canaries, and the Azores that should be imported into his Majesty's colonies. These duties were judged too high by Lord Rockingham; and that Administration had agreed to admit those articles into America direct from the place of their growth, at a much inferior duty, but I cannot recollect what rates they fixed. You may have them from Mr. Dowdeswell or from Mr. Rose Fuller, who took a copy of them at a meeting I was at on the occasion at Mr. Dowdeswell's. Or Mr. Cooper can give them to you. They are necessary for you to see, as they were communicated to the American agents and by them sent to America, or at least by some of them; but they were never proposed in the committee of supply, though Mr. Dowdeswell carried them to the House for that purpose, which was owing to the difficulties which arose about the free ports.

Permit me to remark to you that it is certain that by a regulation of the trade of America for the reciprocal interest of both mother and children, you may have a sufficient revenue to pay all Great Britain's expence for her colonies and in a manner perfectly agreeable to both under your conduct; but be assured no regulation or measure that is to raise money can be agreeable or practicable in the continent colonies till you give them a currency. Till then you are demanding brick without straw. A bill for this purpose was drawn up by Mr. Franklin and myself last year; and I moved to bring it in with the *seeming* approbation of the Ministers; but Mr. Dyson and Lord Clare opposing it, though they knew not one tittle of the plan, or of the nature of a good or bad paper currency, nor never will know any more of it than I do of the Mogul's cabinet, it was carried to postpone it to this session, when to this moment nothing is brought into the House about it.

I have been told today by a gentleman who said he had it from you, that you intended to impose a duty upon *salt* imported into America! Upon this ground and upon knowing that sometimes the greatest pilots may receive a useful hint from a passenger, permit me, sir, to assure you that a more fatal imposition to both Great Britain and her colonies could not be devised. And if ever it does take place it will have the same effect as an Act of Parliament to pluck out the eyes or to tear out the hearts of the people of America would have. I beg pardon, perhaps I have said too much. It is my business only to answer the questions you please to ask, and therefore I shall conclude with saying your account will be finished as soon as I can stand and move without assistance.

With the sincerest wishes for your health, honour, and happiness, I remain, with the greatest deference,

Sir,

Your most obedient humble servant,

J. Huske

St. Martin's Lane
9th April

[Buccleuch MSS.]

APPENDIX B

Preliminary draft of the Townshend duties

[This document, from the Buccleuch MSS., is undated and has no heading. It is docketed (not in Townshend's hand): 'Duties proposed for 1767 Mr. Touchet's writing.' The numbers seem to have been added by Touchet after the rest of the document was written.]

[Sheet 1]

China No. 5
The whole drawback
upon exportation to
America being [blank in MS.]
amounts to £8,000

Glass No. 6
Upon exportation of
white glass is 1d. per lb.
is drawn back
upon green glass ¼d.
the former being valued
at 6d. per lb. — ½d. duty
payable in America is
8 per cent
Green glass valued at
1½d. per lb., ⅛ of a penny
duty to be paid in
America is also 8 per cent
these duties upon what [?]
is exported to the colonies
will produce annually 5,000

Carried over £13,000

[Sheet 2]

Brought over 13,000

Paper No. 7
The excise in England
is estimated as nearly
as can be at 18 per cent
all of which is drawn
back upon exportation.

It is proposed to continue
the drawback and to lay
half the duties or 9 per cent
upon importation into
America, which will
produce per annum 5,000
Red and white lead No. 8
and painters' colours which
are the produce of Britain
and pay no duty upon
exportation will very
well bear 2s. per cent upon
importation into Am-
erica and on a moderate
estimate will produce
annually 2,000

£20,000

[Sheet 3]
Brought forward 20,000
Wines No. 1.
Britain consumes
16,000 tons per annum
The British
colonies may at least
be supposed to contain
$\frac{1}{4}$ of the number of
inhabitants who drink
wine which is 4000
tons, whereof
$\frac{3}{4}$ have been legally
imported from Britain
and the Madeiras the remaining
1000 ton if permitted
to entry will produce
at the intended duty of
£7 per ton 7,000
Fruit of all sorts No. 2
there must be consumed
1000 tons at 2/6 per cent
or 50 s. per ton 2,500

Carried over 29,500

[Sheet 4]

Brought over 29,500

Oranges and lemons pay No. 3
in England 4d. per hundred
upon importation, if
permitted to America
direct from Spain and Portugal
they will bear the same
duty and as punch is used
there instead of beer
the consumption may
be supposed at half the
quantity or [blank in MS.]
thousands and will produce 3,000

32,500

[Sheet 5]

Brought over 32,500

Oil No. 4
It is computed that
one fourth of the inhabitants
or 500,000 persons in America
consume oil with salt fish
and sallads [sic] and that every such
person uses at least one
gallon per annum which
500,000 gallons or 1984 tons
at £5 per ton amounts to £9,920

No. 9
It is proposed to lay
the following small duties on
capers 1d. per lb.
olives 3d. per gallon
~~vinegar~~ ~~40s. per ton~~ [deleted]
and cork wood 1s. per hundredweight
of the consumption whereof
no accurate computation
can be made and therefore
shall state the produce of all these
articles at the very moderate
sum of 1,000

Total 43,420

APPENDIX C

List of Books by Sir Lewis Namier

THE following list of works by Sir Lewis Namier does not include articles, pamphlets, or reviews not subsequently republished in book form.

1929 *The Structure of Politics at the Accession of George III*. Second edition, revised by the author, 1957.

1930 *England in the Age of the American Revolution*. Second edition, revised by Lady Namier and John Brooke, 1961.
Intended as the first part of a multi-volumed work which was never completed. See Namier's foreword to John Brooke, *The Chatham Administration, 1766–1768* (1956).

1931 *Skyscrapers*
A collection of essays on various aspects of modern European history.

1937 *Additions and Corrections to Sir John Fortescue's Edition of the Correspondence of King George III (vol. I)*

1939 *In the Margin of History*
Essays, mainly on eighteenth-century British and nineteenth-century European history.

1942 *Conflicts: Studies in Contemporary History*

1944 *1848: The Revolution of the Intellectuals*
An expanded version of the Raleigh Lecture, delivered to the British Academy.

1947 *Facing East*
Essays, mainly on East European history.

1948 *Diplomatic Prelude, 1938–1939*
A study of the diplomatic origins of the Second World War.

1950 *Europe in Decay: A Study in Disintegration, 1936–1940*
Essays, supplementary to *Diplomatic Prelude*.

1952 *Avenues of History*
Essays on British and European history.

1952 *In the Nazi Era*
Essays, supplementary to *Diplomatic Prelude* and *Europe in Decay*.

1955 *Personalities and Powers*

Essays on British and European history. Includes the Romanes Lecture, *Monarchy and the Party System*, and the Creighton Lecture, *Basic Factors in Nineteenth-Century European History* (both published separately).

1958 *Vanished Supremacies*

Volume I of *The Collected Essays of Sir Lewis Namier*. Essays on European history, 1812–1918. Includes *The Downfall of the Habsburg Monarchy* (contributed to *A History of the Peace Conference of Paris*, edited by H. W. V. Temperley), and essays from *Skyscrapers*, *In the Margin of History*, *Facing East*, *Avenues of History*, and *Personalities and Powers*. Does not include *1848: The Revolution of the Intellectuals*, or essays from *Europe in Decay* or *In the Nazi Era*.

POSTHUMOUS WORKS

1962 *Crossroads of Power*

Volume II of *The Collected Essays of Sir Lewis Namier*. Essays on eighteenth-century England. Includes essays from *Skyscrapers*, *In the Margin of History*, *Avenues of History*, and *Personalities and Powers*; three essays not previously reprinted in book form; the Leslie Stephen lecture, *Charles Townshend*, also published separately; and the first three Ford Lectures (delivered in the University of Oxford in 1934 but never published).

1964 *Charles Townshend*

1964 *The History of Parliament: The House of Commons, 1754–1790*

In 1951, when the plan of writing a biographical *History of Parliament* was revived, Namier became a member of the editorial board of the History of Parliament Trust and editor of the section 1754–1790. To this work he devoted the last years of his life, and on his death in 1960 was succeeded as editor by John Brooke. The section consists of three volumes and is expected to be published in 1964. It contains biographies of Members of Parliament, 1754–1790, accounts of the constituencies, appendices, and an introductory survey. Namier himself wrote about a quarter of the biographies and constituency accounts, but did not live to write the introductory survey.

INDEX

PRINTED IN GREAT BRITAIN BY ROBERT MACLEHOSE AND CO. LTD
THE UNIVERSITY PRESS, GLASGOW